When Children Are Abused:

An Educator's Guide to Intervention

Cynthia Crosson-Tower

Allyn and Bacon

Boston • *London* • *Toronto* • *Sydney* • *Tokyo* • *Singapore*

In memory of Gordon Felton
who took a chance on a young writer,
and in so doing became a mentor and friend

Senior Editor: *Arnis E. Burvikovs*
Editorial Assistant: *Matthew Forster*
Marketing Manager: *Kathleen Morgan*
Editorial-Production Administrator: *Michael Granger*
Editorial-Production Service: *Chestnut Hill Enterprises, Inc.*
Manufacturing buyer: *Julie McNeill*
Cover Administrator: *Kristina Mose-Libon*
Electronic Composition: *Modern Graphics, Inc.*

Copyright © 2002 by Allyn and Bacon
A Pearson Education Company
75 Arlington Street
Boston, Massachusetts 02116

Internet: www.ablongman.com

Between the time Website information is gathered and then published, it is not unusual for some sites to have closed. Also, the transcription of URLs can result in unintended typographical errors. The publisher would appreciate notification where these occur so that they may be corrected in subsequent editions.

Library of Congress Cataloging-in-Publication Data

Tower, Cynthia Crosson.
  When children are abused : an educator's guide to intervention / Cynthia Crosson-Tower
    p. cm.
Includes bibliographical references.
  ISBN 0-205-31962-9
  1. Child abuse—United States—Prevention. 2. Child abuse—Reporting—United States. 3. School social work—United States. 4. Home and school—United States. 5. Abused children—Services for—United States. I. Title
  HV6626.52 . T693 2002
  371.7'8—dc21

2001022872

Printed in the United States of America

10 9 8 7 6 5 4 3 2 1   05 04 03 02 01

Contents

Preface

"Would you be interested in writing a pamphlet for teachers to help them recognize child abuse and neglect?" The request from Gordon Felton, the Director of the National Education Association Publications both pleased and surprised me. He had been given my name by Al Alschuler, who, as a member of my dissertation committee, knew of my interest in child abuse and neglect and knew that I had been engaged for several years in the teaching and training of educators in this area. As a former social worker, who had also worked closely with the teachers of abused children, I felt strongly that teachers, those very important people in children's lives, had been all but neglected in the literature that had begun to appear as the world became increasingly concerned about the protection of children.

I eagerly accepted Gordon's offer, having no idea that that decision would shape my career. The fact that the "pamphlet" became a book with over 100 pages that provided the impetus for a multimedia training package for educators, left all of us in the project stunned at the important need that we had uncovered. Educators were hungry for the knowledge that would allow them to understand and help the abused children whose issues they often felt at a loss to address.

Over the next few years I found myself doing extensive training throughout the country as teachers and other school personnel sought to learn what they could do for at-risk children. The original book, *Child Abuse and Neglect* was revised as *How Schools Can Combat Child Abuse and Neglect*, and continued to be in demand by those who were trying to meet the educational and emotional needs of children.

As so often happens, the magnitude of issues facing education began to overshadow the immediate needs for the attention given to abuse and the book took a backseat to educational reform and the concern about drugs, violence, and a variety of other issues plaguing our young people today. But as I continued to teach and train on child abuse management, I was reminded of how many of the concerns we have about children often have their roots in the abuse or neglect they suffer early in life.

Through my work with the Children's Trust Fund in Boston and the Middlesex Country District Attorney's office in Cambridge, it became clear to me that schools were now concerned with building in protocols that would enable them to address abuse and neglect issues more efficiently. At the same time, the increased concern over quality control and the fear that often exists about lawsuits had convinced many schools that a protocol was not only more effective in helping the child, but also offered increased protection for staff. It was the need for schools to develop protocol that caused me to write *Developing and Implementing a School Reporting Protocol: A Guide for Massachusetts Teachers* (Childrens' Trust Fund, Boston, 1998). Yet the need for direction in creating a reporting protocol was not true just in Massachusetts, but throughout the United States.

It was but a few twists and turns that took me to the writing of this book, *When Children Are Abused*, that blends the original guidance for educators to help them to recognize and respond to the different forms of child maltreatment, with ideas on the formation of a school reporting protocol and a Child Protection Team.

When Children Are Abused is divided into two parts: the first helps the educator to identify the symptoms of abuse, neglect, and sexual abuse as well as acquainting the reader with specific factors that may put a child at risk for maltreatment. The reader is also introduced to the parents or perpetrators who might harm children and why they might be motivated to do so. And finally, in Part I, the educator is aided in his/her consideration of reporting the abuse to the proper social service office by outlining how to validate and prepare for the reporting process.

Part II takes educators through the reporting process from discussing how to set up a protocol and a Child Protection Team through making the actual report and the events that may follow the report. And finally, the book looks at prevention of maltreatment and the long-range picture. Throughout the text and the Appendix are charts and checklists that should make an educator's job much easier.

The path from the beginning to the end of a book is filled with many people who made the writing possible. I would like to thank those who have stood by me and who have provided much needed help along the way. My thanks to Gordon Felton, Al Alschuler, Mary Ann Hanley, Elaine Francis, Cynthia Eselonis, and Bill Leikas and many of my students who have provided suggestions or inspiration. Once again, I thank Judy Fifer who always knew how to direct my talents.

Colleagues on the FACTS Team/Project Alliance of the Middlesex County District Attorney's office and at the Boston Children's Trust Fund are to be thanked for their sharing of ideas that have shaped this book. My special thanks to Kate Schluter and Neal Micheals. My appreciation goes also to the staff of the Perkins School for the Blind in Watertown, Massachusetts who asked me to provide training for them and taught me as much as I taught them. I am especially grateful to Kathy Bull, who persevered and to the talented committee who brought a dream to reality.

I appreciate the time and effort taken by the reviewers who read this text before publication and made valuable suggestions. They are Grisele Casanova, Purdue University; Kimberly McCabe, University of South Carolina; Stephanie Vaugh, New Mexico State University; and Duane Whitbeck, Pittsburg State University (Kansas).

No book that I write would be possible were it not for the patience and love of my family, my husband, Jim, my three sons, Chay, Jamie, and Andrew and my mom, Muriel. Even though there are raised eyebrows and tolerant sighs when I announce that I have signed one more book contract, they are always there when I need them. For this I am truly grateful.

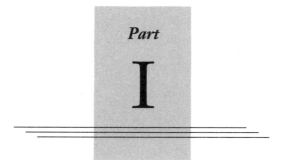

Part

I

Recognizing When Children Are Being Abused or Neglected

Why Are Educators So Important in the Lives of Abused and Neglected Children?

David was not an easy child to like, but Garth Nobel did. David was hyperactive and demanded a good deal of attention. Other teachers told Nobel that David got on their nerves. But David loved gym class. Or was it Garth Nobel's patience and kindness that he enjoyed? For whatever reason, David was always the first to arrive at class and put his whole self into whatever game or activity was asked of him. He wasn't necessarily a team player. In fact, he stayed away from the other children when he was not engaged in an activity. He never dressed with the others or palled around with them. But it was not until David was injured one day in a rather exuberant game of basketball, that Garth Nobel suspected anything. When he lifted David's shirt to check for injuries, he could not believe what he saw. Numerous ugly bruises and burns transversed the boys chest. The different stages of healing made it clear that they were inflicted over a period of time.

"What happened to you, Dave?" Nobel breathed, almost in a whisper. At first, tears ran silently down the boy's face. And then he began to sob, deep heart-wrenching sobs that were hard for the teacher to witness.

"My Dad . . ." Sobbed David but he could not continue. Instead he hugged Garth Nobel with a desperateness that the young and caring teacher would never forget.

He would later learn that David's father had beaten him so badly over the last few years that he had caused internal damage. But that day, Garth Nobel knew that David needed an advocate—someone who cared and could help this boy

3

Continued

through the perils that his future would bring. Years later, David would return to see Nobel with sincere thanks and admiration for standing by him over the next few years when David would be removed from his abusive home and placed in a foster home.

How many of us can remember that special teacher or guidance counselor who had a real impact on our life? As you think back over your own school career, do you remember that educator who made you feel that you were brighter than you thought or who encouraged you and made you feel as if you could accomplish whatever you needed to do. As those who spend our lives interacting with children in educational settings, we are sometimes not even aware of the power we have to influence their young minds. Yet, this is a fact that we must not underestimate. It could be a caring teacher, nurse, or guidance counselor who gives the abused child the will to survive and to become something. As one survivor put it:

> Had Mrs. Jenks (her guidance counselor) not taken the time to recognize that I was hurting, I probably would have killed myself. My father had lost his job and had started drinking and beating my mother. I felt powerless to do anything. My grades suffered and I was so depressed. I knew it was wrong, but I didn't know what to do about it. Mrs. Jenks would see me in the hall and seem so concerned. Sometimes I'd go down to her office after school and we'd just talk. I still couldn't tell anybody. I was petrified that, if I did, Dad would beat her more or take it out on my sister or me. But just having Mrs. Jenks there and knowing that she cared really made a difference. By the end of that school year, when I was so afraid that Dad would kill my mother, I knew I had to tell someone. It was Mrs. Jenks who finally gave me the courage to tell. I wonder if she knows how much I owe her.

Educators do have a major impact on children. This is one of the several reasons, why they must be involved in recognizing and reporting the situation when a child is being abused or neglected. Let us look at these reasons.

Why Should Educators Be Involved in Reporting Abuse and Neglect?

First, *school employees have daily contact with children*. Classroom teachers, especially, see the child in a variety of situations and may be privy to some of the most intimate information about a child's life. As I have already mentioned, with this contact comes a great deal of influence on the developing young person.

Second, educators are concerned with the development of young minds as well as the child's potential. Newer programs that emphasize teaching the whole child have recognized that learning is not just a cognitive activity, especially in the early years. There is so much that goes into the process of learning. By the same token, there is a great deal that can inhibit learning. More and more care is taken by modern schools to understand and remove children's barriers to learning. And yet, *the trauma and residual effects of child abuse and neglect can be as detrimental to a child's ability to learn as are the perceptual difficulties that schools spend so much time addressing today*. Only through relief of the pressure placed on the child by the abuse and neglect can significant learning take place.

And finally, *in all states teachers and other school personnel are mandated by law to report suspected child abuse and neglect*. In fact, they can be held liable for failure to do so.

It took a long time for laws to be passed that protected children from abuse. The process appears to have started in 1874 with a little girl named Mary Ellen. Mary Ellen Wilson lived in a poor section of New York City with her guardians, the Connellys. Neighbors heard the child's cries as she was beaten, and had observed her, ill-clad for the winter weather, huddled on the porch. Concerned, they tried to get help for the child. Finally, they enlisted the support of a neighborhood worker, Etta Wheeler, who met with much frustration and encountered numerous dead ends in her attempts to find relief for this little girl. In desperation, she appealed to the Society for the Prevention of Cruelty to Animals (SPCA). After all, contended Wheeler, Mary Ellen was being treated worse than many animals that were protected by the SPCA. The director of the SPCA, Henry Bergh, did intervene and together with his colleague, Elbridge Gerry, saw that Mary Ellen was removed from the situation. The result of this was the establishment of the Society for the Prevention of Cruelty to Children, an agency that is still strong today (Watkins, 1990).

Why all this history? The fact is that a hundred years elapsed from the time of the first efforts at intervention in the case of Mary Ellen, until there was a federal law to mandate the reporting of child maltreatment by professional. It was not until 1974 that the Child Abuse Prevention and Treatment Act was passed by Congress to insure that abused and neglected children would be protected by law (see Crosson-Tower, 2002). This law ordered each state to carry out child protection by identifying which individuals are mandated to report and to what agency the report should be made. Every state identified teachers and other educators as mandated reporters.

All this is to let you know how long it took for children to develop a voice, albeit through the advocacy of others. Being a mandated reporter enables you to protect children from continued abuse, gives you credibility in your report and protection against being sued for libel (this will be discussed further in Chapter 6). And the fact that educators are included as mandated reporters underscores their importance in the lives of children. Children are in contact mostly with their parents, but if that parent is an abuser, it may be only the educator who has enough contact with and knowledge of the child's life to intervene on that child's behalf.

What If We Do Not Intervene?

The residual effects of child maltreatment are myriad. Adults abused as children attest to the scars that they carry from childhood. Some live their lives in smoldering rage. Most have difficulty trusting. Survivors report having difficulty with relationships, having low self-esteem, and impaired social skills. Some abuse substances, develop eating disorders, practice self-injurious behaviors, or develop somatic symptoms to cope with or hide the pain (see Crosson-Tower, 2002). Children may try to tell adults when they are being abused but, if the adults cannot or will not listen, these young victims assume it must be their fault and stop their efforts to get help. The result is that the hurts of childhood fester into the wounds that the adults carry with them—wounds that may affect their lives in profound ways. Many of these adults seek therapy later in life to deal with the scars they endure. We have learned, however, that if we can intervene when they are still children, there is hope for healing the pain before it becomes overwhelming.

Not long ago, I gave a workshop for educators to help them recognize and prevent child abuse and neglect. Amidst the flurry of questions, one frustrated teacher stood up and said, "Why can't we just forget about all this stuff? Years ago, we just taught and didn't worry about finding out if kids are abused. My teachers never talked to me about abuse and I'm fine. Maybe we are just overreacting!" A hush fell over the audience as the man sat down, sure that his point was well taken by his colleagues. All eyes turned to me expectantly, but before I could respond a woman in the back row stood up—unnoticed until then.

"I'd like to say something," she said quietly. "At six, my father began to molest me. I assumed that all fathers treated their children that way. He beat me too, but no one seemed to notice the marks when I went to school. No one seemed to notice how unhappy I was. I especially liked my third grade teacher and I tried to tell her. I wrote notes and left them for her. But I don't think that she believed that such a thing could happen. No one had taught her that these things do happen. And, we didn't always believe kids back then. She was a good teacher and a concerned person, but she couldn't hear my cry for help. My mother wouldn't listen either. I knew after that that it was useless to try to tell anyone. It never occurred to me that I could say no—that my body was my own—the things we now teach kids. The abuse continued until I ran away and got married at 17—and it has hurt me in so many ways since." By now the woman's voice had risen in volume, and she spoke clearly and with emotion. "As a teacher, I want to know how to recognize other children who are abused. I want to teach them that they have the power to stop that abuse, perhaps with my help. I want them to know that there are knowledgeable people they can go to and who will believe them. I don't want them to suffer in silence as I did!" She took a deep breath and sat down. There was a deafening silence; then the sound of applause came from several sections of the audience. Within a few seconds the whole room resounded with support.

That day, that instance, was a powerful reminder for me of the importance of involving educators in protecting abused and neglected children. The teacher's brave appeal renewed the challenge for me—to continue to teach educators how to recognize and intervene on behalf of children, to teach them to remove the barriers to children's learning no matter what those barriers might be. We can do this by understanding, believing, and reporting as well as empowering children to protect themselves. It is a challenge within our grasp.

How Can We Recognize Child Abuse and Neglect?

Most of us assume that we can recognize the symptoms of a child who is being abused or neglected. In fact, if asked to give a "laundry list" of symptoms, many educators could do it fairly easily. But when faced with a classroom full of children, we often talk ourselves out of recognizing abuse. As one teacher put it:

> I had gone to several trainings and was sure I could recognize abused kids. In fact, I remembered a few in the past and wished I'd known enough about reporting then. There was one child in my class who concerned me, though I didn't know why. There was just something. I happened to come across a chart on the symptoms of abuse and neglect one day—one I had gotten at a training. As I looked down the chart, this little boy's face jumped out at me. No! Could he be being sexually abused? Maybe I didn't think that much about boys being abused, but there it was. He matched all but a few of the symptoms. I later learned that he was being abused by a neighbor. It was a real eye-opener for me!

Children may demonstrate a symptom or two associated with abuse and neglect and not be victims of maltreatment. What we look for is a cluster of symptoms or those symptoms that are especially indicative of a certain type of abuse. For example, a very young child who had specific, and especially tactile, sexual information well beyond his or her years would immediately make me consider sexual abuse. Or sometimes we may notice one symptom and not see others until we really consider. For this reason, I have outlined each type of abuse or neglect and then provided a checklist that can be used to easily see clusters of symptoms.

There are several types of maltreatment: physical neglect, physical abuse, and sexual abuse and exploitation. Emotional or psychological abuse underlies all other types of abuse, but can also be present alone. What is most problematic about emotional abuse is that, unless it is extreme and can be proved, most child protection agencies have difficulty intervening. The reasons for this will be discussed when we consider emotional abuse.

What Is Neglect?

The term *neglect* is much used and defined in a variety of different ways. All children think they are being neglected at some point in their lives. Dinner alone with my husband on a Saturday evening constitutes neglect in the eyes of my twelve-year old. Some people believe that so-called latch-key children are neglected, while working parents argue that they take great pains to make provisions for their children's well-being until they are able to be there. Is a child who is not as clean as most neglected? When you discover that the hygiene habits of the parents are not much different, you begin to wonder if that is really neglect.

Experts agree that neglect falls into several categories. Neglect might be *emotional neglect* when parents fail, in significant ways, to meet the child's needs for attention and affection. *Educational neglect* means that parents do not attend to the schooling and educational needs of their children. *Developmental neglect* involves parents who do not encourage the child's healthy progression through the appropriate developmental stages. *Medical neglect* refers to the failure to attend to a child's medical or even dental needs. Currently, there is also a concern for the neglect of children in-utero (sometimes called *prenatal neglect*) by failure of the mother to care for herself or to expose her body to injurious substances such as drugs, alcohol, cigarettes, or medications when she knows that she is pregnant. Parents might also be accused of failing to provide a safe environment for their children (*environmental neglect*) by not protecting them from unsanitary or hazardous living conditions.

Because neglect is so difficult to define and due to the fact that child protection agencies must employ some concrete criteria, neglect is usually seen as *physical neglect*. Physical neglect refers to *the failure of the child's caretaker to meet that child's basic physical needs*. This definition encompasses or overlaps the other types of neglect mentioned above. One teacher's picture of Robbie is a good example of how such neglect might look.

> My first impression of Robbie was of the dull appearance of his hair, skin, and eyes. Somehow, this was even more striking than the odor emanating from his corner desk. Robbie drifted through my first grade lessons, barely able to find a pencil in his disorganized desk. His lunch usually consisted of Twinkies, which he had bought on his

way to school. Later I learned that he frequently stole them from the market he passed on his walk to school. He eyed the other children's lunches covetously, and once I saw him steal an apple when a classmate's back was turned. Quickly, like a furtive animal, he thrust the apple into his dirty, faded, and torn pants.

Notes and phone calls to his house went unanswered. Robbie was a sad little nomad, drifting into school and listlessly returning home, reportedly to take care of his younger brother and sisters.

Robbie is not unlike many other neglected children. Teachers often remark about their dull appearance or muted affect. In addition, these victims of neglect demonstrate symptoms that might fit into several categories.

Physical symptoms: Neglected children may

- Appear in soiled clothing, significantly too small or too large for them and often in need of repair
- Be inadequately dressed for the weather
- Always seem to be hungry, hoarding or stealing food but coming to school with little of their own
- Appear listless and tired, due to little energy or no routine or structure about bedtimes
- Often report caring for younger siblings when the child caretaker may be only 5, 6, 7, or 8 years old
- Demonstrate poor hygiene, may smell of urine or feces, or have very bad breath or dirty or decaying teeth
- Be emaciated or may have distended stomachs indicative of malnutrition
- Have unattended medical or dental problems such as infected sores or badly decayed or abscessed teeth
- Have lice

Behavioral/social symptoms: These children may

- Exhibit stealing, vandalism, or other delinquent behaviors
- Have frequent school absences or tardiness
- Have poor peer relationships, perhaps because of hygienic problems or a depressed, negative attitude
- Be withdrawn
- Crave attention, even eliciting negative responses to accomplish it
- Be destructive or pugnacious, showing no apparent guilt over their acts
- Have difficulty processing multistatement commands
- Exhibit low self-esteem
- Be diagnosed with conduct disorder or be oppositionally defiant

Intellectual symptoms: Neglected children may

- Have difficulty coping or problem solving
- Exhibit learning disabilities
- Have lower overall intelligence (often due to lack of stimulation)
- Have difficulty with language comprehension and expression
- Have a variety of academic problems

Be aware that all of these symptoms are not always indicative of neglect, but by the same token, are often observed in neglectful situations. Often when older neglected children and adolescents demonstrate these symptoms, they may escape the notice of well-intended educators by dropping out of school. They may also exhibit early emancipation from their families with the promise of drifting into unfulfilled or even crime-ridden lives. As one counselor put it: "Teens in neglectful families do not exit from their families. They ooze out by being absent for a day, back for another and finally the family realizes that they are gone."

Most neglected children of all ages have become accustomed to a life style devoid of routine and organization. They may mirror this in their own lives by the inability to organize themselves, their possessions, or their thinking. Used to single command statements like "shut up," "shut the door," "come here," most neglected children have difficulty understanding more complex thoughts. It is important to realize that many of these children represent just one more generation characterized by their lifestyle and verbal inaccessibility. Their grandparents' teachers may have been concerned with similar problems. Children learn parenting from their parents, who are their role models. Generation after generation of inadequate and neglectful models, with no intervention, will create individuals who are only negatively prepared for parenting (Cantwell, 1997). Because of its pervasive nature, neglect is difficult to deal with. Social workers often describe feeling depressed and overwhelmed when working with neglectful families.

Where does the cycle end in the cases of parents with unmet needs that, in turn, are unable to meet the needs of their offspring? Only through intervention can this neglectful parent be changed. Although we can insist that children be properly fed, clothed, and bathed and given attention and affection, it is only when we also help the parents that we can break the cycle of neglect.

What Is Physical Abuse?

Most of us have an idea that children with persistent and serious bruises are possible victims of physical abuse, but let us look at those symptoms more closely.

Physical abuse can be defined as *nonaccidental injury to a child*. Child protective service agencies usually add that this injury must be perpetrated by a caretaker. The most obvious way to detect this type of abuse is by outward physical signs such as the following:

- Extensive bruises, especially in areas of the body that are not normally vulnerable. On light pigmentation one might observe numerous bruises of different colors indicating various stages of healing. The age of bruises can be approximately determined by the following colors:

  Immediate–few hours = red
  6–12 hours = blue
  12–24 hours = black-purple
  4–6 = green tint, dark
  5–10 days = pale green to yellow (Davis 1982, 8)

  On darker pigmentation, this coloration is not obvious.

- Frequent bruises around the head or face, the abdomen or midway between the wrist and elbow. Although bruises to the knees, legs, and elbows frequently occur in normal falls, the above areas are less likely to occur that way and should be investigated.
- Bruises in specific shapes such as handprints or hanger marks
- Marks that indicate hard blows from an object such as an electrical cord or other whip-like object that makes a burn around the body
- Bruises on multiple parts of the body indicating blows from different directions
- Unexplained abdominal bleeding (could be caused by internal bleeding)
- Extreme sensitivity to pain or complaints of soreness and stiffness or awkward movements as if caused by pain
- Bald spots from severe hair pulling
- Adult sized human bite marks
- Burns, especially from objects such as cigarettes, irons, and other objects

The key thing to look for in physical abuse is an explanation that does not fit the injury. For example, the child reports a "fall" while the bruises clearly indicate the outline of an object such as a belt. Or the child who "fell out of bed" is too severely bruised for such a fall. Another important factor to consider is where the injuries occur, considering whether or not the location or type of injury is feasible or typical. For example, a child may hurt the palm of the hand but is not as likely to sustain an injury on the back of the hand. It is common, however, to see children whacked on the back of the hand by someone else. Likewise, bruising in the genital area, the abdomen, and the back are not as likely to be accidental. Although head injuries can also be accidental, one usually protects the temples, checks, ears, and skull. Injuries in these areas may suggest that harm has been done to the child (Monteleone, 1998). Physicians tell us (see Hobbs et. al., 1998) that when a child breaks a bone, the location of the bone that is broken should be considered. Some bones are more easily broken in accidental circumstances while others are not. Some types of breaks (e.g., greenstick fractures) are also more suspect for abuse than others. Obviously, this would be something left to medical care providers rather than teachers, but it is an important fact of which to be aware.

There are several types of symptoms that can be seen in young school age children, but are more likely to appear in preschool children or infants. The first set of symptoms involve children who are shaken to the point of injury. When a child is shaken, it is possible for them to develop a subdural hemotoma (blood around the brain) or retinal damage or detachment (see Feldman, 1997). These children might complain of dizziness, blurred vision, loss of consciousness, seizures when none had been previously present, or severe headache. Obviously such concerns should be brought to medical attention.

Another concern is over an increasingly-seen syndrome referred to as Munchausen Syndrome by Proxy. This phenomenon usually involves mothers whose children appear to have frequent medical complaints that require hospitalization. The most common of these are breathing problems and vomiting. What actually occurs is that Mom, pathologically in need of attention from someone in a position of authority (usually medical personnel) will actually cause her child's illness through her own actions. Mothers have been known to suffocate children, to feed them poisonous substances, and to inject them with harmful materials so that the child develops a reaction. While her child is hospitalized, Mom seems like the model parent, always at the child's side and very helpful. Their children can be in serious danger as their mother's need for attention brings them more and more frequently to the attention of professionals (see Rosenberg, 1997).

Behaviorally, children also give us clues that they are being abused. They may:

- Be aggressive, pugnacious, or defiant
- Cower or demonstrate fear of adults
- Act out, displaying aggressive or disruptive behavior
- Be destructive to self or others
- Come to school too early or not want to leave school—a clear indication of fear of going home
- Show fearlessness or extreme risk taking
- Be described as accident prone
- Cheat, steal, or lie (may be related to too high expectations at home)
- Be low achievers (to learn, children must convert aggressive energy into learning; children in conflict may not be able to convert this energy)
- Be unable to form good peer relationships
- Wear clothing that covers the body and that may be inappropriate in warmer months (be aware that this may be cultural as well)
- Show regression, or exhibit less mature behavior
- Dislike or shrink from physical contact (may not tolerate physical praise such as a pat on the back)

Kara, Ricardo and Kevin exemplify different extremes in behaviors that might be typical of abused children.

Kara, age 5, always presented a neat, well-ordered picture. Although not expensive, her clothes were well chosen, clean, and pressed. Her long-sleeved blouses and colorful tights seemed a bit strange, especially in the Alabama heat, but the teacher made no comments about them. The child was very affectionate, almost to the point of smothering; her endearing ways made her well liked by all the teachers and staff. It was not until Kara unexplainably wet her pants, that anything became obvious. Kara became extremely overwrought and fearful, cowering as the teacher tried to help her to remove her tights to clean her up. As Kara winced in pain, her small legs revealed numerous bruises in various stages of healing. An examination by the school nurse attested to the abuse that Kara had suffered over her entire body.

*****

Ricardo was not a difficult child, nor was he unlikable. He was just "there" in the classroom with thirty other bubbling, boisterous youngsters. He did his work as instructed and never talked back. His only problem initially was that he frequently fell asleep in class. Ricardo's "accidents"—the bruises in September, the broken arm in January, the burned hands in March—did not even raise the teacher's suspicions. In April, the teacher witnessed some outburst of extreme anger against other children on the playground. Once, Ricardo had to be restrained lest he hit another child. It was not until a younger sibling told her teacher of the family situation that Ricardo's problems were addressed. For years he had been a silent witness to his father's abuse of his mother. Now, at 12, Ricardo had tried to intervene making him the new brunt of his father's anger. Intent upon keeping the family secret, Ricardo had taken great pains to explain away his injuries. But his nocturnal vigil to try to insure the family's safety from a drunk and abusive father, took its toll on this young boy. Ricardo's own suppressed anger was slowly raising its head.

*****

Kevin, a boisterous, unruly, and pugnacious child spent most of his time sitting in the assistant principal's office for some offence or other that he had committed. Most of the teachers in the junior high school dreaded his appearance in class. In the past year, he had run away from home twice. It was not until the social service agency notified the school that Kevin had been removed from the home due to threatening abuse, that the cause of his behavior became apparent.

Each of the above vignettes spoke of a different manner in which a child will exhibit the symptoms of abuse. Kara's story speaks of a well-ordered home where expectations ran too high. Her desire to please within this rigid framework transfers itself to school as well. Ricardo's life had been in turmoil for many years. Experts might be surprised that he had not exhibited more obvious manifestations of the violence he was witnessing earlier. Here was a child who had turned inward, spending his nighttime hours watchful for further abuse to his family and his daytime hours fighting his body's need for sleep. But now he had repressed his pain and anger to the point where he could no longer keep it hidden.

While Kara's and Ricardo's problems might go unnoticed for sometime, Kevin's issues are more obvious. Kevin is striking out at the world, which appears to give him nothing but abuse. He is at the hub of an ever-moving wheel of abuse and misperception. At home he is beaten by a drug-addicted father who spends his sober hours expounding on the virtues of "being a man." His mother, also a drug abuser is not available to help him. Appelstein (1998) suggests that challenging behavior on the part of youth is a cry for help that we, as concerned adults, must learn to decode. Kevin's attempts to cry for help at school translate into disruptive behavior and meet with more rejection from those who are not decoding his message. If his parents are called in, the cycle repeats itself.

The symptoms of abuse mentioned above can apply to adolescents as well as to younger children. Although the abuse of adolescents is also a major problem, it may not be as easily recognized due to some misconceptions that we have about adolescents. First, we do not think of adolescents as victims. We assume that they are stronger, and could fight back or run away if they were threatened by an abuser (Rossman and Rosenberg, 1998). What we often do not consider is that adolescents may have been taught since they were quite young that it is not acceptable to go against their parents. It might take distance from their homes to realize that, in some situation, resistance would have been best. We also assume that adolescents are more difficult or more provocative and therefore "invite" abuse. Yet no one need be a victim of abusive behavior regardless of the apparent provocation. And finally, we assume that adolescents have more access to potential help than do younger children. Yet the reverse may often be true. Because we perceive that adolescents are more capable, we are less likely to intervene or to alert them to the resources available to them. The following example proves the case in point.

I was on a school-based task force to study the needs of children when it came to the prevention of child abuse. We had gotten some prevention packages put out by various groups and had decided to institute prevention training in grades K–8. Someone suggested that we should do something for the high school level as well and the suggestion was voted down. "By the time they are in high school," said one member, "they can fend for themselves pretty well. We'd be better off teaching them to stay off drugs than alerting them to child abuse!"

Had Renata been in this meeting, she might have enlightened the group considerably. From the time that Renata was quite young, she had been physically abused by her mother who pinched her, beat her, and humiliated her in front of others. From early on Renata had been told that she was an evil child and that the beatings she had suffered were because she was so evil. It was not surprising that she told no one. Surely, this would have alerted them to what an evil person she was. The fact that her family moved often helped to keep their secret. So Renata endured years of abuse trying to be a "good girl" and ever hoping that something she did would please her mother. Her teachers found her quiet and compliant, a student who caused no problems. As she began high school, she quietly fit into the crowd. Had Renata not been involved in an automobile accident and been hospitalized, her old bruises and scars might never have been discovered.

Despite the apparent advantages that adolescents have over younger children, in an abusive situation they are still hampered by ties and remnants of family dependence from childhood. Adolescents want to be seen as independent, but their history has probably been one of returning to the family for safety. They, like Renata, may also have come to believe that the fault lies with them rather than with the abuser.

Adolescents who act out behaviorally may often be reacting to the fact that they are being abused at home. Not sure how to tell anyone, or not sure what their own role is in the family, the adolescent may be acting out as a cry for help. Too often we respond to the symptom and neglect to search for the cause. When considering adolescent abuse, the school is decidedly the *most* important link in the helping chain. Teachers and guidance counselors are the professionals most likely to detect abuse in this age group. Younger children may come to the attention of the medical community; as a rule, adolescents do not.

As you review the symptoms, whether visible in an adolescent or a younger child, keep in mind that one or two of these symptoms does not *necessarily* mean abuse. It does mean that one should be watchful, carefully observing the child for additional indicators. Many of the factors mentioned may be indicative of other problems as well. In addition, one must be particularly mindful of the culture from which the child comes. For example, some Vietnamese children may suffer unusual bruises resulting from a common folk remedy called *cao gaio* or "coin-rubbing" that is used to cure colds and headaches. Long-sleeved shirts or pants worn by Moslem girls may be the custom rather than a cover-up of abuse. Documenting strange or unusual behavior can help the unsure educator accumulate a variety of clues and perhaps become more aware of an abusive pattern.

Remember that abuse affects children in different ways. Victims suffer from poor self-image, feelings of having little self-worth, and perhaps, that they deserve the abuse. In addition, they may have learned that adults will hurt them; therefore they are watchful and untrusting. Children reflect their family life.

Those who present a negative, depressed picture may well be mirroring the unrest at home—if not actual abuse, certainly some other kind of family disturbance.

What Is Emotional Abuse?

Emotional or psychological abuse underlies all types of abuse and neglect. In fact, survivors have explained that it was the emotional component of the maltreatment that was the most devastating. But emotional abuse may be present when no other type of maltreatment is obvious. Because children are devalued in our culture and their needs secondary to those of adults, emotional abuse has become so embedded in our child-rearing practices that we do not always recognize it for what it is. Even when this type of abuse becomes so recognizable that it cannot be denied, it is often difficult for child protection agencies to prove that it is abuse or to intervene.

Severe emotional abuse refers to belittling, rejecting, isolating, terrorizing, or ignoring a child. Messages like "you are such a stupid kid" or "you are so dumb, who would want you" (*belittling*) make a child feel that he or she is worth little. Such messages undermine one's self esteem. Some parents convey *rejection* to their children with words such as "I was better off before you were born!" Gabby's parents, frustrated that she was more difficult than the other children to toilet train, made her stay by herself for long periods (*isolating*). "You smell bad!" they would tell her when she would not adhere to their training demands. "The other kids don't want you around!" These messages stayed with Gabby long after she entered school. Her peer relationships were always problematic as she was convinced that "no one wanted her around."

Prejudice can play a part in the emotional maltreatment of children. For example:

> The Roa family, Brahmans (the highest caste in Indian culture), were well-educated professionals, newly arrived in the United States. All light complected, the Roas were extremely distressed when their third child was born. His dark complexion was met by his maternal grandmother with the comment, "Where did he come from? Our family has never been dark! He looks like the village people!" (often from a lower caste). While the Roas at first tried to overlook their son's different coloring, they felt that he was rejected by relatives. The subtle pattern of ignoring this child, which they developed, and their practice of keeping him away from others as much as possible, was detected by teachers when he reached school age. (Crosson-Tower 2002, 257).

Some parents find threats of malevolence an effective way to discipline their offspring. "If you don't behave, the bogeyman will get you!" can be heard in some households. This practice may also have cultural implications. For example, some families from certain African or Native American roots threaten their children with an equivalent of the bogeyman (Crosson-Tower, 2002). Such practices represents centuries of cultural childrearing.

More recently, *corrupting* has also been included in the definition of emotional maltreatment. This occurs when an adult "mis-socializes" a child by encouraging him or her to practice antisocial or destructive behavior, reinforcing deviance and making it difficult for them to fit in with their peers (Garbarino et. al., 1986).

> Harmon's parents were convinced that the world would end and that everyone else was "wicked and would be destroyed." Therefore, no one could be trusted. The parents outfitted their basement as a survival shelter and encouraged their children to spend long periods down there. The children were taught to shoot a shotgun and to threaten to shoot anyone who ventured onto their rural homestead. The mistrust of others that the parents drummed into their children left them ill-equipped to attend school and associate with others. Harmon took every unusual event (e.g., the yearly fire drill alarm) as an omen for the end of the world and would run from school, attempting to make the five mile journey home on foot. Invariably, someone would have to pick him up and bring him back to school. His teacher became so concerned about his strange behavior that she reported the situation to the child protection agency.

In Harmon's case, there was little that the child protection agency could do besides insist that he be in school. While the social service system is not always able to intervene, steps may be taken to support the child emotionally.

How might one recognize that a child is being emotionally abused? Some of the indicators might be:

- Inappropriate affect such as turning negatives into jokes and laughing when in pain
- Extremes in behavior—manically happy or very depressed
- Withdrawal—or no verbal or physical communication with other
- Self-destruction
- General destructive behavior
- Learning disabilities
- Compulsive attention to detail
- Cruelty to other
- Vandalism, stealing, cheating

- Rocking, thumb sucking, head banging
- Enuresis (wetting one's pants) or soiling after an age when such behavior is inappropriate
- Substance abuse
- Eating disorders
- Physical manifestation such as asthma, ulcers, or severe allergies
- Delinquent behavior

Granted, some of the symptoms mentioned above can be indicative of other forms of abuse or some other conflict in the child's life. But emotional abuse is also a factor that must be ruled out.

Parents who emotionally abuse their children may have unrealistically high expectations of their offspring. When the children are unable to meet these expectations, they receive verbal criticism that makes them feel incompetent or generally "bad." Such expectations may be related to the values or ideas held by the parents, as the following example illustrates:

Sally demonstrated her abuse by a perpetually sad expression. She was the child of a former military man and the Vietnamese woman he had brought back with him from Vietnam. She died when Sally was just a baby. Sally constantly looked as if she had just been beaten, but her father never touched her. Instead, he berated her: "How did I ever deserve a girl? One child, and it has to be a girl! Girls are worth nothing!" The father had Sally's hair cut in an unbecoming, boyish style saying that there was no point in trying to make an ugly girl look better. He demanded complete obedience and subservience, including having her stand beside him when he ate to cut and salt his food. He rationalized this activity by saying that her only hope in life was to be of use to a husband, even if anyone in fact wanted her. Even when Sally scored 160 on an IQ test, her father assured her teachers that they were wrong—she was only a girl. Unfortunately, Sally believed him.

Unfortunately, emotional abuse may not be easy to pinpoint. It is also difficult to prove. Teachers may help these victims though with attention and encouragement to express themselves.

What Is Sexual Abuse and Exploitation?

Sexual abuse has always been a human problem, but there has perhaps never been more awareness of it than there is today. Social workers estimate that between 60 to 75 percent of reports of abuse are sexual in nature. News reports are filled with the potential for children being abused through the Internet.

There is no way to know how many cases go unreported due to our society's taboo on sexuality.

Again and again I hear the question, "Is sexual abuse more prevalent today or just more widely reported?" Although some theorists favor the "more widely reported" explanation, others, like Diana Russell (1986), believe that the incidence of child sexual abuse quadrupled from 1900 to 1973. She accounted for this increase by citing several changes in society. First, Russell blamed the flourishing child pornography business as not only a stimulant for perpetrators but also as a means of engaging children in sexuality through their use as subjects in pornographic films and photographs. Second, society began to be tolerant of a variety of sexual life styles. And the sexual equality results in some men being increasingly threatened by adult females and attracted to the pliable, cooperative, adoring faces of young girls used seductively to enhance TV ads. Russell also suggested that the lack of expertise in treating sexual abuse until recently has accounted for the numbers of perpetrators, who, abused themselves as children, have gone on to repeat their victimization by abusing others. Finally, David Finkelhor (1984) demonstrated that the incidence of sexual abuse is higher among families with stepfathers. To absolve innocent stepfathers, it should be noted that abuse is not always at the hands of the new spouse; it may result from two other factors. Statistically, children of reconstituted families have been exposed to a greater number of men if their mother dated before her remarriage. Any of these might have been guilty of abuse. And the male friends of the stepfather may not perceive the same taboo in molesting the stepdaughter of their friend as they would in the case of a blood-related daughter. Whatever the reason given, the increased divorce and remarriage rate had a decided impact on the incidence of sexual abuse.

During the 1980s, there was an increased effort and new legislation that sought to reduce the incidence of child sexual abuse and increase the level of training for treatment. These efforts apparently bore fruit as Wang and Daro (1998) report that the incidence of child sexual abuse began to decline in the 1990s. Despite this decline, child sexual abuse remains a significant problem for children and must be addressed.

There are several factors that can be assumed about the sexual abuse of children. First, it is an act of power usually perpetrated by an individual who does not feel that powerful when faced with adults. The aim is the sexual gratification of the abuser not the child, despite the abuser's rationalizations to the contrary. The power differential involved removes any question that the victim may have consented. And finally, the presence of secrecy makes the abuse possible (Hobbs, et al. 1999).

Child sexual abuse can be defined as *sexual involvement imposed upon a child by an adult who has greater power, knowledge and resources*. Finkelhor (1984), points out that sexuality in our culture is based on an individual's ability to consent. Because children have neither the knowledge nor the authority to make the decision to consent, sexual contact with them is abusive.

The most classic myth is that sexual abuse is perpetrated by strangers. We were probably all told as children not to talk to strangers or not to take candy from strangers. While this may still be good advice, the fact is that between 70 to 85 percent of sexual abuse is committed by someone known to—and often loved by—the child. Most perpetrators are male although female perpetrators are now becoming more widely recognized and reported. One reason for this tendency to recognize males and not females as perpetrators, is that our society allows females more opportunity for intimate activities with children (e.g., bathing, sleeping with, and so on) in the guise of mothering. This may give women more chance to bond with children and not be inclined to abuse them, but it may also allow female perpetrators to hide their abusive activities in their mothering duties. For example:

> George reported that he remembers his mother bathing him when he was ten and eleven. Because he was uncircumcised, she would often pull back his foreskin to bath him. George, as a child, assumed that all mothers did this, but when his own children insisted at 3 and 4 years old that they could bath themselves, he began to wonder. As he thought about his times with his mother, other memories began to emerge of her touching him inappropriately. He soon began to realize that what he thought was her motherly attention was in fact blatant sexual abuse that had engendered in him feelings of shame and difficulties in his relationship with other women.

Children may be sexually abused at an early age or as preadolescents or adolescents. Finkelhor (1984) identified the period between ages 8 and 12 as the most vulnerable time, but much younger children have also been abused. Boys are often abused at younger ages than their female counterparts. This is probably because sexual abuse is an issue of power. As a boy becomes an adolescent, he is seen to have more power and therefore is less likely to be a target for abuse. Girls, on the other hand, as "little women" share the assumed powerlessness that our society still attributes to the female gender. In addition, the type of abuser who preys on boys prefers younger, more vulnerable children. Abusers of girls are often attracted to females but see younger females as less threatening.

Sgroi (1982) identified a progression of sexual activity that characterizes the sexual abuse of children. It may begin with disrobing on the part of the perpetrator, or close observation of the child during bathing, dressing, or elimination rituals. Many sexual encounters begin with seemingly innocent "horseplay" or kissing and progress to fondling, genital exposure, and mutual masturbation. For example, Terry recounts:

> My sister and I used to spend the summer at my Uncle and Aunt's farm. My Aunt used to be doing farm chores while my Uncle fed us

breakfast. He would sit at the table in his bathrobe, which would seemingly accidentally flop open. Once, my sister went under the table to get something she had dropped and was faced with a full view of my Uncle's lower body. We both tried to ignore this. Then I used to feel his hand on my leg, working its way up. Later in the summer, he cornered me in the barn and kissed me in a way that felt really strange. He rubbed my breasts as he was doing it and it upset me. But I dared not say anything. My Mom worked all summer and this was our chance to be outside and have fun. Only recently my sister told me that he did the same thing to her and eventually took all her clothes off and made her do things to him. He never went that far with me, but I was more outspoken than she was.

Oral genital contact, as well as anal manipulation, may follow. This progression from less intrusive to more intrusive behavior on the part of the perpetrator, is called *grooming*. Through a slow methodical progression, the perpetrator is testing the child's readiness and trust of him or her. Experts are discovering, however, that these first stages of grooming can create guilt and shame and can be almost as damaging as the more intrusive behaviors. Vaginal penetration with the fingers or penis usually happens only after the perpetrator has the child's trust, full compliance, or he or she is assured that the child will not tell.

Why don't more children tell that they are being abused? First, we instill in children from an early age that they are subservient to and even at the mercy of the adults in their lives. In the case of parents, they may depend on these adults for their very survival. And, children may not have another context. If the adult is a parent, they may not realize that parents should be anything other than abusive. Children may also enjoy the attention that they are receiving from the abuser. Perpetrators tell us that the easiest child to abuse is the one who is starved for attention. These children may do almost anything to achieve the attention that they crave.

Secrecy is a very important part of the whole picture of sexual abuse. Our societal view that "sex is private" gives the perpetrator an excuse to justify his insistence that the child tell no one of the abuse. By the same token, society's seeming phobia about sexual deviance (while paradoxically condoning it in the media and print) creates a need for the perpetrator to be especially careful in compelling quiet in the victim. Although special attention or threats may be enough to ensure the child's silence, sexual abusers may also use gifts, money, edible treats, or other forms of "blackmail." Some children report being given money, clothes, or other gifts in exchange for their compliance and silence.

Children retain this need to keep the secret in many parts of their life. For example, a child may refuse to undress for gym, feeling that the teacher or peers could detect the sexual abuse just by seeing the unclothed body. It should be noted that failure to report sexual abuse can actually perpetuate the secrecy by aiding the perpetrator rather than the child.

Children who have been sexually abused exhibit a variety of symptoms including the following:

- Frequent urinary tract infections
- Difficulty in walking or sitting
- Torn, stained, or bloody underwear
- Genital/anal itching, rashes, pain, swelling, or burning
- Genital/anal bruising or bleeding
- Frequent yeast infections
- Pain in urination
- Excessive bathing
- Frequent vomiting
- Excessive sore throats (may be indicative of gonorrhea)
- Excessive masturbation
- Other symptoms of venereal disease such as vaginal or penile pain or discharge, genital or oral sores, genital warts
- Early pregnancy
- Frequent psychosomatic illnesses

Granted, many of these symptoms might not be observable in the classroom, but may come from reports by the abused child or peers. Behaviorally, children may exhibit:

- Exceptional secrecy
- More sexual knowledge than is appropriate for the child's age (especially in younger children)
- In-depth sexual play with peers (in younger children, different from the normal "playing doctor" form of exploration)
- Overcompliance or withdrawal
- Overaggressiveness or acting out
- Inordinate fear of males (or females)
- Extreme seductiveness
- A drop in school performance or sudden nonparticipation in school activities
- Reported sleep problems or nightmares
- Crying without provocation
- Sudden onset of enuresis (wetting pants or bed) or soiling
- Sudden phobic behavior
- Feelings of little self-worth, talk of being damaged
- Appearing much older and more worldly than peers
- Suicide attempts or ideas of wanting to kill self
- Running away from home excessively
- Extreme cruelty to animals (especially those that would normally be pets)
- Fire setting

- Eating disorders
- Self mutilation (cutting, scratching to draw blood)

It may become obvious that many of these symptoms could be indicative of a number of conflicts that do not involve sexual abuse. This often makes it easier to deny the presence of sexual abuse. Many experts believe that the only indicators that are usually indicative of sexual abuse are too much sexual knowledge for the age of the child, and when the play of children is especially explicitly sexual. Cunningham and MacFarlane (1996, 184) reported that in their study of children being treated for sexual abuse, 80 percent were fire setters. If we look at sexual maltreatment as an abuse of power and control, we may also consider attempts to take control over those weaker (e.g., cruelty to animals) as an abused child's way of seeking the control he or she has lost. It is important, however, that if a cluster of this list of symptoms is seen, the educator should at least consider the possibility of sexual abuse.

For sexual abuse to occur, several contributing factors are necessary. The first is *opportunity*. Often we see the profile of the mother who works in the evening or at other times when a child is most vulnerable. Our high divorce rate may also expose children to a variety of adults who are not their own parents and who might not feel the same taboo against sexual contact as most parents would. An increasing number of young babysitters, some with their own abuse histories, have been reported to be abusing their charges. Over the last few years, we have been shocked at the stories of priests and ministers who have abused their position with young children. Video arcades, so popular to entertain the children while the parents get a few undisturbed shopping moments in another part of the mall, are known to be prime targets for the perpetrator looking for prey. And lurking in most homes is the seat of opportunity for many sexual abusers today . . . the computer and the Internet (to be discussed later). In our culture, there are numerous opportunities for perpetrators to have access to and to engage children for the purpose of sexually abusing them.

Another contributing factor to a child's abuse, especially in the home, is *change*. Families who abuse have frequently undergone some recent stress such as relocation, unemployment, job changes, or illness that make family members feel vulnerable. Feeling out of control of one's life is a factor, which is prevalent in the histories of sexual abusers.

The profile of the abused child has been much studied. Unfortunately there is no classic profile so that we might say, "this is the child to protect." However, we have learned a few things over the years. We know that often a child who is sexually abused is a child who is more needy and has a poorer self-concept than his or her peers. In addition, we still teach children that adults are to be obeyed unquestionably and this message does a disservice to the potentially abused child. This is the child who does not perceive that he or she has the power to resist, to run, or even to tell. We also know that boys are more often abused at younger ages than girls. If we are reminded that abuse involves power and control, we again recognize that boys are assumed to have power sooner than girls. This brings us to our misconceptions about the abuse of boys.

Over the last few years, the literature has been reminding us that boys are victims of sexual abuse as well as of physical abuse and neglect. Yet, for several reasons, we tend to forget that boys are as vulnerable as their female counterparts. First, in our culture, it is difficult for us to see males as victims. The female is the perennial victim. According to this conscious or unconscious argument, the male should be able to protect himself or run. While this concept of the male as powerful and the female as vulnerable has been an underlying assumption of our culture for years, the concept of male power has been augmented as cultures that value male infallibility (e.g., concept of *machismo*) increase in population.

Second, boys have learned that admitting to being victimized subjects them to being seen as "sissies" which often invites teasing or more abuse from peers who see them as vulnerable. Joel was a good example of this:

> Joel, at 13, was sexually abused by a middle school coach. He had been raised by his older grandmother who taught him that one should always respects ones elders and do what one is told. To make matter worse for Joel, the coach was a well-liked but very loud and overpowering man. Most of the players were in awe of him. When Coach started keeping Joel after practice and ordered him to perform sexual acts, Joel was afraid to refuse. When a teammate returned one afternoon and found the coach sodomizing Joel, one would think that it would have been reported. Instead, the teammate told others, who protected the coach but taunted Joel about what a "sissy" he was for "getting it in the arse." Joel's humiliation was finally stopped when another coach heard the taunts and, with suspicions of his own about his colleague, took the matter to the principal.

Third, another reason why we overlook boys as victims, is the fact that our society has a double standard about victimization. While girls are theoretically to be protected from sexual relations before adulthood, there is often an expressed or unexpressed feeling that early sexuality for boys is almost a rite and therefore expected. This is what I have termed the "Summer of '42 Syndrome." The movie, *Summer of '42*, popular several decades ago, followed several young boys in their infatuation with a military wife whose husband is fighting in World War II. When the husband is killed she turns to one of the boys in her grief. With all the lighting, music, and romantic mood that Hollywood can muster, she takes him into her bed. At no point did the movie recognize that the seduction of a young boy by an older woman was abuse. It is assumed that boys want the sexual experience however coercive it might be. For this reason, many boys may have had early sexual experiences with adults but do not feel harmed by them (see Finkelhor, 1984). Others admit that they fear that by calling a sexual experience with a female abuse, they will label themselves as less macho.

Are boys abused significantly less often than girls or is it just less talked about? Although there are somewhat fewer reports of males being abused, the number of victims of men who abuse boys is usually greater than the numbers of victims of perpetrators against girls (see Chandy et al, 1997). So where are all these victims? They are probably not talking. Not only do boys feel that they will be branded "sissies" if they talk about their abuse, but they have concerns about homosexuality. If they were abused by a male, they wonder if there was something about them that appeared gay. Was that why they were singled out? And, I have already stated that if abused by a female, they have been taught by the culture that it is not abuse, but "an experience any boy would want." In either case, the abused boy fears being labeled homosexual and therefore tends not to tell others. His fear often makes him unwilling to face the victimization in his own mind as well.

> A mother approached the counselor concerned about her nine-year old son. Shawn had been behaving strangely. Very moody and uncooperative with his parents, he was also bossy with his younger sister, almost to the point of abuse. He had also developed an interest in guns and war toys—playthings that his parents did not encourage. His mother described him as "suddenly tough—a professional macho." After seeing Shawn for several therapy sessions, the counselor began to suspect sexual abuse and asked him if he had ever been touched sexually. The boy began to deny it vehemently and finally broke into almost uncontrollable tears. He was finally able to disclose that he had been sodomized by the adult brother of a friend. The brother had continued to abuse Shawn, suggesting that he tell no one lest people think that Shawn was homosexual. So concerned was this boy about this, that he had adopted his pseudo-macho manner.

Another factor prevents boys from telling about their abuse. In our culture, boys are given much more freedom in everyday life than girls. Male children are less closely supervised and are allowed to be without adult supervision much earlier than are girls. Most parents who learned of their son's victimization outside the home would try to protect him from future occurrences. This protection would mean curtailing his activities, perhaps, but certainly giving more supervision. Thus the boy perceives that he would lose more than he would gain.

It is important that educators be alert to the signals given by boys, as well as by girls, that they are being abused. Intervention can save a boy from growing up with the scars of abuse. Since many perpetrators have a history of victimization in their childhoods, teachers may also be protecting future generations by breaking the cycle *now*.

As we consider the above symptoms, we wonder, "how will I really know if it is abuse?" This question will be answered as best anyone can as you read on in the text. However, it is important to note here, that one's ability to recognize abuse and neglect may be influenced by two important factors: how we see behavior and how we see ourselves.

Behavior as a Clue to Abuse

Mandatory reading for any teacher, guidance counselor, or other educator is Charles Appelstein's book *No Such Thing as a Bad Kid* (published by the Gifford School, 177 Boston Post Road, Weston, MA 02193). So often, abused and neglected children get the reputation of being "bad kids" or at least those who are extremely difficult to understand and control. Appelstein (1998) explains that what we are seeing is a message that this child needs help and it is our job to decode that message. When students "rub us the wrong way" by their language or behavior, two things happen. First, the message often gets lost in our response to the symptom. As Appelstein puts it:

> When our buttons are pushed, the natural tendency is to focus our attention on what the child did and what should be done about it, rather than on why he did it. . . . To grasp the difference between the symptoms and the core issues, imagine an athlete who has torn the cartilage in his knee and is experiencing pain. A strong painkiller, may temporarily ease the situation, but it will not remedy the underlying problem. The pain is a symptom—a message that something is wrong. If the athlete's doctor treats only the symptom, the condition may in fact worsen. Good treatment entails appropriate symptom management (pain relief) and sophisticated problem resolution (surgery). Both are essential. . . . Disciplining children without considering the cause of their problematic behavior is like dispensing medication to people without searching for the cause of their symptoms. (8–9).

Likewise, how many times have we, as educators, dealt with a child who exhibits out-of-control or difficult behavior by consequences that may go as far as suspension or expulsion? Yet, it is often this child who needs to be in *school* rather than in an abusive home, but also needs to be understood. This is not to say that we should not interrupt the behavior, but there are many ways of responding rather than reacting, and some more functional than others.

The second result of troubling behavior by a student can make the adults involved feel psychologically attacked and then inadequate. Attacked? Of course you feel attacked! After all, doesn't Johnny calling you a variety of colorful names casting doubt on your parenting skills and confusing you with various parts of the anatomy, imply disrespect? We often take these insults personally. Not only this, but our competence as educators can also be affected. Why can't we reach this child? Thus the self-esteem of the adults in charge may also suffer when children act out. As Appelstein (1998) puts it: the fact that "something isn't right, does not necessarily imply that you are doing something wrong" (10). Yet, often it feels that way.

Appelstein (1998) also suggests that these young people tend to be labeled as difficult children, with tags that do them a discredit. The child who has learned at home that telling the truth may meet with a whack or who is so ashamed of his poverty that only fabrications can get him accepted by his peers becomes the "liar." The child who is depressed, or withdrawn, or who has learned that it is safer to fade into the woodwork, becomes the "lazy kid" or the "loser." The girl who has learned through sexual abuse to bargain with her body becomes overly provocative or even the "tramp" or "slut." And children who have learned to control their environment to try to minimize the effects of their abuse are seen as manipulative. In fact, the very behaviors that may be criticized in children are the ways that they have learned to *survive* in dysfunctional families.

Thus, as we are considering the symptoms of abuse, it is important to remember what these symptoms tell us. They tell us that this child has enough spunk left to cry out for help. It is up to us to hear their cries and decode these messages.

Understanding Ourselves

Each of us is unique and that uniqueness is a compilation of, not only our genes, but the experiences we have had throughout our lives. These experiences color all that we do—our relationships, our perception and even the way that we teach or perform our jobs. The experiences of educators themselves, can influence the way in which they see and deal with children. Given the high statistics of those who were abused or neglected as children, it is certain that there will be educators who have themselves experienced maltreatment as children. Individuals have a variety of reactions to an abusive past at different points in their lives. Some survivors may want to search for answers, working out the hurt and anger they feel through understanding. Other past victims want only to completely forget what happened. Discussing abuse and neglect in prevention programs or making one's self aware that a child has been abused may be difficult if one is trying to put abusive memories in the past. In general, the reactions of survivors seem to fall into several categories. First, a survivor may ignore the symptoms of abusing because it is too painful for him or her to recognize them.

> I spent 17 years being abused at the hands of my father. When I left home to get married, I couldn't wait to be away from it. I later put myself through college and started teaching. I had a little girl in my class who frequently came in with bruises. She always had some

plausible explanation and I believed her. I wouldn't let myself consider the alternatives. It brought up too many memories. Now, I realize that I did that little child a real disservice. When she moved to the next grade, her teacher reported the bruises and it was found that she was being abused by her father. Déjà vu. For a time I had a really hard time thinking about it, mixed with my own guilt. I finally realized that I had to face my own abuse if I wanted to be there for my students.

Other survivors think they must be slightly paranoid when they believe a child is being abused.

Quite a few of my colleagues knew I had been sexually abused as a child. I had actually told some of them when I was in therapy. When I began to have suspicions about Suzie, I felt like some of them thought it was my imagination. Because I had been abused, I read abuse into everything. I wondered about myself too for a while. But another teacher convinced me that it was not just paranoia. Suzie had some real symptoms of abuse.

Educators from abusive background might want to consider the importance of understanding their own reactions to their abuse in order to help children. They owe it to themselves as well as the children they serve. There are many excellent books available today and competent therapists skilled in working with past trauma issues. To find such therapists, call a local agency that deals with child abuse and neglect (the child protection agency, a rape crisis center, a family service agency) and ask for resources for adult survivors. The Internet may also be a source of discovering written materials.

For educators who were never abused, the reality of maltreatment in a child's life may be so far out of their frame of reference that it does not occur to them. Because you would not sexually molest your child or beat him or her, it is hard to imagine how another adult would do such a thing to someone he or she loved. But we all know that abuse does exist and by recognizing the symptoms, we can be more available to the children in our care.

Teacher's Checklist for Recognizing Neglect

Does the child:

— come to school in soiled clothing, significantly too small or too large for them and often in need of repair?

—inadequately dressed for the weather?

—always seem to be hungry, hoarding, or stealing food but coming to school with little of their own?

—appear listless and tired, due to little energy or no routine or structure about bedtimes?

— often report caring for younger siblings when the child caretaker may be only 5, 6, 7, or 8 years old?

— demonstrate poor hygiene, smell of urine or feces, or have very bad breath or dirty or decaying teeth?

— seem emaciated or have distended stomachs indicative of malnutrition?

—have unattended medical or dental problems such as infected sores or badly decayed or abscessed teeth?

—have lice?

— exhibit stealing, vandalism, or other delinquent behaviors?

—have frequent school absences or tardiness?

—have poor peer relationships, perhaps because of hygienic problems or a depressed, negative attitude?

—appear withdrawn?

— crave attention, even eliciting negative responses to accomplish it?

—demonstrate destructive or pugnacious behavior, showing no apparent guilt over his or her acts?

—have difficulty processing multistatement commands?

— exhibit low self-esteem?

—have a diagnosis of conduct disorder or act oppositionally defiant?

—have difficulty coping or problem solving?

—exhibit learning disabilities?

—have lower overall intelligence (often due to lack of stimulation) with no apparent organic cause?

—have difficulty with language comprehension and expression?

—have a variety of academic problems?

Remember that these factors are not always indicative of neglect. Look for clusters of symptoms, but remember that these symptoms may also point to a variety of other problems?

Teacher's Checklist for Recognizing Physical Abuse

Does the child have:

- extensive bruises, especially in areas of the body that are not normally vulnerable? The bruises may be of different colors indicating various stages of healing.
- frequent bruises around the head or face, the abdomen or midway between the wrist and elbow? Although bruises to the knees, legs, and elbows frequently occur in normal falls, the above areas are less likely to occur that way and should be investigated.
- bruises in specific shapes such as handprints or hanger marks?
- marks that indicate hard blows from an object such as an electrical cord or other whip-like object that makes a burn around the body?
- bruises on multiple parts of the body indicating blows from different directions?
- unexplained abdominal bleeding (could be caused by internal bleeding) which might be observed as discoloration under the skin or blood-filled lumps?
- extreme sensitivity to pain or complaints of soreness and stiffness or awkward movements as if caused by pain?
- bald spots from severe hair pulling?
- adult sized human bite marks?
- burns, especially from object such as cigarettes, irons, and other objects?
- injuries for which the explanation given is inadequate?

Behaviorally, does the child:

- demonstrate an aggressive, pugnacious, or defiant attitude?
- cower or demonstrate fear of adults?
- act out aggressive or disruptive behavior?
- demonstrate destructiveness to self or others?
- come to school too early or not want to leave school—with a clear indication that he or she fears going home?
- display a fearless attitude, often taking extreme risks?
- have a reputation of being accident prone?
- cheat, steal, or lie (may be related to too high expectations at home)?
- exhibit low achievement, perhaps having difficulty converting aggressive energy into learning?
- have an inability to form good peer relationships?
- wear clothing that covers the body and that may be inappropriate in warmer

Continued

months (be aware that this may be cultural as well)?

— demonstrate regression, or exhibit less mature behavior?

— dislike or shrink from physical contact (may not tolerate physical praise such as a pat on the back)?

Remember that all these symptoms do not always mean physical abuse. Look for clusters, cultural explanations, and organic causes as well.

Teacher's Checklist for Recognizing Sexual Abuse

Does the child:

—have frequent urinary tract infections?

—have difficulty in walking or sitting?

—complain of or exhibit genital/anal itching, rashes, pain, swelling, or burning?

—complain of genital/anal bruising or bleeding?

—have frequent yeast infections?

—complain of pain in urination?

—complain of excessive bathing in the genital area?

—frequently vomit without organic cause?

—have excessive sore throats (may be indicative of gonorrhea)?

—excessively masturbate?

—complain of other symptoms of venereal disease such as vaginal or penile pain or discharge, genital or oral sores, genital warts?

—become pregnant at a young age?

—have frequent psychosomatic illnesses?

The above symptoms might not be observable in the classroom, but may come from reports by the abused child or peers. Behaviorally, children may exhibit:

—exceptional secrecy?

—more sexual knowledge than is appropriate for the child's age (especially in younger children)?

—in-depth sexual play with peers (in younger children, different from the normal "playing doctor" form of exploration)?

—compliance or withdrawal?

—overt aggression?

—an inordinate fear of males (or females)?

—extremely seductive behavior?

—a drop in school performance or sudden nonparticipation in school activities?

—sleep problems or nightmares?

—crying without provocation?

—a sudden onset of enuresis (wetting pants or bed) or soiling?

—sudden phobic behavior?

—feelings of little self-worth, talk of being damaged?

—a much older and more worldly appearance than peers?

Continued

—suicide attempts or ideas of wanting to kill self?

—desire to run away from home excessively?

—extreme cruelty to animals (especially those that would normally be pets)?

—setting fires and enjoying watching them burn?

—an eating disorder?

—self mutilation (cutting, scratching to draw blood)?

All of these symptoms do not always mean sexual abuse although the final four are very strongly correlated with this type of maltreatment. Look for clusters.

What Factors Put Children at Risk for Abuse and Neglect?

Child maltreatment does not happen in a vacuum. There are many factors that can contribute to the fact that a child is abused. A few of these are worth special mention and will be discussed here.

Children and Attachment

Most of us assume that the birth of a child is a joyous event. We anticipate caring for the child, nurturing it, and watching it grow. At birth and during the child's early days, we bond with it. As we care for him or her and meet this child's needs, the child begins to develop a relationship with us. This reciprocal relationship based on met needs—the child's for food, warmth, and nurturing and ours for some reciprocity, if only a facial expression that can be interpreted as a smile—is referred to as *attachment* (Hughs, 1998; Hewitt, 1999). The ability to attach sets the stage for all aspects of an individual's life. It has influence on self-esteem, autonomy, resiliency, relationships, coping skills, the ability to trust, the ability to empathize, and all aspects of a person's life (Levy and Orlans, 1998). The poorly attached child has difficulties in all of these areas.

We sometimes forget that all infants are not welcomed into the world with positive sentiments. Parents who are overwhelmed by responsibilities or who never had their own needs met in childhood may have a difficult time giving to their children. Attachment difficulties can actually be transmitted from generation to generation as poorly attached caretakers raise individuals who in turn will have difficulty attaching to their own children. Parents who do not have the emotional energy to give to their infants will often ignore them or respond only to *some* of the child's needs. Some parents, especially some idealistic teen mothers, expect that the child will be more fun and less responsibility and resent the baby's demands. They may expect "to be loved" before the baby has the capacity to show this emotion. The parent's frustration, disillusionment, or disinterest teaches the child that having his or her needs met is not a predictable event and thus he or she withdraws from the caretaker emotionally. The caretaker, expecting some type of response from the child, reacts to the infant's withdrawal by further pulling away and the results can be disastrous for this small developing person.

Hewitt (1999) identifies several patterns of attachment. These might almost be seen in a continuum based on parental behavior. The healthy relationship between parent and child fosters *secure attachment* characterized by a child who sees the parent figure as someone safe to whom he or she can return to in times of trouble and be nurtured. Hewitt estimates that about 65 percent of American children fall into this category (p. 21). Some children experience inconsistent parenting when the parent does not properly read the child's signals and adapt his or her behavior to the child's needs. For example, such a parent might overstimulate a child who needs calming or not soothe the child properly. The child of such a caretaker may develop *anxious resistant attachment*. These children may be too fearful to explore the world, yet be overly attached to a caretaker who does not meet their needs. They appear to have lower self-esteem, be less flexible, and more dependent than others with a more secure attachment.

Anxious avoidant attachment refers to a child who has been exposed to indifferent or emotionally unavailable caretakers or those who reject physical closeness with their babies. The child quickly gets the message that the parent will not "be there" for him or her and does not look to that parent for comfort. Becoming inwardly centered, this child may seek ways to dissociate or find self need-fulfilling methods. Hewitt (1999) estimates that 20 percent of American children are anxious avoidant attachment styles (22). At the far end of the continuum are children whose caretakers have been unable to respond appropriately to the child, often as a result of unresolved trauma in their own lives. Their children develop *disorganized or disoriented attachment*, characterized by changeable, inconsistent, and contradictory behaviors (Hewitt, 1999). One minute they might behave one way and the next they might behave in the opposite. They often confuse and frustrate the adults around them.

Difficulties with attachment lead to problems in later life and difficulties in our way of responding to these children. Levy and Orlans (1998) comment that

> *Compromised attachment early in life not only leads to aggression and antisocial acting out, but also has contributed to the current disorganized and overwhelmed state of our foster care system. Over the past generation, the number of children with severe attachment disorder in out-of-home placements has increased, while the number of foster parents has*

decreased. . . . large numbers of children with attachment disorder are moved aimlessly through the system, their problems increasing in severity even more (5).

Attachment has a great influence on the abuse and neglect of children. Parents who are not able to meet the basic needs of their children let alone bond with them fall under the category of neglectful. The child who is abused rather than neglected in early life might experience interrupted attachment. When we recognize that children who have disturbed or poor attachment demonstrate such behaviors as poor impulse control, clingy, needy, whiney behaviors, aggression, antisocial behaviors such as lying, stealing, and disregarding socially acceptable norms and negativity, it stands to reason why their parent's frustration would also make them candidates for physical abuse (Levy and Orlans, 1998). These are also the children that, in our classrooms, are a never-ending source of frustration. It does help, however, to recognize that it has often been the child's first negative contacts with the world that have created the individual we see before us.

Attachment also has cultural implications in that there are differences in the frequency and patterns of attachments among various cultures. For example, Asians try to minimize stress for their children, resulting in many fewer anxiously-attached children. Asians, Hispanics, and Native Americans all stress community, and therefore attachment with the parents happens with variations. Northern European children, whose culture stresses independence may tend toward more insecure attachment (Hewitt, 1999). But for each culture, the type of attachment experienced by the majority of their children will be the norm and this must be taken into consideration when assessing the child's attachment behavior.

It is difficult to separate the concept of attachment from abuse and neglect. We do know that a large number of the children coming to the attention of social services have attachment problems. This may make them difficult to reach. How does this pattern get interrupted? Certainly children with severe attachment disorder will require in-depth therapy, but some children have the ability to learn attachment through consistent, nurturing but structured behavior on the part of the adults around them. This is where the school has an important role to play. How many neglected or abused children have bonded with a special educator despite a fractured homelife? It is the child who seems the hardest to reach who may be in the most need of help.

Substance Abuse in the Home

Every year thousand of children grow up in homes where alcohol and drugs are a significant problem for their parents. Hobbs et al. (1999) point out that substance abuse can affect children even before they are born. Alcohol, when abused during pregnancy, can cause congenital malformations, impaired fetus growth, prematurity, low birth weight, and withdrawal symptoms. Fetal alcohol syndrome (FAS) or fetal alcohol effects (FAE) describe a set of conditions resulting from the abuse of alcohol during pregnancy. These conditions may include mental retardation and central nervous system disorders. Marijuana, another much used drug, may stimulate premature birth and result in withdrawal symptoms for the infant (p. 284). A variety of other street drugs may cause similar symptoms in a newborn. There has been a move, over the last decade, to define substance abuse in pregnancy as child abuse. The trend appears to be taking us in that direction.

Even if a parent does not abuse alcohol or drugs when the child is in utero, the effects of these substances on the ability of the parent to function have a significant impact on the child. For example:

> Joanne married young and had three children in quick succession. Her husband, Herbie, worked in an automotive factory and would often take an extra shift. He made good money so Joanne could not understand why he worked overtime. Perhaps he just didn't like coming home to her and the kids. That would not surprise her. Jason, Georgie, and Sam, all a year apart, were a handful and the house was so noisy. She felt tired and frustrated all the time. When her Aunt died and left her a small inheritance, Joanne was overjoyed. She begged Herbie to travel and do other "fun things" with the money. He said that it was her money and refused to use it. And furthermore, he said, he wasn't going to travel with three little kids and who would watch them if they didn't go along? Frustrated, Joanne complained to a friend. "Have you ever tried coke?" the friend asked. "It makes you feel great and you have the energy to do anything, even be alone with three kids." After a bit more encouragement, Joanne started using cocaine and discovered that she liked it. But instead of putting her energy toward the children she preferred to find new pursuits. She joined a health club, shopped for new clothes, and went to movies which she adored doing. At first she dragged the children with her. But they were a pain. Increasingly, she began leaving them home with eight-year-old Jason, making excuses to keep him out of school. When at home, she became annoyed that they were keeping her from what she wanted to do. She would often scream at them and send them to their rooms. The children began to see Mom as someone who was unavailable to them and their frustrations began to be seen in acting out behaviors that came to the attention of the school.

Joanne's addiction to cocaine affected her parenting to the point that children's protective services had to intervene. Other drugs also hamper a parent's abilities, making them ineffective caretakers. Often their children become their caretakers. Different substances can cause dulled reactions, euphoria, sleepiness, and a general lack of the ability to function and parent. In addition, drugs or alcohol left within the reach of small children can cause illness or even death.

Substances lower the parent's frustration tolerance, vigilance in childcare, and can also be used as an excuse for abusive behavior. How many abusive parents have pleaded that they never would have beaten or sexually abused their children had they not been under the influence of alcohol or drugs. With our society's tolerance for drugs, this excuse is often believed, leaving the children to be victims of further abuse. There are many factors that contribute to children being abused and neglected. Certainly substance abuse can play a large part in the equation, and though not the total problem, it is a contributor to a variety of abuses perpetrated against children.

Children Who Witness Domestic Violence

The home should be a place where children feel safe and nurtured. And yet, every year, more and more children grow up in homes where domestic violence threatens them in a variety of ways. Research indicates that children who witness violence between their parents suffer from fear, depression, delays in development, acute anxiety, and violent acting out against others (Asbury, 1999; Edleson, 1998; Barnett et al. 1997) as well as hyperactivity, defiance, and delinquency (Stephens, 1999). Children growing up in violent homes may well carry this interactional style into the next generation.

Tamica tried to block out the memories of her childhood when she heard Mama's screams and the ringing of Papa's slaps as he beat her into submission. She did remember when seventeen-year-old Abraham had tried to intervene. Papa beat him so badly that Abe had been in bed for a week. When he was better, he ran away and she had never seen him again. Tamica heard that he was in jail but she wasn't sure. She missed him and remembered how he used to hold her and tend to Mama after Papa had left the house. Now at 17 herself, Tamica had left home when she got pregnant with Emmanuel. The baby's father, Clem, had let her live with him. Clem was gone a lot but Tamica didn't care. Then one day, Abe appeared at the doorstep. He had a woman with him and said that they had no place to go. Tamica let them stay, not knowing what Clem would say when he returned. It was that first night she regretted her decision. From the next room, she heard the woman's screams as Abe smashed his fists into her. Tamica put her hands over her ears. Why didn't he stop? Didn't he remember those nights during their childhood? How could he do this? But she felt totally powerless to intervene.

For Tamica, the violence she had experienced was a recurring nightmare. Eventually she went on to abuse Emmanuel, an outcome that Edleson (1998) suggests is not uncommon for adult children who have witnessed violence. Not only are these adults more likely to physically abuse their children, but some theorists feels that they are also at higher risk to neglect them (Simolinski, 1997).

Recent research has also considered the relationship that children in violent homes have with their mothers. Usually the primary caretaker, the mother has a significant influence on the child's life. When the child sees Mom as the constant target for abuse and Mom sees the child as an onlooker to her humiliation, this vital relationship can be damaged. Stephens (1999), in her study of how battered woman view their children, found that several types of patterns emerged. Mothers tended to see their children as "adultified" in several different ways.

Typically, adultification involves inputting motives of adult complexity and (usually) malice to children out of frustration when the child literally does not have the neurological capacity for impulse control expected of them. Adultification is all the more pernicious and dangerous when the child of a conflictual marriage is viewed by one spouse as embodying the hated characteristics of the other (735).

Thus some mothers see the child as similar to her batterer with the qualities of that protagonist and therefore must share some of the blame.

Another way that children are adultified is for them to take on the role of parent to their parent (referred to as *parentification*). The mother may develop a close relationship with this child, expecting that the child will give the mother emotional support and nurturing. Sometimes the battered wife even expects protection from her vulnerable child. This premature thrust into an adult role has significant implications for the child, who often becomes withdrawn and depressed by his or her inability to meet the mother's expectations (Stephans, 1999).

A third type of adultification results from a mother who sees her child as the "bad" side of herself, projecting her own self loathing and hatred onto the child. This child can rarely please the mother and often becomes a scapegoat for the family. And finally, these women may adultify their children, often adolescents, by assuming that he or she is old enough to protect him or herself from the abuser and therefore does not need the mother's protection (Stephens, 1999).

There may be variations in the incidence of family violence from culture to culture. Segal (2000) cautions that it is also important to realize that some cultures may not report violence, even when studied. This may result from the fact that some cultures value keeping family issues firmly encased within the family. Asbury (1999) concludes that many minority women do not seek help until the abuse becomes severe and therefore may be underrepresented in statistical analyses. Although some cultures are more prone toward violence than others, the fact remains that domestic violence and its accompanying impact on children is possible in any culture.

Special Needs as a Risk Factor for Abuse

Over the years researchers and practitioners alike have found that one population that is particularly vulnerable to being abused or neglected are children with special needs (see Whetsell-Mitchell, 1995). Special needs encompass a wide range of conditions related to children but usually include children who are physically disabled, developmentally delayed, learning disabled, have attention deficit disorder, or other disabilities that set them apart from their peers. Although we know that abuse and neglect are high among such children, little research has been done to document the extensiveness of this problem. Further, Kelly (1992) comments:

> *Apart from not knowing how common abuse of children with disabilities is, we know even less about how those who are abused cope with it. . . . How can safety and protection be developed for children and young people with different/limited communication. . . . (p. 165).*

There is a common misconception that children with disabilities will not be abused as frequently as other children. Some people do not feel that they are as attractive, especially to sexual abuse for example, due to their disability. Surely they would arouse sympathy rather than exploitation. Many adults just cannot fathom that anyone would abuse a disabled child, so deny that it could happen and are blind to it when it does occur. And finally, some have argued that even if such children were abused, the effects could not be discerned from all their other problems (Marchant, 1991; Hobbs et al. 1999). Such arguments are particularly disturbing when we recognize that there are still fewer services for disabled children who have been abused and much less research done on the issue, while the numbers of those abused and neglected rival or surpass their able-bodied peers.

Children with special needs, whether in community schools or residential programs, are particularly vulnerable to abuse and neglect for a variety of reasons. First, many *special needs children must rely on others—especially adults—for care, help or even companionship.* Because many need this help, *they are encouraged by those around them to be submissive and cooperative.* Further the need for the most intimate care in some children (i.e., toileting, bathing, and so on) robs them of a sense of privacy. *The concept of privacy becomes meaningless.* Often children with special needs are *segregated from their peers* either in school or by placement in institutions. There *is a stigma attached to not being in the "normal range" of mobil-*

ity, intellect, and development and those who fall outside of that range may not be given the same respect or be seen as being as reliable in their perceptions or responses. In addition, families of these children may *see them as an embarrassment and ignore them* to the point of neglect. Some special needs children in their naivete or inability to perceive and *communicate may not recognize that the treatment they are receiving is abusive.* Those with severe physical limitations may not be able to get away if threatened with abuse. And many of these children *lack the ability to communicate their distress even if they feel it* (Whetsell-Mitchell, 1995). Some, due to low self-esteem resulting from their disability, do not feel that they will be believed (Hobbs et. al. 1999).

In addition to characteristics of the child or the environment that his or her disabilities necessitate, special needs children are at risk due to the effect they may have on parents. For example:

> Queenie felt that she did okay with her four kids especially since her man had left her after the last one was born. Joe was born with a cleft palate and a had great difficulty in talking clearly. The doctors had repaired it at birth but he needed more operations and she just couldn't afford it. He made himself understood with his three older brothers so she figured that he'd be okay without the operations. As Joey grew, he became more and more difficult to handle. He was so active that sometimes Queenie just couldn't stand it. A couple of times she shut him in the closet just to get some peace but he banged on the door and screamed so much that the neighbors started pounding on the wall. And he was so destructive. He would break anything he could get his hands on. And when she asked him what he thought he was doing, he's babble at her with that gibberish that he used to talk. It was so aggravating. One day when he broke her mirror and just laughed, Queenie couldn't stand it anymore. She whacked him, and threw him in the closet with a great deal of force to make her point that he should shut up and behave. To her surprise, he didn't make a sound. When she opened the closet, he was pretending to be sleeping and that made her madder, until she finally realized that he wasn't play-acting!

Quennie's severe abuse of her disabled son who was later found to also have Attention Deficit Hyperactivity Disorder (ADHD), resulted in a concussion for which he had to be hospitalized. The resulting investigation culminated in the placement of the child in foster care. For parents like Queenie, who was already overstressed and whose parenting skills were minimal at best, a child with special needs may serve to tip the delicate balance in her ability to cope, resulting in abuse. For overwhelmed parents who feel that they are already out of control, the inability to control or normalize a child with disabilities may be more than they can handle.

It is not only discipline that sometimes is beyond these parents. They may feel inadequate when they cannot comfort a crying disabled child or when they realize that he or she is not like his or her peers. These feelings of inadequacy may get taken out on the children. Parenting a disabled child is not an easy task. Many need constant physical or emotional energy. For example;.

> As Cleo got older it seemed like it was harder and harder to care for her. She had to be lifted out of bed and into her wheelchair. Her catheter had to be changed constantly. If it got too full, she would try to do it herself. Invariably, she would spill it all over everything. I felt like we were constantly bathed in urine. It seemed like everything smelled. I got so that I hated it all. I was always tired and then she would get cranky and that added to the stress. Some days I wondered how I could continue.

This young, overwhelmed mother called the crisis hotline before she abused her daughter, but her feelings echo those of many parents of disabled children. Parents who are at the end of their patience may neglect the needs of their offspring.

Some parents, in their misguided attempts to shield children from an unaccepting world, jeopardize their health.

> Mrs. Wichenski was devoted to her son, Max, who was born with cerebral palsy. She saw her life as dedicated to his care. When her husband complained and finally left her she decided that it was "God's will" so that she would have more time for Max. Max went to a special school where he was learning to talk and to use a letter board to communicate. But as Max got older, he began to resent the intensity with which his mother cared for him. School had taught him that he could have more independence and he enjoyed that feeling. But when Max began to resist Mrs. Wichenski's ministrations, she became convinced that it was the school's fault. She removed him from school and felt that she could do better with him at home. At home, she took away his letter board and encouraged him to once again become compliant. When a nurse visited a few months later, Max's condition had so deteriorated that she felt that the child was a victim of mother's unknowing abuse.

Depriving children of necessary treatments or of therapeutic devices can also be seen as abusive. Some parents do not feel that their children need these devices and some lack the initiative or motivation to supply them.

Despite the dearth of literature on the subject, children with disabilities who are abused suffer just like any other child. It is equally important that we recognize their symptoms and not confuse them with the myriad of other problems that they might have.

The Impact of Abuse on Children and Multiple Victimization

If someone were to assault us in the street, we would probably be incensed. We would most likely call the police and wonder "why me?" We have learned that this type of thing is not supposed to happen to us and therefore we are angry when it does. Ronnie Janoff-Bulman, in her excellent book, *Shattered Assumptions* (1992), explains that most of us grow up with three assumptions. From our early years each of us learns that the world is meaningful, the world is benevolent, and I am a person of worth. We go to great lengths to protect these illusions once we believe in them. We come into the world expecting to be cared for, expecting to be nurtured, and expecting that our lives will meet our expectations. Trauma begins when we can no longer explain away the betrayal of these beliefs. Children whose needs are not met cease to expect them to be. Children who are constantly battered begin to expect this type of assault from life. Therefore, it is not surprising that young children who are neglected often withdraw and older children may come out of every situation fighting. It also should not surprise us that children's ability to recognize the danger signals becomes hampered. One adult survivor explained that her father's severe sexual abuse of her had robbed her, both figuratively and literally of her ability to scream. Thus, in later life, when someone attempted to rape her she did not initially perceive the danger nor was she able to physically scream when he grabbed her to rape her (Tower, 1988). For this reason, it is not uncommon for abused and neglected children to experience what is referred to as *multiple victimization* or multiple incidents of being a victim often over time (see Rossman and Rosenberg, 1998). Victims of abuse may experience more than one abuse by different abusers in a short period of time and/or be victimized later in life as well as during childhood. Roberta was a classic multiple victim:

> When I was 6, my Uncle started sexually abusing me. My father had died and my mother worked long hours. He used to spend time with me and then he started touching me. His attention was so important to me that I did not know how to stop it. He abused me until I was 10 when he moved away from the area. When I was 12, my cousin, Rufus, who was 16, used to come over to watch me when Mom went out. I figured I was too old for a baby-sitter but she thought I needed someone. When Rufus came into my room one night and started to fondle me, it almost seemed natural that it would happen again. He

told me that if I told my Mom he would tell her that it was my fault. I already thought that my Uncle's abuse must have been my fault, so I just kept quiet. In high school, I was at a party and a couple of my classmates took me outside and raped me. We were all drinking and I was sure that it was my fault as well. I started working at a factory right out of high school. This nice guy asked me out. He was a real gentleman . . . at first. Then one night we were at his house, drinking and he said he wanted to have sex with me. I said no, but he dragged me into his bedroom and raped me. I wasn't even surprised. By then it just seemed like it was my lot in life . . . to get used by any guy who wanted me!

For this survivor the fact of being abused had become so commonplace that she no longer knew that she had the right to resist. It is not uncommon for children who have been abused to be abused again and again. Do these victims ask for the abuse? Of course they do not. But the fact that they were abused once makes them more vulnerable. The abuse has often further impaired their self-esteem and robbed them of their ability to trust themselves, their perception of danger, and their confidence in their own ability to prevent another assault. The sooner the cycle of abuse can be interrupted and the victim helped to heal, the better the chance of creating a survivor rather than a multiply abused victim.

How Has the Internet Put
Children at Risk for Abuse?

In the writing of this book, I had initially included a brief section on the Internet and the potential danger to children in the previous chapter. I soon began to realize that the threats posed by Cyberspace are actually of major proportion when discussing sexual abuse, child pornography, and child prostitution. Therefore, I decided to devote an entire chapter to the Internet, discussing how it might represent a potential threat to children and some steps that educators can take to prevent this. Rather than talking about perpetrators in the next chapter on why people abuse children, I have chosen to deal with the entire cyberspace issue in one chapter.

The Lure of the Internet

Today's children have never known a time without the computer. The computer and the Internet open to all of us a new world of unlimited resources. The Internet refers to a vast network of computers, linked together through phone lines, cables, and satellites in a manner that enables them to share information with each other. Being "on-line" means being hooked up to this network and to have at one's fingertips a magnitude of web sites and the ability to converse with others through chat rooms. In many cases, children have become more adept at the use of the Internet than have their parents. But along with the games and the educational resources can come a magnitude of sites that have a negative impact on children. Since the network of computer is often referred to as *cyberspace*, the exposure to a variety of sexual stimuli and exploitation on the Internet has begun to be referred to as *cybersex*.

There are basically two ways in which children might fall victim to sexual stimulation or abuse via the Internet. First, *they might be exposed accidentally or intentionally to pornography* and second, *they might be solicited by sexual offenders* via the Internet.

Exposure to Pornography

The use of pornography has been a much-debated topic. Is there any harm in viewing sexually explicit materials? Hughes (1998) suggests that we are influenced in our debate about pornography by several myths. The first myth is that obscenity is a matter of opinion. Perhaps this may be true to some degree, but most would agree that pornography refers to ". . . graphic material that contains reccurring sexual activity and/or sexual violence that is unmistakably offensive and lacking in serious value" (p. 78). Second, many viewers of pornographic material argue that it is protected by the First Amendment. But, in reality the Supreme Court has ruled that obscenity is outside of that protection. Third, fourth, and fifth, some people believe that pornography is harmless entertainment and that it reduces dangerous impulses (p. 79) and, if legalized, would decrease sex crimes (p. 80). However, research shows (see Finkelhor, 1984) that it is far from harmless and can be correlated with more extreme forms of sexual abuse. Pornography is often part of a perpetrator's escalation toward acting upon what he or she sees by victimizing others, often children. Other myths suggest that morality is something that cannot be legislated. Rather, many feel that one can make a choice not to access pornography. But we all know that, where children are concerned, this may not be that easy. Children may choose to access pornography because they are curious or may be exposed inadvertently.

Is pornography really harmful for children? In fact, pornography influences children negatively in several ways. It *gives children distorted view of sexuality* often before they have had an opportunity to learn about healthy sexuality. And it is *often used by perpetrators to desensitize children to sexuality and groom them for being sexually abused.* Further, *this glimpse into adult sexual practices may overstimulate children to the point that they choose to act out their fantasies.* For example:

> Tony was the son of a police officer in the vice squad. Tony's father. found some of the pornographic materials that he confiscated appealing and would bring them home. Despite his wife's admonishments, the father was not careful about keeping these materials out of the way of his young son. Tony remembers hiding some of the magazines and videos in his room and viewing them when his parents were at work. Soon he began to use them to masturbate. So stimulated did he become that he eventually sexually abused a young neighborhood girl using the acts he had seen on one pornographic video. Tony's father became livid, screaming at the boy that he had come from a "good home. What was wrong with him!" Tony's

mother angrily protested that she knew the source and pointed to the pornographic magazines and tapes. For Tony, the result was treatment and eventual placement in a program for sexual offending youth.

In addition to stimulating a child beyond his or her years, exposure to pornographic material can, in some instances, *lead to sexual addiction in adulthood* (Hughes, 1998).

How might children be exposed to pornographic materials? First, children might find pornographic sites accidentally through seemingly innocent searches for other materials. Pornographic sites are often named in such a way that one might easily pull them up. One survey showed that 63 percent of the students polled unintentionally pulled up and downloaded pornography while searching for another topic (Hughes, 1998, p. 58). For example, a term as innocent as Beanie Babies to search out information on the popular stuffed toy might bring up a variety of child pornography sites that reference "babies." Sometimes the use of ".com" rather than ".org" can put a viewer into a different site than he or she intended. Many children actually pull up these sites on a school computer as well as at home.

Children may also accidentally access USENET news groups that are often used to trade illegal materials such as pornography. Through E-mail, instant messages, or chat rooms, perpetrators may offer to send young people pornography in an attempt to get a reaction and lure them into abusive situations (Hughes, 1998; Finkelhor et al. 2000; Mc Laughlin, 1998, 2000).

Some children discover how to pull up pornographic sites and pass the information on to others. When Nancy's ten year old developmentally-delayed son was openly viewing nudes in the act of sexual intercourse, she was upset. When she asked Frankie about this, he eagerly told her that he knew several other addresses for such materials. "One of the kids at school showed me!" he eagerly volunteered. For other children, the natural developmental curiosity about sexuality influences their intentional choice to access what seems to them like a forbidden gold mine.

Solicitation Via the Internet

Currently anyone—group or individual—has a right to have a Web page giving rise to a variety of pornographic sites. These sites may be accessed by children whose parents are not as vigilant as they might be or have not taken the opportunity to put a block (a mechanism that prohibits access to certain sites) on the home computer. In addition to Web sites, children can be engaged in chat room or E-mail conversations with perpetrators whose eventual goal is to meet and sexually abuse these children.

A recently published study by the National Center for Missing and Exploited Children (NCMEC) estimated that one in five children has received sexual solicitation over the Internet in the last year, and one in four was exposed to sexually explicit pictures in the last year. One in thirty three was aggressively solicited—that is when a solicitor asked to meet them , called them, or sent gifts or money to the child. Of the children solicited in any sexual manner, only about 40 percent told a parent and of those, less than 10 percent reported to an agency that might deal with the complaint (Finkelhor et al. 2000). All this would indicate that Internet solicitation has become a major problem for our children and many do not know how to appropriately respond.

What is it that gives the Internet such a potential to be used to sexually abuse children? There are several significant issues that figure into this phenomenon. First, *computers and the Internet are available to many children*. And, the *Internet is a medium that youths understand* due to their exposure to it. They feel as comfortable using on-line resources as their parents may have been in watching television as children. Since the Internet is usually used in the safety of the home, *youths feel safe, protected, and impervious to harm*. At the same time, they feel that *between themselves and the screen is a degree of seeming secrecy*. They may feel that *Mom or Dad will never find out* what goes on between the computer and themselves. The days of cloistering one's self in one's room talking furtively to a friend on the phone has been replaced by E-mailing.

What makes the Internet especially appealing to teens is that they may feel protected from the developmental inadequacies that make them feel so vulnerable with others at this age. Conversing on the *Internet requires a minimum of social skills*. The teen *need not worry about his or her appearance*. After all, when you meet someone on-line, your pimples do not show. The *Internet provides relative anonymity, which may encourage youths to take more risks than they might have outside of their homes*. It is fun, for example, to talk to a stranger on-line. And the *budding sexuality of teens makes them vulnerable to being caught up in seemingly harmless flirtations on-line*. They may even be *flattered to realize that the on-line attention they are receiving is from an adult*. And suddenly, without even being aware of it, the young person is engaged in a sexual dance that often leads to meeting and being molested by the perpetrator (Hughes, 1998).

The Internet also provides an excellent opportunity for the child molester for several reasons. Being on-line *provides the opportunities for access to children* that he or she might have had to work much harder to get without such a resource. For example, look at the experience of a pedophile who now makes use of the Internet to engage his victims.

Before I got a computer, getting to know kids took a lot of work explains Harry, a 42-year-old molester of male children. I used to go down to the malls on weekends and evenings and just hang around, looking for kids. I had to be careful that the shop clerks didn't pay too much attention to me and report me to security. I'd alternate malls, just so that my face wasn't too familiar. I liked the ones with arcades. That kids hang around there. When I found a kid that I thought might be good, I'd start a conversation with him. I like the ones who are about eight or nine and who are kind of laid back and shy. If the kids talked to me, I'd give him some money to play some games. Sometimes they backed off at that, but a lot of them didn't. When I got them playing, I'd make idle talk, just finding about more about them. I always had to be on the lookout for the arcade guys. If they knew I'd just met a kid, sometimes they would come over and hang around, like they were suspicious. It was always a pain.

If I got the kid really relaxed, I might offer to buy him something. I tried to find out who was with parents and who really needed attention. It would sometimes take me a while to get a kid to trust me and to go along with what I wanted. Sometimes I had to hang around for several weekends just getting to know a kid. And all the time, I was aware that he's seen me and could identify me if anyone found out or he got suspicious.

Now it's so much easier. I just get on-line and I can be talking to several kids at the same time. I get to know them and get an idea about how cooperative they will be before I even have to let them know who I am. I don't have to worry about security guys and if I think that a kid is too much of a risk, I just don't talk to him anymore. What a change from the old way!

The wide scope of the Internet also *allows the pedophile to meet many more children regardless of geographic location*. While Harry was once limited to the malls within a few hours of his home, he now, through cyberspace, has access to children across the country, and may victimize children in an area as far as he is willing to travel. McLaughlin (2000 b) reports arrests of perpetrators who have traveled significant distances to meet him when he posed as a young boy who they had then solicited and lured into a meeting.

In addition to the access, the *Internet provides perpetrators with anonymity*. They need not identify themselves until they are ready to meet a child. They also have the *luxury of time during which they are able to groom the child*. Being in conversation with the child exclusively *provides them with some protection from the scrutiny of adults*, unless of course, the child's parent recognizes what is happening. And finally, the Internet provides perpetrators not only with access to children, but also *puts a variety of types of pornography at their fingertips*. Pornography is used to fantasize and excite the pedophile but also as a way to desensitize children to sexuality.

Al enjoyed the wide range of pornographic sites available to him over the Internet. He downloaded some of the most stimulating pictures he had found. As he began to talk with various children through chat rooms and E-mail, he soon learned that he could

E-mail stimulating pictures to them. In this manner, he could test their reactions and even suggest that they might like to try some of the things that were pictured. He would start with less explicit pictures. If the child liked them, he would graduate them to more graphic images. It gave him an excellent tool not only to desensitize them to sex, but also to show them some of the things he hoped to do with them.

Who Abuses Children Through the Internet?

When one considers how easy it is for perpetrators to have access and abuse children through the use of the Internet, one wonders who would use this resource in such a way. Detective Jim McLaughlin of the Keene, New Hampshire Police Department has dedicated the last few years to just this type of work. He has coined the use of the Internet to gain children as *technophilia* (*pedophilia* is the sexual interest in children) (1998). From his extensive work with this type of offender, McLaughlin suggests a likely profile:

> *A 35-year-old man anxiously watches the clock on his office wall in anticipation of ending his workday. His coworkers would describe him as a person who tends to isolate himself from others. He really doesn't have a friend, just acquaintances, and these relationships are shallow at best. He has withdrawn over the years from his extended family and often turns down social invitations. He spends considerable time alone. He leaves work as soon as the clock strikes four. Without any delay he heads straight home. If waylaid in any manner, he experiences anxiety. He has a compulsion to follow through with his daily routine of leaving work at the same time and going straight home to his computer. He arrives home and doesn't even take his coat off before turning on his computer. After a few key strikes he has his modem logging on to the Internet. Around his computer is evidence of his long hours in front of the monitor. The last microwave meals he has eaten are stacked nearby. The rest of the apartment appears unlived in. The computer, which he has set up in his bedroom, is the central feature of the residence. He double clicks on the special icon he has set up as a shortcut to his favorite chat system. He selects one of his many fictional characters, deciding on this day to be a 14-year-old boy, "Donny14". He enters a chat room called "#littleboysex" and joins a cyber community of persons with similar interests. The hunt begins (McLaughlin, 1998, 1).*

McLaughlin goes on to explain that this man may or may not be married, have children, may or may not have been in the service, or have a job with children. In short, there is no adequate profile of the men (and some women) who use the Internet to set up children to abuse. Arrested for this activity have been college students, computer technicians, teachers , laborers, engineers, military personnel, truck drivers, retired people, and a variety of other representatives of various professions. The typical scenario is that he will enter into conversation with a child, sometimes posing as a peer, sometimes as an adult. Once he engages the child in conversation and even friendship, he will know a good deal about the child by having asked seemingly benign questions about him or her. The offender becomes increasingly aroused and may even masturbate while in discussion with the child. Eventually, he will introduce pornographic pictures and monitor the child's response. Some may even set up meetings with their victims for the purpose of sexually molesting them. By the time this happens, the child is usually so emotionally engaged that the offender finds an easy prey.

McLaughlin (2000) identifies four types of cybersex offenders: the *collectors* are interested in developing their collection of child pornography. They may begin by accessing pictures of children in sexual poses and positions that are already on the Internet, but will eventually make contact and trade with other offenders. The *travelers* are those who engage children on the Internet with the idea of meeting them for sexual purposes. These offenders rationalize that they are not hurting the child but rather empowering them. The *manufacturers* may also be collectors but not all collectors are manufacturers. The manufacturers will produce their own pictures of children through taking photos of children at parks, playgrounds, and beaches or will engage in sex with children on camera. The films will then be sent over the Internet. And finally, the *chatters* are not interested in pornography collection. Instead they will just talk with children on the Internet and engage them to the point that the child feels the offender is the only one he or she can trust. They may choose to escalate into phone contact, but usually do not try to meet the child (3–9).

The story of Peter presents a picture of a pedophile who used both the Internet and pornography to sexually abuse his victims.

> Peter was a 24-year-old man who had returned to college after a brief and unsatisfactory career in the Marines. He was lonely and kept to himself, preferring to spend his time on the computers in the basement of the Computer Science building. He had always had an interest in pornography and enjoyed cruising through the various sites on the Internet. When his appetite for this endeavor became too time consuming and he feared that other students would observe his addiction, Peter bought a computer for his apartment. He had lived on his own since he was a teen, when he had left his alcoholic and abusive home and fled to an uncle's. The uncle was glad to set him up in an apartment but made it clear that this was in return for sexual favors. Sex was not new to Peter. He had been sexually abused by a priest when he was ten and had vague memories of earlier sexual encounters with a female babysitter. At 18, Peter was recruited into the Marines. He hoped that it would "make a man of him" as the recruiter promised, but he was met only with taunts from the other men because of his somewhat effeminate manner. He had had a brief but discouraging relationship with a high school girl but when he was transferred, it ended.

Now he was once again on his own, but very lonely. Between his frequenting pornographic sites, Peter began to go to various chat rooms. He found that there were often children talking on-line and began to talk to several of them. One girl, who said that she was 14, was especially engaging. She sounded as if she too was lonely. They began to E-mail and posted long letters to each other. Her mother was also an alcoholic and she understood Peter's own history. He began to share love poems with her—poems that began to have extremely erotic themes. He also began to E-mail her some of his favorite pornographic pictures. She seemed to enjoy these, too. He learned where she lived, where she went to school, and the places she frequented. It was not long before they had arranged a meeting.

Peter traveled the several hours to meet this girl and carried on a sexual relationship for several months with her. They found secluded spots in the woods where he taught her about sexuality. When she became frightened of pregnancy and put pressure on him, Peter retreated. Because he had told her little of himself including where he lived, he was able to disappear from her life with relative ease. He found another victim of twelve and had a similar sexual relationship with her until she became concerned that her parents had found out. Once again, Peter disappeared. On Peter's third attempt at finding a girl on the Internet and arranging a meeting with her for sex, he found himself face to face with an undercover police officer. But, there are many Peters who are never apprehended.

Finkelhor et al. (2000) suggest that the increased incidence of on-line victimization should send a message to teachers, parents, and others who work with children. It is vital that we alert children to the dangers of this type of perpetrator and give them tools to use if and when they encounter one.

Why Do Such Perpetrators Have Access to Children?

One would think that our knowledge of abuse through the Internet would go a long way toward protecting children from this type of victimization. Yet, because this type of abuse is relatively new, parents and educators are not always as aware as they might be of the potential danger. This lack of awareness may result from the lack of education about the potential dangers.

When I attended a school-sponsored workshop on sexual solicitation over the Internet, recounted one mother, I could not believe it. Sure, I had told my children not to go with strangers or get into strange cars, but warning them about having a stranger approach them at home on the Internet—it never occurred to me!

This mother is not alone. Each year numerous parents express surprise and guilt when they learn that their child has been victimized through the Internet. In the study done by Finkelhor et al. (2000) for the Center for Missing and Exploited Children, the researchers found that 64 percent of the 1,501 youths interviewed lived with two parents in the home (p. xii). Most of the youths (61%) spent an hour or less on the Internet in a typical day and the highest percentage (40%) were on only two to four days a week (p. xiii). Many of their parents had occasionally supervised. But a high percentage of youths did not report when they were solicited or exposed to pornography. Even when they did tell their parents, only 10 percent of the parents knew how to report such crimes (p. xi).

Although this study was based on at-home use of the computer, numerous sources (see also Hughes, 1998) also discuss children being solicited at school computers. Thus, it becomes obvious that perpetrators have access to children on the Internet not only because it is a wide network of contact potentials, but also because neither children nor the adults in their lives are sufficiently well versed in how to ensure that children are safe while using this resource.

Protecting Children From Sexual Abuse Through the Internet

Making the Internet safe for children has been an ongoing battle. SafeSurf (at <http://www.safesurf.com/time.htm>) provides an historical overview of these efforts. There are several ways that children might be protected from abuse via the Internet. These can be divided into precautions, reporting, and proposed research and legislation.

Precautions for Children and Educators

Every child or teen who has access to the Internet should be made aware of some basic safety rules regarding its use. There are a variety of sources that suggest what youthful users must consider. "Guidelines for Student Safety on the Internet" provides a compilation of these suggestions from various sources. These should be reviewed with students periodically. In addition, some schools have created contracts for computer use that must be signed by students before they are allowed to access the Internet. Hughes (1998) uses the example of the Baltimore school system that insists that students follow certain written procedures (based on safety guides like the one provided here) and requires that both the student and his or her parent sign a contract saying that they have read the contract and will abide by it (see page 169–170).

In addition to contracting with students and parents, some schools use blocking tools to prevent access of unacceptable sites. There are two types of blocks: end-user and server-based. End-user blocks are installed on an individual computer and act on that computer only. Examples of this blocking tool are: Surfwatch, Net Shepherd, Cyber Snoop, CYBERsitter, Net Nanny, and Cyber

Patrol (Hughes, 1998). For the most part, these are designed for home computer use. Server-based systems are designed to be installed at the server level rather than on each computer. This allows blockage of specific material throughout the entire server network. Names often associated with this type of blocking are Net-filter, I-Gear, AME, GuardiaNet, WebSENSE, EdView, and X-Stop's Shadow (Hughes, 1998). New filter and blocking systems are constantly created and brand names are too extensive to name.

Some people complain about these blocking mechanisms, saying that they may prevent students from accessing valuable resources. For example, information about something like "Middlesex County" might be blocked due to the "sex" in the title. In addition, such bars create a false sense of security. Others argue that the precautions served by these devices outweigh the drawbacks. In general, the best course is to educate children about the Internet risks and be conscious of how they are using this resource.

It is important to recognize that children are more vulnerable to solicitation by pedophiles when they feel alone, isolated, and depressed. If they feel that they have no one to whom they can talk, they will be especially susceptible to someone who wants to talk with them on-line and appears to be especially caring. One way to combat this is to offer students opportunities for personal time and for expressing their feelings and opinions. The child who feels "heard" and cared about is less likely to need an on-line confidant.

A child who accidentally accesses harmful material or begins an ongoing conversation with an adults who may have ulterior motives, may return to the site either out of curiosity or because he or she enjoys the experience. What might be some cues for educators that a child is involved in intentionally accessing pornography or having secret conversations over the Internet?

- Be aware if a child prevents you from viewing his computer screen
- Be aware if a child is hiding disks that he or she will not allow you to see
- Be watchful when a child uses files that end in .gif and .jpg. These are picture files that might be quite innocent or could be pornography
- Be aware if the child's use of the computer takes significant time away from his or her other school work (Hughes, 1998)
- Be aware if a student begins to exhibit furtive or secretive behavior when using the Internet (<http://www.missingkids.com.>)

For classroom use, computers should be in the open and arranged so that a quick look can tell you what most of your students are doing on the computer. If you are using computers in your classroom or teaching, it is important that you make yourself "computer literate."

Reporting and Other Resources

Children might be reluctant to tell teachers or parents when they accidentally access pornography or are solicited over the Internet. In fact, Finkelhor et al.

(2000) and his colleagues found that 49 percent of the youths in their study did not tell anyone of being solicited. Only 10 percent reported the incident to an adult (p.4). Youths exposed to uninvited pornography did not tell 44 percent of the time (p. 15). If almost half of the young people are not telling about these type of experiences, how can we intervene? In addition to adequate supervision and teaching children the safety rules (as mentioned above), young users must be educated about reporting and encouraged to do so. Adults who let children know that telling them will not result in getting into trouble or curtailed use of the Internet will have a better chance of compliance. In addition, children can be taught that there are places to report this type of sexual offense. For example, the National Center for Missing and Exploited Children in conjunction with the Federal Bureau of Investigation, the U.S. Postal Service, and the U.S. Customs Service features a Cybertipline (www.missingkids.com/cybertip or call 1-800-843-5678) where anyone can file a report about any type of child exploitation via the Internet. There are also Internet sites sponsored by such organizations as Childnet International (www.chatdanger.com), Coalition for Children (www.safechild.org), SafeSurf (www.safesurf.com), and Enough is Enough (www.enough.org) that offer a variety of resources about safe Internet use for parents, educators, and children. Other safety sites will turn up a wealth of important information.

Research and Legislation

In addition to education and reporting, the report by Finkelhor et al. (2000) suggests more research in several areas and increased legislation to control Internet abuse.

What intervention strategies will really work with youth? We all recognize that youth, especially the teen years, is a time of testing limits and often becoming involved with secret endeavors just because they are secret from parents. How then can we convince young people that something that seems as benign as being on-line in the safety of one's home or school may have dangers? This is one area that is ripe for further research to determine what will provide an adequate deterrent to prevent children and teens from becoming the targets of cyberspace abuse.

In addition, Finkelhor et al. (2000) suggests that more attention be given to understanding the impact of on-line victimization on young people. We have learned about the residual effects of sexual abuse in general, but does solicitation or exposure to pornography pose threats to the psychological health of children? Research is also needed to understand the type of perpetrator who uses the Internet to solicit children for abuse. Is he or she different from the pedophiles we have studied over the years? Or is this merely the same pedophile who has found a new technological method to lure children? Answers to such questions will enable us to do a better job of protecting children in the future.

It is clear that the Internet must have more safeguards than it does. Finkelhor and his colleagues (2000) also suggest that legislation should be proposed that will further define and prohibit the type of criminal acts on the Internet that harm children. There is a great need for social planning and social policy in this area.

Using the Internet can be a very rewarding and educational experience for children. It will, therefore, be up to us as the adults in their lives to ensure that they have protection from the abuses that can come along with this useful tool.

Guidelines for Student Safety on the Internet

1. Never give identifying data such as your name, address, phone number, school name, and so on to anyone on the Internet unless you check with a parent or teacher first.
2. Never share your password with anyone, even a best friend.
3. Never tell anyone on-line where you will be or what you will be doing at a certain time without a parent or teacher's permission.
4. Never give out your picture over the Internet.
5. Choose a name that is not your own name for an E-mail address.
6. Check with a parent or teacher before you enter a chat room.
7. Never agree to meet in person anyone whom you have met on the Internet. If someone asks to meet you, tell a parent or a teacher.
8. If you receive pictures or messages that make you uncomfortable, tell an adult at home or school immediately.
9. If someone makes suggestive comments to you on the Internet stop talking to him or her immediately. Tell an adult at home or at school.
10. Never fill out a questionnaire or give a credit card number on-line without checking with a parent or teacher.
11. If you unintentionally pull up nude or obscene pictures, tell someone immediately.
12. Never open or respond to an E-mail message from someone you do not know.
13. Be open with parents or teachers about what you are accessing on the Internet.
14. Be careful when anyone offers you anything free on the Internet.
15. Do not do things on-line that you would hesitate to do in real life.

Adapted from Hughes, 1998; Monteleone, 1998; http://encarta.msn.com/schoolhouse/safety.asp; and http://www.missingkids.com.

Why Do People Abuse and Neglect Children?

Newspapers and magazines are filled with statistics attesting to the "vicious mal-treatment of children by their parents." Yet, the sensationalistic drama of these statistics distorts the picture of the distraught human being behind the abuse.

Neglectful Parents

The neglectful parent shares certain characteristics with the abusive parent such as poor self-image and role reversal with the child. In other areas, there are marked differences. While compulsive order or control may characterize the life of the abusive parent, the life of the neglectful parent is devoid of routine or consistency, and issues such as cleanliness have little importance. The over-whelming desire of neglectful parents is to have their own unmet needs met, which are tragic remnants of their own dysfunctional and often neglected child-hoods. The most obvious characteristic of these individuals is a lack of con-structive energy. They may present a face to the world that is apathetic or hostile but at home they lack the ability to parent constructively. Neglectful parents may or may not have a support system. For those who do, however, it is often a deviant subculture of other neglectful parents.

Neglectful parents have been a too-little studied group. Garbarino and Collins (1999) suggest that there are several reasons for this lack of attention by researchers. First, neglect is less dramatic than abuse and the problems less easy to identify. Our culture's failure to effectively address poverty may make people hesitant to uncover any more stones linked to this problem. And finally, there are clear and obvious interventions for abuse—stop the abuse—while neglect necessitates a very long process of helping people to relearn how to identify and meet their own needs and finally meet those of their children. It is easier to ig-nore issues for which there are not quick and measurable solutions.

The most extensive study of neglectful mothers (because most of the fathers were not available) has been the work of Norman Polansky and his colleagues, which culminated in the book, *Damaged Parents: An Anatomy of Child Neglect*, in 1981. From their studies of mothers in the rural south as well as several urban areas, they devised a typology of parental categories: the apathetic-futile; the impulse-ridden; the mentally retarded; the woman in reactive depression; and the psychotic woman. Many social workers describe working with mothers who would probably fit best into the apathetic futile category. These women . . . "appeared passive, withdrawn, and lacking in expression" (39). They were also characterized by:

- A feeling that nothing was worth doing (for example, "What's the point of changing the baby's diaper when he'll only wet it again?")
- An emotional numbness or lack of affect that may be mistaken for depression.
- Superficial relationships where the needy individual desperately clings to another
- A lack of competence in basic daily living skills compounded by fear of failure if they tried to learn these skills
- A passive expression of anger through hostile compliance
- A generally negative attitude
- A hampered ability to problem solve, making verbal accessibility to others difficult .
- A perhaps unconscious ability to make others feel as negative and depressed as they do (Polansky et al. 1981)

Consider the following example:

Mrs. Barber was the 25-year-old mother of five children: Ralphie, 6; Eddie, 3; Susan, 20 months, and Terry and Gerry, 6 months. The Barber family was reported by Ralphie's teacher who was concerned about his rotting teeth, his extremely dirty appearance, and the fact that he appeared to have a good deal of the childcare responsibility despite his age. The Barber house was in extremely poor condition with a strong urine smell and little visible evidence of food. Mrs. Barber greeted the social worker's visit at 2 PM in a torn, dirty housecoat and although she talked to the worker, she did so with an air of passive hostility. Susan was standing at the bars of a nearby crib, clad only in a soiled undershirt. When asked why the baby was not diapered, Mrs. Barber explained that she would only have to be changed. The crib sheet was torn and had been urinated on several times.

Although Mrs. Barber was apparently highly dependent upon her live-in boyfriend, their relationship consisted of watching TV and frequenting the local bar—leaving Ralphie to care for the other children. Mrs. Barber had little sense of housekeeping or childcare and no idea how to use the food she received from a community agency. Any attempts to help her cook creatively or to clean or care for her children were met with the sullen response of noncompliance. Only the threat of the children's removal eventually elicited some positive response.

Polansky and his colleagues (1981) also found that the neglectful parents they studied exhibited the following traits:

• An inability to recognize or meet their children's needs
• An attempt to escape through alcohol, drugs, or sexual promiscuity
• Frequent instances of single families
• Possible history of deviant or criminal behavior
• Isolation from the larger community and its resources
• Childlike demeanor
• A burden of physical or psychological ailments

Crittenden (1999), writing more recently about neglect, suggests that it might be better to identify categories of neglectful parents according to how they process information. She felt that there are three types of neglect: disorganized neglect, emotional neglect, and depressed neglect. The family of *disorganized neglect* is a multiproblem family that lives from crisis to crisis. Feelings determine what the behavior will be. The facts pale next to the feelings about them. Thus, the parents' response to the child is totally unpredictable. The child who makes the loudest noise or is in the most crisis gets the attention. Children learn to be demanding and dramatic. They refuse to accept delay or compromise or take time to process explanations. Polansky would call them impulse-ridden. The child of this home is all affect and a challenge to have in a classroom. In essence these children have spent their homelives having their negative behaviors rewarded by maternal attention. They expect that it will be the same at school. Thus their failure to recognize the importance of problem solving and talking about ones feelings rather than expressing them spontaneously must be taught to them. This may be quite difficult as they will return home each night to an environment that values affect, not reason.

Emotional neglect crosses socioeconomic lines and can be seen in any type of family. Their chaotic lifestyle and inability to plan has not placed them in poverty like their disorganized cousins. Instead, the neglect in these families results from the tendencies to place more importance on things than on people. These families use their heads and their cognition rather than their feelings or affect to process the information given them to relate to the world. They often live highly-structured lives and may thus escape the scrutiny of being seen as neglectful of their children. As babies, infants of these parents may have expressed displeasure at the lack of empathetic response from their caretakers.

Their displeasure, often in the form of cries or misbehavior, was punished, making them feel a need to isolate from the harmful stimuli. As the parents have little interest in caretaking, soon the children become emotionally isolated and do not reach out to others. Competence is cognitive; emotion or affect is negative. We often see these children as the achievers without recognizing that they exist in a world that has robbed them of the ability to feel.

The families of *disorganized neglect* are often those we think of when neglect comes to mind. These families who appear dull, depressed, and as if nothing is worth doing are not unlike Polansky's apathetic-futile. They have ceased to feel that either feelings or behavior makes any difference. They feel that they have no impact on any part of their lives, so why try. Because of their lack of interest in living, they often fall into poverty and isolation. Their children learn early that neither feelings nor behavior will move Mom or Dad to pay them any more attention. Thus, they too stop trying. They are difficult to reach in school as they do not believe that they can succeed, and furthermore, they do not care. In fact, the most obvious trait of these children is that they seem to care little about anything at all. But they can be helped. The following story proves this point:

> Jared was a new member of the preschool group. All that Jean, the toddler-age teacher, knew about him was that he had recently been adopted. She sought out Jared's friendly vivacious adoptive mother for some help. Since coming to preschool he had seemed withdrawn and listless. Nothing seemed to reach him. His mother was optimistic. "We knew he had a rough time at home," she told Jean. "The social worker told us that his parents gave him little attention. They were pretty depressed themselves and apparently just couldn't get it together to change. But we know that we can get through to Jared. Just give us time." The care and stimulation in his adoptive home did it's magic. By the end of the year, Jared was a different child. He was more outgoing and could express feelings openly. He was interested in books and in toys—a fact that had not been true when he first came to his adoptive home.

Not every story has the successful ending of Jared's, but these children can be taught to enjoy feelings and to learn. It is worth the extra time and effort..

Neglected children frequently come from parents whose own histories speak of generations of living in disorder, poverty, and neglect. These parents have not learned during their childhood how to parent effectively. Perhaps they have never felt that anyone outside their own little network cares for them. With Mrs. Barber, for example, the social worker's task will be a difficult one. If the decision is made to allow the children to remain in the home, it will be necessary to communicate to the mother that someone does care; that her problems will not totally overwhelm her helper and she will once again be left alone. Beyond the establishment of trust with a representative of the community, she can be put in touch with other visiting resources such as visiting nurses, day care, fuel assistance, and teaching of homemaker skills that will enhance her lifestyle. In other words, treatment of neglectful parents consists largely of "parenting the parents" so that they can learn to parent the child.

Physically Abusive Parents

Libby Carter was a neat, well-dressed young woman whose house appeared immaculate—to the few who had seen it. Libby, her husband, and two children had recently moved and she reported knowing few people. Deeper exploration of Libby's family background would have revealed that she had married young and had had an extremely difficult time in her pregnancies, especially with Tommy, her first child. As a baby, Tommy had been colicky and difficult, and Libby, an only child, had felt at a loss to know what to do. Her husband, Mike, a hard-working, conservative man, expected her to know what to do. He often brought work home and was annoyed when Tommy's crying made it difficult to concentrate. In addition, the couple never seemed to be able to make ends meet which caused a great deal of friction between them. This may not seem to be an unusual scenario in an age of unpredictable economy and increased mobility. However, Libby Carter was brought to the attention of the local protective agency because five-year-old Tommy repeatedly came to school with unexplained bruises.

Any parent will readily admit that there are times when a child becomes so exasperating that it may be difficult not to lash out in anger. Most parents, however, are able to maintain control so that they do not abuse their children or punish them excessively. Somewhere they have learned how to maintain control. Dr. Ray Helfer described physically abusive individuals as those whose experiences with their own parents have not provided adequate preparation to become parents themselves. In short, they have not learned five vital elements (Helfer, 1979).

   1. *Abusive parents have not learned appropriate ways to have their needs met.* Helfer used the scenario of the child who asks a question while the parent is on the telephone. The parent continues the conversation and the child becomes more insistent. Instead of simply answering, "I'll be with you in a minute," the parent continues to ignore the child until the request becomes a tantrum. As an adult, this translates into overreactions to have needs met.

   2. *Abusive parents have not learned the difference between feelings and actions.* If a parent consistently strikes out in anger rather than verbalizing the anger, the child learns that anger equals aggression or hitting. As an adult this individual may strike out when angry instead of recognizing the anger and treating it in a different way.

3. *Abusive parents have not learned to make decisions.* It stands to reason that if control is an issue in abusive situations, the abuser feels out of control. The feeling of being in control or not can evolve from early experiences of decision making and problem solving. Most parents give their children chances to make decisions without even thinking about it. "Would you like peanut butter and jelly or bologna in your lunchbox tomorrow?" Children whose lives are so thoroughly structured that they are not allowed to make decisions begin to feel powerless and this feeling may transfer into later life. By the same token, children who live in chaotic homes where crisis is the only motivator, may never learn how to make a conscious decision and may spend their lives never acting unless spurred on by crisis.

Helfer pointed out that for healthy development, children should be given opportunities for choices but only when appropriate to their role. For example, it is not so much, "Do you want to go to bed?" as "What animal would you like to take to bed now?" Children deprived of the chance to make appropriate decisions or those thrust into inappropriately mature roles in which they are expected to respond, are robbed of an important task along their developmental path.

4. *Abusive parents have not learned that they are responsible for their own actions and not the actions of others.* Have you ever known a child whose parent communicates in grief and bitterness that an absent spouse (perhaps too immature to handle the problems of parenting) would not have left home had it not been for the child? Or the disgruntled parent who tells the child that his or her life would have been much more exciting or successful had the child not come along when he or she did? In such cases the child begins to feel responsible for the pain others are experiencing.

At the same time, if not taught otherwise, the child may begin to deny responsibility for deeds or misdeeds. The classic response of the two- or three-year-old that "the dog did it!" becomes internalized so that as an adult the individual feels powerless and becomes convinced that whatever the offense, it was in fact caused by the action of another person.

5. *Abusive parents have not learned to delay gratification.* Children naturally want instant satisfaction of their desires. But as they are guided through their development, they come to realize that some pleasures must be delayed. Granted, we live in a world where a piece of plastic can immediately get us some of our material desires, but there are still things in life that necessitate waiting. Adults who have not learned to delay gratification want instant results—immediate obedience from their children or immediate solutions to their problems. When the act or solution does not ensue directly, the individual feels out of control and may react negatively.

Parents who have not learned these tasks in their own childhoods have difficulty teaching them to their offspring. Thus a pattern emerges; many abusive parents came from dysfunctional families themselves, often those in which they were abused. One of the keys to interrupt the cycle seems to be insight and learning these above-identified tasks in later life. Helfer contends that the learning of these tasks should be a necessary part of any treatment program.

In addition to inadequate preparation for parenting, environmental factors may play a part in the drama of abuse. Often physically abusive parents experience many of the following:

- Frequent geographic moves
- Financial stresses such as uncertain employment, changes in employment, or underemployment
- Other types of stresses such as failed relationships, extended family arguments, community isolation, or prejudice

Also at high risk are parents in situations that include

- Marriage at an early age
- Pregnancy before or shortly after marriage
- Difficult labor and delivery
- Abusive families during their own childhoods
- Marital difficulties

In short, the lives of abusive parents are characterized by a great many stressors. The parents themselves usually present a picture of

- Social isolation
- Excessive neatness
- Unrealistically high expectation of children
- Role reversal with children (i.e. the child parents the parent and often does a great many parental tasks such as housework or childcare)
- Poor control of children (especially older children)
- Great difficulty coping with crises, often to the point of feeling immobilized

Unusually high expectations are frequently seen in abusive families. Parents look to their offspring as extensions of themselves and as somehow responsible for proving that they, the parents, are worthwhile. Failure to meet these parental expectations convinces the children that they are of little worth—a feeling that, with ripple effect, creates a feeling of failure in the parents as well. Diagram 1 of the vicious cycle of physical abuse demonstrates this self-perpetuating phenomenon.

The abuse of adolescents may, in some ways, differ from the abuse of younger children. And the motivations of the parents, in turn, may differ as well. There are three types of adolescent abuse:

1. Abuse that begins in childhood and continues through adolescence.
2. Abuse that may begin in childhood, such as spankings, but intensifies in adolescence.
3. Abuse that begins in adolescence and is directly related to the problems of adolescence (Fisher, et al. 1980).

The first type of adolescent abuse is based on too high, unmet parental expectations. Because these unrealistic expectations are not being met, the parents feel that they are failures as parents. The abuse that is perpetrated against the young child up to 7 years of age may let up slightly in the otherwise quiet latency years (7–11) but be stimulated again during the turbulent teens. Thus there is a pattern of continuing, though fluctuating, abuse.

The second type of adolescent abuse is related to control. During childhood, the family accepts and uses corporal punishment, which appears to compel the child into acceptable behavior. As the child grows in stature and independence, however, this type of punishment is ineffective. At the same time, the older parent begins to feel more and more out of control of the situation. While the younger child could be subdued by threats, belittlement, or a swat or occasional spanking, the adolescent tests, to the point that the parent feels that only more severe physical means will suffice. Emotions by this time have usually reached a fever pitch and abuse is the outcome.

The third type of adolescent abuse becomes obvious in the following:

Mary had been a model child and an excellent student just as her mother before her had been. Mary's mother, from an alcoholic family, had delighted all her teachers in the small town school by overcoming her family problems and going on to college. She had forged a brilliant career and had married later in life. An only child, Mary had always been doted upon by her parents. Now in high school, her popularity was assured by her open, jovial manner. She was confident and appeared very much her own person. At the beginning of her junior year, however, teachers were surprised at the change in Mary. She became sullen, difficult, and verbally abusive to her peers and teachers alike. So concerned was the school counselor that she asked Mary's parents to come to school. Sensing a definite change in the family atmosphere, the counselor asked the family to seek counseling. The counseling eventually revealed that Mary's mother, once an outgoing, popular girl like her daughter, was feeling emotionally unsupported and worthless. Watching her daughter's beauty and sexuality wax as her own waned became too much for this insecure

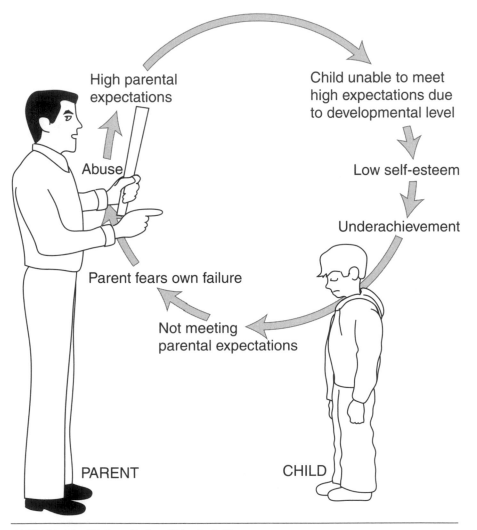

FIGURE 5.1 *Vicious Cycle of Physical Abuse*

woman. Feeling totally out of control of the situation, she struck out at Mary, who in her distorted view, appeared to cause her turmoil.

While the adolescent is blossoming into adulthood, the parent may feel stuck in a mundane existence devoid of the excitement of youth. Some parents who had their children later in life may feel that they have only retirement to look forward to. They may also see their lives being lived again through their child but feel powerless to control it.

Emotionally Abusive Parents

The parent who emotionally abuses a child may have some of the same characteristics as the physically abusive or even the neglectful parent. The most obvious trait shared by all these individuals is an extremely poor self-image that manifests itself by striking out verbally as well as sometimes physically against someone closest to him or her—in this case, the child. Even more obvious than the other types of abusers, emotionally abusive parents come from all socioeconomic levels. Frequently, they too have been victims of childhoods that have prevented them from growing emotionally. Their family experiences—from life with a skid-row alcoholic to life with a wealthy public figure—may have been as different as their personalities.

Emotionally abusive parents include not only those who belittle, criticize, or even torture the child, but also those who fail to provide any of the support or affection that promote the child's healthy development. The latter condition is sometimes referred to as emotional neglect. Parents who have had little physical touching, affection, or encouragement from their own parents may have been deprived of a great deal of the emotional satisfaction that young children need. As a result of their own childhood experiences, they may neglect very vital needs of their offspring—by not wanting the child, by overcompensating for their fear of spoiling the child, or by not having time for the child.

In other words, emotionally neglectful parents may not comprehend the importance of reassurance, encouragement, and endearments to their offspring. If they do not feel comfortable about their own strengths and accomplishments, it will be difficult for them to recognize and acknowledge those of their child.

Emotionally abusive parents who are aggressive rather than neglectful in their acts are more difficult to understand, but perhaps they are more in need of understanding. These are individuals whose lives have taught them not to expect success, affection, and attention. Often they have a bitter attitude toward the hidden disappointments of the past. They may see the child as an extension of themselves, with the deficiencies painfully obvious. Or the child may be a symbol of a hated spouse, a parent perceived to be unfair or cruel, or an unfulfilled dream. Frequently, because of their own problems, these parents have little ability to realize the profound effect their criticisms, threats, or tortures may be having on the child. Therapy to improve their view of self may be the only way to help the child.

Sexual Abusers

Although parents may still teach their children to beware of strangers, it is not the stranger who presents the greatest danger for children today. In fact, seventy to eighty-five percent (depending upon the source) of sexual abusers are known to the child, and more than one half of these are probably family members. We usually think of sexual abusers as being male. Although it is most often males who are reported, females certainly do abuse children. There may not be as many female perpetrators, however, for several reasons. First, when women abuse, they are more likely to do so within the role of the nurturer and these actions may not be perceived as abusive. For example, the male child whose mother washes his genitals long after his peers have taken on this task themselves, may not recognize when the act is becoming abusive. On the other hand, in our culture, we are not likely to condone a father washing his little girl's genital area after she is able to do so herself. And secondly, women are enculturated (taught by the culture) in ways that make them less likely to abuse. Because women have traditionally been victims over the years, they recognize what that feels like and are less prone to victimize others. Women are also more often responsible for the total child including cleaning and toileting, while traditionally Dad was given the child cleaned up and ready to be presentable. And, men are taught by the culture to prefer younger and weaker partners while women are enculturated to enjoy older and stronger partners. And finally, several studies have pointed out that men tend to sexualize affection more than their female counterparts (Finkelhor, 1984). Women who break out of the cultural pattern and abuse children are often more pathological than men.

In addition to there being fewer female abusers, women are also less likely to be reported for their abuse. Women who abuse their daughters usually bring to the relationship a pathology that infects the daughter as well. Unable to separate herself from her victim, the abusive mother often hampers her daughter from emotionally separating from her. The result is a profound confusion in the victim who knows that she will never be believed if she tells anyone (Crosson-Tower, 2002; Rosencrans, 1997). When women abuse boys, the boy's own fears get in the way of reporting. First, because our society is so caught up in what was earlier referred to as the Summer of '42 Syndrome, boys may assume that what is happening to them is not abuse. If they perceive it as abuse, they may wonder what is wrong with them or if they are homosexual.

To date, and probably because of the relatively infrequent reports of female perpetrators, there are very few typologies to describe them. Faller (1988) characterized sexually abusive women as polyincestuous (women who joined with other family members in abusive situations of more than one victim); single-parent abusers (where a single mother often used her oldest child as a surrogate partner); psychotic abusers (whose severe mental health problems gave rise to the abuse); adolescent perpetrators (who targeted children for whom they cared, usually through babysitting); and noncustodial abusers (mothers who did not have custody of children but abused them during visits) (Faller, 1987; Whetsell-Mitchell, 1995) . Matthews, Matthews, and Speltz (1989) suggested that female abusers could be broken into the categories of teacher-lover (an older female who targets adolescents); intergenerationally-predisposed (who came from families where abuse was prevalent and who probably had an abuse history themselves); and male-coerced (women who were co-abusers with males and who usually felt "forced" by these males) (Whetsell-Mitchell, 1995). Most theorists agree that the female abuser manifests more pathology than a male abuser.

> Joyce remembers that her mother was diagnosed as schizophrenic early in her childhood. In and out of mental hospitals, her mother spent much of Joyce's younger years away from home while Joyce went from aunt to aunt. Finally, it was felt that the mother's medication was stabilized and Joyce was returned to her. At first, Joyce remembers her mother as being warm and loving. At 9, having been cared for by relatives who found her a burden, Joyce so wanted her mother's attention. The mother would often crawl in bed with Joyce and the child found this comforting. Then Mama began to stroke her all over and at first it felt good. When mama began to masturbate her, Joyce did not know how to respond. Finally she just gave in to the pleasurable sensations of her body. When the mother was again hospitalized, the abuse ended only to be raised in Joyce's nightmares for many years to come.

Over the years, three typologies have endured, with variations, to describe the male who sexually abuses children. A. Nicholas Groth, well known for his work with sexual offenders, developed a way to describe male abusers that has been much copied and adapted. Groth (1982) cites several characteristics that he has seen demonstrated by these offenders. Such an offender may:

- Appear more submissive than assertive, especially in relationships. He may see himself as a victim and not in control of his life.
- Feel isolated. He may seem like a loner who does not belong in relationships with others. Even though some offenders appear to have people around them, these are usually acquaintances rather than intimates.
- Feel fearful, depressed, and doubtful of his own worth, and rejected by the outside world. A few offenders express this insecurity by overcompensating or acting like they "know it all."
- Not seem to be able to derive pleasure from or feel security in life—thus causing him to replace adults with a child who symbolizes his own immaturity (229–230).

Groth explains further that the offender's insecurities appear as either aggression and dominance in his family, or passivity and dependence. For example, Mr. Daniels and Mr. Walker, both members of the local PTA, were in direct contrast with each other.

> Dave Daniels, long-time PTA president, was outspoken, aggressive, and highly verbal. He ruled his retiring wife and two daughters with a stern hand. In fact, they all acted afraid of him. For those who had

more than just a passing acquaintance with him, Mr. Daniels' aggressiveness masked a profound sense of insecurity. Anyone who tried to get close to him found him cold and aloof. It became obvious that beyond a superficial directing relationship with adults, he could not cope with any more equal liaison. His unrelenting overstrictness with his eldest teenage daughter was eventually brought to the attention of school officials, resulting in the final disclosure of an incestuous relationship.

*****

Elmo Walker was the new husband of Thelma Walker, another assertive individual. He was as shy as his wife was outgoing, creating an interesting contrast. Through marriage, he had inherited several young sons who were unlike their mother and as retiring as their new stepfather. It was not until several years after the marriage that school officials learned that mild-mannered Mr. Walker was sexually abusing his eight-year-old stepson.

Although there is recognition in the field that sexual offenders are both male and female, the male perpetrator is more often reported and appears to be in the majority. It is, therefore, this type of offender who is most often the subject of research. Groth (1982) divides male sexual offenders into two categories: fixated and regressed. Those in the fixated category exhibit the following characteristics:

- An interest in children that started during adolescence
- Main interest in being with children rather than adults
- More likely to molest boys
- Great difficulty in relating to other adults
- Overwhelmed by the logistics of living
- Often sexually victimized at about the same age as their child victims (although some deny ever being victimized themselves)
- Any relationships they have with women are either initiated by these women or because the offender has an interest in her children
- Chaotic childhood with numerous moves, illnesses, or parental problems
- Frequently seem like children to their wives, if married
- Show little or no shame or guilt for having abused a child
- Is not that likely to abuse drugs or alcohol (99–104)

The fixated offender usually chooses boys because he sees himself in them and he mentally and emotionally lowers himself to their level. He perceives himself at the same maturity level as his victim and therefore as a peer. This makes him especially engaging for young boys who feel misunderstood by the other adults in their lives. Although this offender may choose a girl as victim, he views her in much the same way. Usually the girl victims tend to be tomboys.

In short, he tries to join with his victim, seeking the undemanding love that he feels he did not receive as a child.

A frequent misconception about a fixated offender, due to his choice of male victims, is that he is homosexual. This is not the case. Most of these offenders are intimidated by adult males rather than attracted to them while most gay men would be quite offended at being confused with child molesters. Although an occasional offender will be attracted to men as well as to boys, it is the exception rather than the rule.

The regressed offender may have developed seemingly normally as far as his sexual preference is concerned, but has found the adult lifestyle and relationships beyond his ability to cope. Most often this offender is married, has done fairly well with peers up until this point, and has carried out his role as an adult adequately. For this reason, onlookers are often surprised when the regressed offender is uncovered as a child molester. However, his current life at the time of the abuse may be wrought with stress such as unemployment, marital problems, moves, crises, sudden sexual dysfunction, new disability, or change such as retirement or aging. Unlike the fixated offender, he does not necessarily premeditate the abuse. It is more a case of something in his mind that "just happened." That is not to say that future abuses with his individual victim will not be planned. Thus the scenario is of a man who:

- Has primary interest in agemates
- Has more recently developed an interest in children because relations with them are less conflictual than with adults
- May have begun abusing impulsively
- Is under stress
- Often continues to have sexual experiences with adults as well as with children
- Is attracted to girl victims
- Is usually married or involved with the opposite sex
- Is more likely to be involved with drugs or alcohol (104–109)

The regressed offender chooses children because they offer a nonconflictual, undemanding relationship of warm, mutual dependence and love. He elevates the child to his age level, seeing her as more mature and womanly. He too is seeking the all-loving relationship that will give him a feeling of importance.

Although not every offender fits neatly into Groth's or any other categories, his typology is widely used, in various forms, and at least helps us to begin to understand the complex personality of the abuser.

Some researchers (see Carnes, 1992) feel that the sexual abuse of children falls within the category of a sexual addiction. From this view, sexual addiction to children would be seen from the same perspective as addiction to drugs or alcohol where the addict develops delusional thought process supported by a distorted belief system. He denies that he has a problem, rationalizes that the child likes the abuse or led him on, and eventually he begins to believe that he is a victim of a powerful and unconquerable urge.

The third body of research considers that in order for children to be abused, four preconditions must be met. The first of these preconditions has to do with the *motivation of the perpetrator* to abuse a child. Motivated perpetrators feel an emotional congruence or affinity for children sometimes based on either their own insecurity or their identification with the child due to their own problems in childhood. In addition, these offenders must be sexually aroused by children. Arousal may come because of their own past sexual trauma that has *imprinted* on them an idea that adults and children can be sexual together. Our culture, and the availability of child pornography and the suggestive use of children in advertising stimulated this offender who may then feel aroused. But in order to complete the motivation of the perpetrator, his normal sexual outlets are usually blocked. For example, he may not feel that he can attract women, or he has marital problems, or he is afraid of women. By the same token, he does not see himself as a homosexual interested in other adult males (Finkelhor, 1984).

The second precondition involves the *lack of internal inhibitors*. An internal inhibitor is like a voice inside our head saying, "That's not okay to do!" Alcohol or drugs, an impulse disorder, or an experience of sexual abuse in childhood that makes it seem normal, all have the ability to impede the internal inhibitors for the sexual offender. Thus he rationalizes that what he is about to do—sexually abuse a child—is all right to do. These first preconditions involve the personality and makeup of the offender, but the third and fourth precondition suggest ways in which we can intervene so that a child is not abused. The third precondition is that, in order for abuse to occur, there must be an *absence of external inhibitors*. External inhibitors refer to those factors that prevent an offender from having an opportunity to abuse. For example, when a child is closely supervised or has a good relationship with the adults around him or her, that child is less vulnerable. Children who are protected by their parents from social isolation, unusual sleeping arrangements, or unsupervised contacts with unknown adults are also less likely to be abused (Finkelhor, 1984).

And finally, in order for abuse to happen, the offender must *overcome the child's resistance*. Children who are uneducated about the dangers of abuse or who have poor self-esteem are much better targets for abusers (Finkelhor, 1984). Thus, we are learning the importance of sexual abuse prevention and enhancing the self-esteem of our children.

It is important to note that no one—sexual abuser, male or female— fits neatly into a framework that explains fully his or her behavior. But, understanding the various attempts that have been made in the field to explain the behavior of abusers may help us to get some insight into their motivations.

There is less known about female offenders. Some researchers believe that many women who sexually abuse are either convinced or coerced by the men in their lives. But some women do abuse on their own. Researchers who compare male and female abusers generally agree that their pathology is greater than their male counterparts (Crosson, 2002).

Parents of Sexually Abused Children

What part does the abuser play in the child's life? In fact, about 75–85 percent of all sexual abusers (depending upon the source used) are known to the child and a high percentage of these are parents or parent surrogates. Why would a parent abuse a child in this manner? Hopefully, it is obvious that the abuse of a child is caused by the parent's own pathology. The parent may deny the abuse or rationalize that it is part of parenting or that he or she is teaching the child about the body. Often the abusing parent is the nurturer which further confuses the child who learns to equate affection with sexuality.

But how does the nonabusive parent fit into this domestic puzzle? If the mother is the abuser, research has discovered that the father, if not an abuser along with her, is usually absent either literally or emotionally. But what of the mother in father-child abuse? She is a figure who has puzzled those who are interested in children. Does the mother know the abuse is happening? There has been much debate on this question. Some mothers know on some level and are afraid to intervene, sometimes because they too have been abused by the father. Other mothers deny any suspicions they might have, either because they were abused as children and do not want to believe that it could happen again or because abuse is so far out of their frame of reference that it is not believable to them. Deidre describes this feeling well.

> Donald was what everyone considered a real catch. People saw him as successful and outgoing. I never realized until much later that it was a facade to cover up incredible feelings of insecurity. I was doing well in my career. I had just become the nursing supervisor and I thought that Donald was really proud of me. He was out of work again, but he always convinced me that there was a reason, like the company was downsizing, and I believed him. I was so busy at work and worked long hours. Gina was little, only 3 years old, and we decided that Donald would stay home and watch her. I had a great salary and we could live on that for a while. Donald became Mr. Mom and was the talk of the neighborhood. Everyone thought he was God's gift to a working mother. He seemed so good with the baby. When Gina developed this funny rash on her genitals, I was puzzled. I mentioned it to a colleague and we talked about what it could be. It turned out to be a yeast infection. And then she started getting urinary tract infections. I took her to the pediatrician and he finally told me that he was concerned. She had these little tears around her rectum, too. He told me that the symptoms were all suspicious of sexual abuse. No! I insisted. She hasn't been out of our sight. She is always with Donald or me. Even when

it became more and more apparent that Donald was the one abusing
her, I couldn't believe it! He was her father! How could he do that to
her? And to me?

Eventually Diedre realized that, for Gina's sake, she could no longer deny what
was happening. But it is often difficult for mothers like Diedre to accept what
appears to be happening. Current thinking in the field of child protection is not
to be as concerned with whether or not Mom knew the abuse was taking place,
but rather, how does she protect the child or intervene when she learns that it
is happening.

The nonabusing mother often has other characteristics. She may

- Participate in role reversal with her daughter so that the girl takes much
  of the responsibility that should belong to the mother
- Satisfy the basic needs of the children, but not participate that much in the
  nurturing
- Be seen by older daughters as having failed the father
- Have a strained or unsuccessful relationship with her daughter
- Be absent a good deal especially at prime nurturing times such as bedtime
  (her absence may take the form of long work hours, illness, or being in-
  volved with activities outside the home)
- Have a poor self-image
- Fail to set limits at home
- Have unreasonable expectations (sometimes called magical expectations)
  of her husband and children
- Have been abused as a child herself
- Be very dependent on her husband financially or emotionally
- Not be that interested or enjoyably involved in a sexual relationship with
  her husband (Johnson, 1992; Sgroi, 1982)

Like her husband, this mother may be either dominant or dependent. In
incestuous families, no matter if the abuser is the father or mother, the families
tend to demonstrate other recognizable characteristics. They often:

- Are overly secretive in almost all of their activities.
- Demonstrate what appears to be a closed nature of interaction and lack of
  communication with the outside world and even within the family. Siblings do not share confidences and it is not unusual for one not to know
  that the other is being abused.
- Are overly possessive or restrictive with the abused child (usually a daughter and especially on the father's part).
- Demonstrate blurred generational boundaries (generations do not have
  clear cut roles—parents and children seem more like peers in their behavior).
- Live in an atmosphere where siblings show marked jealousy toward the
  child who is favored (and abused).

- Have a family where the marital pair once had magical expectations—that is, each spouse expected the other to meet all his or her needs. When this did not happen, each may have looked to the children to fulfill needs. Now disillusioned, the parents live in a state of ever searching to have their needs met.
- Live in an environment where the abuser and abused have a good deal of time to be alone (e.g., mother works nights, or abuser is for some reason home alone with children) (Sgroi, 1982; Crosson-Tower, 1999).

The Bryants were a family that would be recognizable given the above profiles:

> Debra grew up the youngest of four girls. She was sexually abused by an uncle who lived with her family for a year and then disappeared. She never told anyone. She met Harry Bryant at a party. After a few drinks they began talking about their childhoods. Harry's father was an alcoholic and all of the children were petrified of him. Harry suspected that he may have abused a sister, but said that he couldn't really remember that much. To Debra, overconfident Harry seemed like a "knight in shining armor." Harry loved the way she seemed to listen to him and care about him. When Debra found herself pregnant and they married several months later, each was convinced that they had found the perfect mate, one quite unlike childhood memories.
>
> Early married life was far from idyllic for the couple. Harry changed jobs several times. His arrogant know-it-all attitude was not popular with employers. Debra had a difficult pregnancy, couldn't work, and was frightened that Harry would not support them. The birth of Joshua compounded their troubles when he was born with multiple medical problems. Harry blamed Debra for not taking better care of herself in pregnancy, and Debra blamed Harry for making her constantly worry about finances. Despite these differences and the disillusionment each was feeling, the couple had two more children, both daughters, in quick succession. Now Debra and Harry rarely communicated. Much of Debra's time was spent taking Joshua to various medical and therapy appointments. Harry became the caretaker for the two girls. As the years passed, it was almost as though there were two families—Harry and his girls in one and Debra and Joshua in the other. Harry continued to bounce from job to job. In fact, he preferred being out of work and home with "his girls." the neighbors who saw little of the family did realize that Harry cared for the girls and thought he must be a "truly caring man." It was much to everyone's surprise and shock that the youngest girl's first grade teacher learned that she was being sexually abused by her father. An investigation later uncovered that the older girl was also Harry's victim.

So isolated was the Bryant family that no one suspected the abuse. In later years, both daughters would tell a therapist that they had no idea that the other was being abused. And paradoxically, Debra, when she learned of the abuse, said that Harry had never gotten over having a disabled son. He was "just needing her," she said. The girls, with whom she had never gotten on, must have made it all up to get more attention from her, so resentful were they of the attention she had had to give to Joshua. Such a case demonstrates the distorted thinking often present in incestuous families.

It is always a danger when discussing the causes of behavior to use frameworks that appear rigid. Being human, people do not fit neatly into any framework. It is important to note therefore, that the knowledge we have about abusers and their families has been gleaned from research but it is still important to recognize that not every abuser or family is the same. One may see the above characteristics, but there will be variations as well. Mentioning what abusers and families *might* look like is designed only to heighten our awareness.

Abusers Outside the Home

Although the purpose of discussing abusers in a book for educators is to help you to deal with the parents of the children you see everyday, many of us wonder about the abuser who is not a parent. By definition, the only abuser who fits into this category is the one who sexually abuses children who are not his or her own. Although I have used both the masculine and feminine pronoun here, it is males who are more widely reported as sexual abusers. Earlier we discussed the fact that this is not to say that women do not abuse. On the contrary, woman may also be abusers both as incestuous parents and as relatives, friends, and surrogate caretakers. But other than in surrogate childcare situations (babysitters or daycare providers) women are less likely to be found abusing outside the home.

The abuser who targets children outside the home often does so in the context of relationships. We often hear of coaches, youth group leaders, and even priests and ministers who use their contact with children to gain an opportunity to abuse them. They might fit Groth's profile of either fixated or regressed offender, be sexual addicts, or fit Finkelhor's precondition model to explain their behavior. In other words, despite what was assumed at one time, experts now believe that there is nothing about the abuse of a child outside the home that differentiates the offender from an incestuous abuser.

When Children Sexually Abuse

Increasingly we are hearing reports of children abusing other children sexually. Many of these children have themselves been abused and their acting out sexually represents their attempt to make sense of what has happened to them. Johnson and Feldmeth (1993) suggest that juvenile abusers fit into one of several categories. The *sexually reactive child* is one who has been sexually abused or exposed to some type of sexuality (e.g., sexually explicit videos or witnessing sexual behaviors) and as a result " . . . their focus on sexuality is out of balance in relation to their peers" (44). Because these children have been stimulated beyond their years they do not know how to integrate this information. They feel shame, intense guilt, and anxiety about sexuality, and in their attempt to understand they act out sexually, either as an individual activity through masturbation or exposing themselves, or against other children. However, they do not coerce, force, or threaten their victims. The children whom they target are more likely to be peers and the interaction could be confused with normal sexuality except that the acting out is far more than what would be expected of children at that age. For example, a six year old who observes another child is quite different from the six year old who attempts oral genital contact with a younger child. In the latter situation the child is reacting to something that was seen or was done to him or her.

There are some children who engage in *extensive mutual sexual behaviors.* They have a ". . . more focused and pervasive sexual behavior pattern" than sexually reactive children (47). They use a full range of adult sexual behaviors from oral-genital activities to anal and vaginal intercourse. Their partners are often similar ages although they may use force as well as persuasion to ensure cooperation. They are also intent upon keeping their activities a secret. The most striking difference in this group, however, is that they do not demonstrate the spontaneity of "normal" children in sex exploration nor do they feel the guilt of sexually reactive children. Instead they are very matter-of-fact in their sexuality toward other children. This attitude appears to stem from the fact that their homes are highly chaotic and sexually charged. For these children, the sexual behavior serves as a coping mechanism—a connection in a world that they see as dangerous, abusive, and unfriendly (Johnson and Feldmeth, 1993).

The last group of children identified by Johnson and Feldmeth (1993) refers to those *who sexually molest other children.* Again, they use a full range of adult behaviors and these intensify in intrusiveness and severity over time. Their behavior is impulsive, but also compulsive and aggressive in nature. There is rage, loneliness, and fear underlying their abuse of others. They can physically harm their victims and seem to feel no empathy toward them. Even when caught in the act, they will usually deny responsibility or rationalize their reasons for abusing. Rarely described by teachers as a "normal kid," these small offenders often seem frightening as their affect is so devoid of feeling and guilt while anger seethes shallowly below the surface (Johnson and Feldmeth, 1993).

Every discussion of abuse by other children brings to light the question "what is the difference between abuse and healthy sexual exploration?" The latter usually occurs between agemates and is considered a normal sideline of sexual awakening. It is also mutually agreeable to both children and reflects their normal sexual knowledge and development. Abuse, on the other hand, more often involves children of different ages, or different levels of power, knowledge, and resources. In addition, this type of sexual interaction is more often than not coercive so that the older or more powerful abuser compels, threatens or tricks the more vulnerable child into being abused (Gil and Johnson, 1993; Crosson-Tower, 1999). Sometimes, abuse may begin as exploration and curiosity, but when one child chooses to cease the activity, the other begins to apply pressure often to the point of coercion or threat. Then the situation becomes abusive.

Abuse of a sibling may add an extra set of dynamics to those of exploration-turned-abuse or repetition of past abuse. Some authors (Caffaro and Conn-Caffaro, 1999: Weihe, 1997; Weihe and Herring, 1991) suggest that some older siblings have a need to dominate their younger siblings to demonstrate their own power. These older siblings may lack the feeling of power in the rest of their lives or see the younger sibling as someone against whom they need to take revenge, be it for some slight or for just being born and usurping parental attention. That sex becomes the vehicle for power or humiliation usually means that sexuality has played a negative part in the older siblings life (e.g., his or her own abuse) (see also Worling, 1995; Laviola, 1992).

When we think of young abusers, we usually assume that they are teens. Although many younger children abuse, developmentalists suggest that adolescence in and of itself is a difficult time for children sexually. During these years, teens are at the height of their sexual curiosity. Risk and the socially unacceptable is something they often enjoy in their attempt to re-form their own set of values. Many are experiencing too much conflict in their activities and may have difficulties with peers. Add to this equation a history of sexual abuse and you may have an adolescent who acts out his or her conflicts on siblings or peers. How does one know when a teen is vulnerable to become an abuser? Some experts suggest that a healthy balance between an interest in children and an interest in peer relationships and activities should be a key sign of health. It is often the isolated teen who may seem to turn to children rather than chance relationships with peers who can get into difficulty.

Acquaintance Rape.   The sexual assault of a teen by a peer, often a date—is another phenomena we hear of more and more today (see Warshaw, 1994). Although the pressure to have sex while dating is nothing new, the increased violence of today has led more young men to force their partners into having sexual intercourse. Although boys are not thought of as being physically forced into having sexual relations, they too are vulnerable to being cajoled or forced into having intercourse by a variety of verbal blackmail statements. A somewhat dated, but unfortunately still viable study (see Adams and Fay, 1984) asked teens when it was "okay for a boy to hold a girl down and force her to have sexual intercourse." Respondents were asked to consider if rape was justified (although it was not referred to by name) in several types of instances. The percentage of males and females who answered "NO" were recorded.

Granted, the percentages of teens who do not feel that these circumstances justified rape are high, but they are not high enough. Consider that 54 percent of boys who perceived that a girl had "led him on" felt that rape was justified and 51 percent percent of boys and 49 percent of the girls felt that rape was acceptable if the boy had "gotten so excited that he couldn't stop." Since

	Percent Answering "NO"	
	F	M
He spent a lot of money on her.	88%	61%
He is so turned on that he can't stop.	79%	64%
She had intercourse with other boys.	82%	61%
She is stoned or drunk.	82%	61%
She says that she is going to have sex with him, then changes her mind.	69%	46%
They have dated a long time.	68%	57%
She has led him on.	73%	46%
She gets him sexually excited.	58%	49%

Adapted from Adams and Fay, 1984, p. 14.

this study was completed over fifteen years ago, one would hope that the statistics would be different if such a survey were taken today. But the increase in violence and the decrease in sanctions against such violence casts serious doubts on the outcome were such a study to be repeated.

It is important to realize that the abuser in date rape usually does not fit the profiles of other child sexual offenders. Granted, acquaintance rape can result from acting out prior victimization, but it is also a product of the values of our society. Adolescents today are trying to form values in an era of confused morals, an era in which they are surrounded by media messages that imply that violence is the method by which one gets what one wants. These half-children/half-adults are also exploring their own sexuality at a time when society's views on sexuality are conflicting. The teacher's role is to open the channels of communication to enable adolescents to undertake this exploration with guidance.

What About Abuse by Another Educator?

When you are in a profession, especially one that gives you responsibility and pride, it is difficult to imagine that a colleague would use his or her position to harm rather than help children. But every year some teachers and other educators are accused and some convicted of abusing children, usually sexually (see Rubin and Biggs, 1998). Although some child protection agencies have been called in to investigate reports of physical abuse, it is usually sexual abuse involving school personnel that comes to their attention. Physical abuse by definition is committed by a caretaker. Physical harm committed by a noncaretaker is usually seen as assault. Many states ban the use of physical punishment of children. In those that do not ban physical punishment, it becomes a judgment call as to when the discipline becomes too severe. For example, one teacher was reported to a child protection agency because she ". . . yelled at the children constantly and hit them with rulers when they would not respond." Although she was initially suspended by the principal, she was eventually reinstated and continues to teach.

There may be fewer questions when a child is sexually abused, but not always. For example, the girls in one high school complained of suggestive comments, gestures, and looks from one male teacher. Some of the female students felt that he stood uncomfortably close to them and questioned if he had accidentally brushed against their breasts. The teacher protested that they were just too sensitive. Rather than calling it abusive behavior, the school decided to pass a sexual harassment policy and suggested that anyone who was concerned could voice his or her concerns claiming sexual harassment. Whether by coincidence or reaction, the male teacher took a job in another school soon after the policy was enacted.

Some sexual abuse is much less obvious but more problematic. One guidance counselor recounted her experiences with a teacher at her school.

> We all thought that Jerry was a little strange, quiet and sort of shy, but he was a nice enough guy. He taught music and the sounds he could get from some of those kid's voices or from the band were amazing. The kids liked him. In fact, I think he preferred being with them to being with his colleagues, and we were a close group. There was one male student, Kirk, who played a number of instruments. He was always in Jerry's office practicing or just talking. Jerry took him to the symphony in the city a couple of times. It was a small town and no one thought much about the special attention Jerry gave Kirk. Then rumors started being passed around. They said that Jerry and Kirk "had a thing." At first we passed them off as rumors, until Kirk's father got wind of them. He was a lawyer in town, a real macho guy. He had little time for Kirk, but when he thought someone else did, he was right there. It finally came out that Jerry had been molesting Kirk for several years. Then several other boys came forward and said that he had done things to them. We were all in shock. We couldn't believe that one of our colleagues would be guilty of sexual abuse!

It is common for us as educators not to want to believe that one of our own would be abusing a child. First, it is out of our frame of reference. If we would not abuse, we assume that our colleagues could not do such a thing either. It is easier often to believe a colleague than it is to believe a child. We often assume that the child is making it up just to get even or to get attention.

This brings up the question, "How often do children make up stories about educators abusing them?" We have all heard about situation where children have claimed abuse and later admitted that they were lying. Granted it can happen, but not as often as we would suppose. And even if a child does eventually deny his or her allegations that does not mean that they were not true. Children often feel compelled to recant their stories by either the perpetrator or those around them who believe the perpetrator and not them.

But let us say for the sake of argument that your colleague is accused of abuse and did not do it. What should he or she do? First, the natural response is to be reactive, often trying to hide what is happening to the last possible moment. One might do better to be proactive. Were I in this situation, I would want to know that the child protection investigator was a skilled, experienced investigator who would competently and objectively interview the child, me, and anyone else involved in the case. If I felt that a lawyer would better protect my rights, I would make sure that the person was familiar with child welfare law and had had such cases in the past. Competent professionals are trained to see through false accusations, and I would do everything in my power to enable this to happen.

But what if we suspect that a colleague or fellow educator *is* abusing a student, how many of us would know what to do? Larry Lindquist had just such a problem.

> I began to suspect that this female teacher was a bit too friendly with some of her male students. She was really flirtatious with the middle school boys. She acted almost like a teenager herself. Finally I caught her in the bleachers and I had some real questions about what they were doing. She had her hand on his leg and the kid looked scared silly. I finally said "Pam, could I see you a minute." I told her that I had some real concerns. She broke down and said that this kid had been after her. That was too much. I knew this kid and there was no way! I told her that either she would tell the principal and get some help or I would tell him. It wasn't an easy thing to do. I had always liked her, but I felt that I owed something to the kids too.

What kind of educator would jeopardize his or her career to abuse children? It should be noted that it is not necessarily that educators are prompted to abuse children sexually, but rather people who do or might abuse children sexually are attracted to a profession where they have access to children. And, these perpetrators are no different from those we have discussed earlier. Most are insecure, have poor self-esteem, and are battling with control problems. Some are seeking a nonconflictual partner and see in the child someone who will not question them but only admire them. The child is a mirror into which they look to feel better about themselves. But for this child, the implications can be life-changing. It is important that there be intervention for the child's sake.

Whether the abuse or neglect is physical, emotional, or sexual, abusive and neglectful parents and other abusers need help. They live in a world filled with pain and frustrations with which they have never learned to cope. The first step in helping all perpetrators, be they parents or not, and in helping the children they abuse, is to see that their problems come to the attention of someone who can help them.

6

Is It Abuse or Neglect or Not?

You suspect that a child in your classroom is being abused. You know that you have the responsibility to report the abuse. Nevertheless a variety of questions may run through your mind. Was the parent just disciplining the child? Are there cultural implications? Could it just be my imagination? How much information do I need to report? These questions are answered in this chapter to enable you to feel more comfortable in your role as reporter.

Discipline versus Abuse

What is the difference between abuse and discipline? To determine this, we must consider the role of adults—especially parents—with children. It is the role of the adult in a child's life to guide him or her to grow up to be a healthy, functioning adult. To do this, there are rules that we give children to follow. Failure to follow these rules, we may feel, means that children are less likely to reach the goal of healthy adulthood. Therefore, we must find a way to discourage deviance and encourage cooperation. It is for these purposes that we use discipline.

Studies have found that effective discipline is preceded by well-defined rules and when administered is consistent, fair, and understood by the child. The goal is to deter the child from breaking the rules again, while at the same time, helping him or her to recognize alternative methods to getting his or her needs met. Discipline should be directed at the behavior that was problematic and not make the child feel that it is he or she who is "bad." For example, the wise parent might say, "That was a naughty thing to do" rather than, "You are naughty." Thus the goal of discipline is to redirect rather than to shame the child or diminish his or her self-esteem.

Defining discipline in this manner helps us to understand how it differs from abuse. While discipline is directed toward helping the child to learn through redirection, abuse is more often a response on the part of the adult without concern over the child's feelings, self-concept, or need to see another solution. For example, whenever Sam got out of hand, his father would "take the belt to him" which meant that Sam would wear the marks of his father's displeasure for days. This action made no attempt to show Sam what he had done wrong, have him think about it, or help him plan alternative solutions. Rather, it was a quick and painful way for the father to demonstrate his displeasure. The result for Sam, over the years, was a seething anger and hatred of his father. Instead, methods like a verbal reprimand, a time-out, withdrawal of desired privileges, or even standing back and allowing the child to experience the negative consequences of his or her own actions (provided safety was not a risk) might have been better teachers.

Does every parent who hits his or her child commit child abuse? Of course not. Although child development specialists have found that physical punishment is not an effective manner of discipline, some parents will still use it. How then do we separate physical punishment from abuse? Most child protection agencies distinguish abuse by identifying it as physical punishment that leaves marks. A slight slap or a whack on a well-padded bottom does not leave lasting physical marks. When a healthy child is slapped hard enough to leave a mark, the parent has hit too hard. This, in most circles, would be considered to be abuse.

Culture and Child Abuse

Earlier, we discussed the fact that many cultures use physical punishment often to the point of what we might call abuse. Many educators and others working with children have a great deal of difficulty when cultural practices appear abusive but have a cultural basis. For example:

> Hazel was born and raised in Haiti but came to the United States to attend college. During her final year as an education major, she was placed as a student teacher in an urban school in a neighborhood housing a good many immigrants. Soon after she began her placement, a young girl in the class began coming into school with badly bruised and cut knees. When the teacher questioned her, the child said that she had been naughty and her parents had made her kneel on stones for several hours as punishment. The teacher was horrified and reported this to the child protection agency. She then mentioned it to Hazel. Knowing that this child was Haitian, Hazel told the teacher that kneeling on stones was a common discipline used in Haiti. When the protective worker arrived, she confirmed Hazel's

claim saying that she had worked with other families who had used this technique. Together, the worker and Hazel talked to the family, letting them know that in the United States, such discipline would be considered abusive.

Many advocates for the rights of newly-arrived immigrant families have argued that individuals should have a right to practice their cultural values. But when these conflict with the laws of the states and country, this can be problematic. To date the argument still goes on, but laws remain the same. In these instances of culturally-based behaviors that could be seen as abusive, it is usually the practice of child protection agencies to try to educate the parents about the laws and mores of their newly-adopted land.

Because of the variations in culture and the fact that cultures have such widely different methods of bringing up their children, it is vital that the educator learn as much as possible about any of the cultural groups represented in his or her school. Books like *Developing Cultural Competence: A Guide for Working with Children and their Families* (Lynch and Hanson, 1998) or *Communicating for Cultural Competence* (Leigh, 1998) might be particularly helpful. Crosson-Tower's *Understanding Child Abuse and Neglect* (2002) offers a chapter on working with different ethnic family groups. In addition, many colleges and universities offer courses that might help the educator to develop an understanding of minority populations.

Some Tips Related to Validation and Reporting

Even after pursuing a list of symptoms, one might wonder, "Is this really abuse/neglect or just my imagination?" There is no definite answer to this question. But if one recognizes the symptoms and knows a few basics about validation, one might feel more confident in reporting.

There are some things that one should know before a case of child maltreatment ever comes up. First, one should know the child abuse reporting laws of the state in which you teach. These can most easily be obtained through the local child protection agency. Second, one should know the school reporting policy or procedure if one is available. These are the steps that should be taken when an educator suspects abuse or neglect. (This will be discussed in much more depth in Chapters 6–8.) It is also helpful to know something about the child protection agency that serves the community.

Armed with this knowledge, you find yourself faced with your first case of suspected child abuse. The good news is that you need only suspicion in most states to report child abuse and neglect. This means that it is not up to you to "be sure," but rather you need only suspect that abuse/neglect is present. But even with this in mind, your sensitivity to validation will enable you to help the child protection agency either to create a more pressing reason for opening the case, to build a stronger case for court, or to provide additional information to help the social worker to work with the family to devise the best treatment plan. If, on the other hand, the state in which you teach requires proof of your suspicions, the suggestions here will help you supply the proof.

Documentation

It is important to have as much information as possible when reporting. Documentation greatly helps. For example, every time a student comes into class with bruises, jot down the date, the type of bruises, and the child's explanation for them. Also note the contacts that you have had with parents, including their reactions to you as well as their interaction with the child. When you report, or at the time of possible court intervention, such documented, factual information will be extremely valuable.

If whatever is going on at home is impeding the child's ability to learn (which is often the case), one way to learn more facts and involve the parents initially, is to treat whatever problem the child exhibits as one that requires special assessment. According to Public Law 94-142, the teacher can request a CORE evaluation through the Special Education Department of the school. This evaluation consists of a series of tests and assessments focusing on educational needs and describing what the child can or cannot do. It usually culminates in a conference of parents and the professionals concerned with the evaluation. Since the child may also be exhibiting learning disabilities, such an evaluation can easily be justified. Closer scrutiny often allows professionals to recognize abuse, and some cases have then been handled voluntarily without court intervention.

Consulting with Other Professionals

Sometimes teachers and other staff members find consultation with other colleagues and professionals helpful in the decision to report child abuse or neglect. Although it is important to do this, be aware of the child's need for confidentiality with a difficult issue in his or her life. Thus you may want to consult those people who you feel might have pertinent information rather than bringing the child up as a topic for teacher's room chat. Have other teachers noticed the bruises or the behavior about which you are concerned? The physical education teacher or the coach, for example, may have noticed bruises as the child changed clothes for gym. If so, you will have additional support. It is also important to consult with other professionals within the school system. School nurses have the medical expertise to examine bruises, burns, and untreated medical problems. They may be the only ones who have the right (varies from state to state) to remove a child's clothing; they may also have a right to take photographs of any bruises they uncover (again, check state regulations). In addition, nurses are in an excellent position to teach the neglected child some basic rules of personal hygiene.

School psychologists are trained not only in testing, which can be helpful in detecting children's problems, but they are also schooled in human motivation, and possibly in counseling. They may not only help the child through diagnosis and counseling, but may be of help to you as a consultant. School social workers or school adjustment counselors, who are trained in counseling, are frequently the professionals most likely to act as links between the child's family and the school, perhaps even making home visits. Valuable information can be gathered by observing the family's attitude toward the child. Are the parents responsive to school intervention? Do they want to help the child or do they see the child as an unwanted responsibility?

Special education teachers also see a large percentage of child abuse and neglect victims. There is documentation (Hobbs et al. 1999; Crosson-Tower, 2002; Araji, 1997; Whetsell-Mitchell, 1995) that having special needs puts children at higher risk for abuse and neglect. By the same token, abuse and neglect can result in a variety of psychological and behavioral problems that might come to the attention of special education.

Depending upon the size, some schools may or may not have these professionals available, or their duties may be assumed by others. Any careful observer can, in fact, be of help in detecting problems of abuse. In one school, for example, a librarian who had great sensitivity to children and their needs uncovered more cases of maltreatment than any other faculty member. Another teacher told me that in their school, they always talk to the custodian. A very observant, caring man, this individual who seems to just go on about his duties observes a great deal about the children in his school. Often, in a brief interchange with a child, he will perceive that something is wrong and will often tell a teacher or a guidance counselor. Now the staff automatically checks with him if they feel that he may have had an opportunity to observe a child about whom they have some questions. "He may never have had a course in psychology," explained one teacher "but he sure knows people!" Secretarial staff, too, may see children at a variety of times and be able to make their own observations. When your school trains staff in abuse issues, it might be wise to include these individuals as well, encouraging them to come forward when they see something in a child that concerns them.

Whatever the school situation, as you attempt to validate your concerns about a child, do not be afraid to use your colleagues as valuable resources.

Analyzing Data

The next step is to analyze your data. For example, for the child who frequently comes to class with bruises, usually with seemingly plausible explanations, is there anything else about the child's behavior that fits the clues for abuse given in Chapter 2? Have you observed the parents and children together? Do the parents' expectations for the child appear to be too high? Or are there other factors related to the parenting that concern you (see Chapter 4)?

One teacher invites all parents, with their children, for a visit early in the school year. At that time she asks each child to demonstrate a task (usually one necessitating adult help), and then she observes any interaction between parent and child. How involved does the parent get in the task? How does the parent react when the child completes (or cannot complete) the task? This teacher finds that the observation of interaction gives her invaluable information. An example she cites is an interview with Teddy and his mother:

> Mrs. Kelsey greeted me as follows: "I'm not surprised that you asked me to come in. Now you know that Teddy is nothing like his older brother, Dan. Dan was good in school and so cooperative. Then there's Teddy." She indicated the 11-year-old boy standing sullenly behind her. I asked Mrs. Kelsey to sit and suggested that Teddy hang their coats in the back of the room.
>
> "For goodness sake, Teddy! Don't drag my coat!" Mrs. Kelsey admonished. "And hang it up right. Don't just heave it like you do at home." Teddy did not acknowledge her but continued to complete his task. As he walked back to us, his mother barked, "Stand up straight, Theodore!" And then to me she said almost conspiratorially, "It's so tough with these kids! Being a mother is no picnic! In fact, will we be long? I have to pick up my son, Dan at a friend's house. Teddy, come over here and sit down!"
>
> Teddy was quietly observing the fish in their tank—moving in endless circles with no hope of escape in their monotonous search for variety in the confines of the tank. Suddenly I saw Teddy's life much like theirs.
>
> Mrs. Kelsey's further comments to me made it clear that no matter what Teddy did, he could never meet her expectations. Was the abuse we observed a symbol of her own frustrations?

Not every teacher has an opportunity to observe either the parent or sometimes the student so closely. At the high school level, a teacher may see the adolescent for only brief periods. As one instructor noted, "My geometry class is not exactly the arena for sharing feelings. How do *I* know if a child is being abused?" In such situations, teachers need to be observant—that is, aware of peculiar behavior or unusual appearance on the part of the student. Further, they can demonstrate an attitude of openness. A chemistry teacher, for example, in spite of her no-nonsense facts and figures class, inspired students to come to her after class because of her open, accepting attitude. Although high school teachers who do not have homeroom or advisory responsibility may not be in a position to report because of lack if information, through observation, they may be able to provide valuable support to colleagues who do report.

Alternative Steps

A frequent problem in validation for teachers is student hygiene and its probability of being neglect. For example, a student may come to school very poorly dressed, unkempt, dirty, and eliciting complaints from other children about body odor. It is easy to assume that this is a case of blatant neglect. If a child neglect report is filed, however, it may well be screened out when it is discovered that an otherwise caring parent has similar habits of personal hygiene.

This type of situation can provide an excellent example of alternative steps to take before reporting. Poor hygiene is not an uncommon problem, and for the most part, is not life-threatening. You might consult with the school nurse or perhaps call the parent in a nonthreatening, informal way. Sometimes a well-meaning parent who discovers that a child is having difficulty with peers due to an odor problem will gladly attempt to remedy the situation. For example:

> Mrs. Daily came in readily when called by the teacher. She was a very large, obese woman who manifested a strong body odor. The teacher was almost hesitant to delicately talk about her daughter's teasing from others about her body odor, but she did. Mrs. Daily was most concerned. She assured the teacher that Lollie would be "washed within an inch of her life!" for school. Indeed she was. Later contacts with Mrs. Daily, however, proved that she did not consider the advice for herself.

If, after talking to the parent, there does appear to be neglect, you will feel more secure about reporting the situation. As far as talking to all parents about your concerns, it might be wise to refer to Chapter 7 before deciding on this course.

Why Educators May Not Report

Despite the fact that educators have extensive contact with children and may suspect that they are being abused long before other adults, many school personnel are hesitant to report. First, they may *lack the knowledge or the confidence in their knowledge*. Hopefully Chapters 1–3 will give you an idea of what to constitutes abuse, what aggravates maltreatment situations, and when people abuse and neglect children. Some educators *do not want to make waves*. Administrators, especially, are concerned that their school will get a reputation for turning parents in. But the fact is that a concerned school system is dedicated to helping children learn and to removing the barriers to their learning. It is also not a matter of turning parents in, but rather trying to get help for them in the difficult job of parenting when they seem not to be doing it effectively.

A third reason why educators are hesitant to report may be because they *fear repercussions from violent parents*. With few exceptions, it is not the abuser of children who you should worry about jeopardizing your personal safety. This is usually not an individual who feels competent or assertive around other adults. This is why they pick on children. Children will usually not fight back. Granted, there may be an abuser who sounds tough and their hostility might seem frightening. But it is probably easy to diffuse this anger by voicing understanding of them and the difficulty they are having. As one guidance counselor put it:

> I was absolutely amazed when I met Mr. Hobbs! He came in screaming and yelling and threatening me. I was really nervous and was sure I would be assaulted. But when he told me that I had no idea what it was like to be a parent to Johnny, I remembered my counseling training and started to empathize with him. I told him that it must be very difficult for him especially since his wife left. And suddenly he was in tears in my office, sobbing like a child! Once he realized that the vibrato that he always used would not work with me and that I was trying to understand where he was coming from, he was most cooperative.

Educators may also be afraid that *the parent will remove the child from the school* if the abuse/neglect is reported. This is certainly a possibility, but careful handling of parents and their feelings can prevent this. If the child protection agency does intervene, the worker may recognize the child's need for consistency and recommend that the child remain in the school. More abusive parents "school-hop" with their children in an attempt to avoid disclosure than the number of removals once a report has been made. If the parent does remove the child, another school will need to send for records and they can be alerted about your concerns.

School staff may feel a need to report child maltreatment but *fear that they will not receive support from administrators*. One way to circumvent this problem is to have a Child Protection Team (discussed in detail in Chapters 6–8). The Child Protection Team takes the responsibility and the decision off the administrators, a fact that might be a relief to many in these positions. Most administrators also want the best for children, but also have the reputation and running of the school in their minds. Careful education of administrative staff is sometimes the key. If the administration understands that competent reporting will make the school more effective rather than less so, and that they have a legal obligation to see that the report is made, they will often institute child abuse reporting policies.

It concerns some potential reporters that *they might be wrong in their allegations of abuse against a parent*. They worry about wrecking people's careers and reputations by falsely reporting. It is certainly possible to be wrong. But protective service workers are trained to detect the false allegations from the real ones. As an educator, you are only mandated to report your suspicions. It is up to another professional, trained specifically for that purpose, to investigate and determine if the individual did perpetrate the abuse. No one wants to be wrongly accused, but look at the other side of the coin. If you are a child who is being abused, a concerned teacher, guidance counselor or school nurse may be the only person who is in a position to intervene. For you the child, the issue might be more than one of reputation; it might be an issue of life or death.

Those not familiar with intervention in child abuse and neglect situations *may have little idea of the process involved after the report has been made.* The unknown is always frightening especially when we think about exposing a child to it. The solution is to learn more about protective services and how these agencies intervene on behalf of children. Chapter 9 relates in some detail what the interface between protective services and the educator might be. In addition, one can always contact the local child protection agency and arrange to talk with a worker about the procedures specific to your state or area. Social workers are usually glad to talk with educators. An educator knowledgeable in reporting procedures will make their jobs much easier.

And finally, I have never given a lecture or workshop to educators that I have not heard the familiar cry, "I reported once and the child protection agency did nothing!" Many in schools *fear that nothing will be done after they have taken the risk of reporting.* There is always a reason why the protection agency does not act. There may not have been sufficient information or evidence to prove that there was abuse. There may not have been abuse/neglect despite the signs. The case may already have been open and was just moving slowly. The agency may be investigating and you do not know it. (Despite the fact that most protective agencies are supposed to get back to the reporter, this does not always happen due to the time and crunch of huge caseloads.) Or the court may have decided that the child would remain in the home. There are a myriad of reasons why it would appear that nothing was done. The solution to this fear is to know how to make an effective report, to understand what child protection can and cannot do, and to know the channels to access for more information about what is happening with the case. All of these issues will be addressed in the following chapters.

Now that we have explored the recognition and validation of child abuse and neglect, it is important to look at how we as educators can intervene. Part II is dedicated to the exploration of this question.

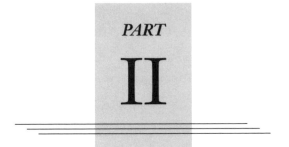

PART

II

How Can We Intervene?

How Can Our School
Be Proactive?

Difficult situations are always easier when we are prepared. Intervention in child abuse and neglect situations is no different. When you know and understand the reporting laws in your state and have familiarized yourself with the symptoms for which one should be alert, you will feel much better able to intervene when the need arises. But there is one additional piece of information you should know in order to be fully prepared. Does your school have a child abuse reporting protocol?

Having a Reporting Protocol

What is involved in a reporting protocol? A protocol is basically a guideline that lets you know how to act in a certain situation. Thus, what does the administration expect you to do if you feel that a child is being abused or neglected? This sounds quite basic and easy, but there are a multitude of decisions that must be made when thinking of a child abuse reporting protocol. For example, to whom does an educator report within the school? The principal? The nurse? The guidance counselor? What if that person is not available? What if a child comes to you after school hours and says that he or she is being abused? Who do you call then? Who reports to the child protection agency? What if you do not want to be the one to report? What should you tell the child?

The following example suggests the need for a protocol:

Jon Forrest was the type of teacher whom children sought out when they wanted to talk. Warm, caring, and concerned, Jon valued his middle school teaching and coaching activities because he valued the children with whom he worked. At the end of one school day, Jon was cleaning up his classroom with one eye on the clock. He had ten minutes to get to basketball practice. At first, when 12-year-old Kevin stole quietly into the room, Jon hardly noticed him. When he did notice that the youth was sitting in one of the back seats, it was obvious that there was something wrong. "What's up, Kev?" Jon quipped. With a somber expression Kevin responded, "Mr. F., we've got to talk." What followed was Kevin's account of his physical abuse by his father. Rolling up his sleeves, he showed Jon the welts and bruises from the latest beating. Now Kevin was afraid to go home and begged Mr. F. to "Take me home with you." Jon had never encountered this before. What should he do? Whom should he tell? What would he do about basketball practice?

What Jon did do was cancel practice and attempt to figure out how to proceed next. Since most of the administrative staff had left school, he did not know where to turn. He wasn't even sure what agency he should call to report. He had Kevin sit with him while he tried to figure out exactly how he should proceed. Several hours later, before Jon had solved the problem, Kevin's irate father, discovering that his son had not returned home, stormed into the school. He had obviously been drinking and berated Jon before he took his son away. Kevin never returned to that school (Crosson-Tower, 1998).

Obviously Jon Forrest needed help. How much easier his life might have been if the school had had a protocol or if he had known about the one they did have. And what about Kevin? How differently his situation might have turned out had Jon had some effective tools at his disposal. A clear effective protocol gives the educator support and direction in a crisis.

As you consider the above, it becomes more obvious how important a clear protocol can be. Some schools provide a listing of their protocol to faculty and staff on a regular basis, often adding this information to training sessions. In other schools, there may be a protocol but no one knows of its existence until someone asks for it. How do you know if your school's protocol is adequate or effective?

The first role of a protocol is to ensure that information is disseminated to staff. The most effective way to do this is to provide staff with *regular training*. Training on child abuse and neglect should include not only familiarizing trainees with the symptoms of maltreatment but also letting them know what to do when they suspect abuse/neglect, how they report it, and a discussion of some of the feelings that are engendered.

The protocol should also *indicate at what point a teacher should report*. These decisions are usually based on the regulations of the state in which your school operates. For example, does the state law indicate that the reporter need only have "suspicion" to report? Or, some laws say "reasonable cause to believe." Remember, and it cannot be overstated, that it is not up to an educator to investigate a child abuse situation. It is for this reason that many states indicate that you need only a suspicion to report. It will be the job of the children's protection agency to do a thorough investigation should they determine that it is warranted. It is helpful for a protocol *to spell out the specific information that the educator should have when reporting.* The child protection agency will need specific kinds of information (discussed in Chapter 8) and it is useful if the educator knows how to prepare to report.

The next role of a protocol is to *spell out to whom, within the school, one should report* suspected child abuse/neglect cases. Usually an administrator will take the report. Some prefer that it go to the nurse or to guidance. *What then does this person do? Does he or she tell you to go ahead and call the child protection agency or will that person do the reporting for you? Whose decision is it whether or not a report will go on to the child protection agency?* If a teacher feels strongly that a case should be reported and the administrator does not, there is often a conflict. The law in most states indicates that the educator who saw or suspected the abuse is still responsible for reporting it even if his or her superior says not to. You need to know *what recourse you have if you still want to report over the objections of your superior.* Although an educator could not be fired for making the decision to report over a superior's head, the reality is that life could become difficult or the relationship strained. If an educator's right to report despite disapproval is outlined in a protocol, the situation can be made much easier.

A protocol should also *emphasize the child's need for confidentiality* during the process of reporting. We often do not realize when we make a comment to a colleague, often about our own discomfort about our role, that we may be violating the child's right to confidentiality and perhaps making his or her situation worse. In addition, a protocol should *spell out where the information about the report may be recorded and who has access to this.*

Many schools have discovered that an extremely effective way to handle child maltreatment reports is through a Child Protection Team (CPT). The Child Protection Team will be discussed in more detail in the following section. Suffice it to say in our discussion of protocol that the formation of a Child Protection Team will greatly enhance a school's ability to handle these cases due to the delegation of duties. In addition, when there is a Child Protection Team, the reporter feels supported and guided in his or her role as someone who wants the best for this abused/neglected child.

To determine if your school's individual protocol provides these necessary components consult "Assessing Your Protocol" which is included here.

The Advantages of a Child Protection Team

The concept of a Child Protection Team is not necessarily a new one. Some schools long ago instituted crisis teams that were responsible for any type of crisis that took place in the school. As one teacher explained:

Assessing Your Protocol

If you already have a protocol designed or in place, you may want to evaluate it for effectiveness. The following is a checklist which will help you to do so.

❑ 1) Does our protocol designate that staff will have training and who will be responsible for arranging training?

❑ 2) Will this training include how to recognize the symptoms of different types of child maltreatment, staff reporting responsibilities, the school protocol, reporting procedure, Child Protection Agency (CPS) procedure, and their obligations once a report has been made?

❑ 3) Does the protocol include the formation of a CPT?

❑ 4) Does the protocol spell out who is responsible for the formation of this team, whom the members will be, and how often the team will meet?

❑ 5) Does the protocol stipulate that all school staff will receive notification of the protocol?

❑ 6) Does the protocol designate how many hours of training each staff member is expected to receive?

❑ 7) Does the protocol reference your state law which requires that, as a mandated reporter, an employee of the school who has "reasonable cause to believe" that a child is being abused or neglected must report such suspicion to the local child protection agency?

❑ 8) Does the protocol spell out the role of the CPT in making a report?

❑ 9) Does the protocol specify who actually contacts CPS? Who completes the required written report within 48 hours after the oral report?

❑ 10) If the CPT is responsible for filing the report, does the protocol spell out what happens if the team is not available?

❑ 11) Does the protocol inform staff that if the staff member who referred the case to the CPT does not agree with the Team's decision not to file a report, he/she can contact CPS directly to file a report?

❑ 12) Does the protocol indicate that all reports must be kept confidential and in a separate file from the student's regular school file?

❑ 13) Does the protocol indicate who is responsible for monitoring (receiving feedback from CPS, etc.) after a report is filed?

❑ 14) Does the protocol mention that once the report has been made, the child will no longer be questioned by any member of the school staff?

❑ 15) After the initial dissemination of the written protocol, is it (will it be) made available to all new school staff and reviewed periodically with veteran staff?

Adapted from *Designing and Implementing a School Reporting Protocol: A How-To Guide for Massachusetts Teachers.* by C. Crosson-Tower, Boston: Children's Trust Fund, 1998. Reprinted with permission.

Our crisis team consisted of the principal, five teachers, the nurse, and someone from guidance who all met together when a child was in crisis. If we found a child smoking, the team might meet with him or her for a disciplinary decision. We planned drug training and worked with the DARE officer. If a child's parent was ill or died, we met together to decide how to help him or her. It was good support, but the crisis team model was too diverse. There were too many things that we felt that we had to attend to. So eventually we all burned out. Now we have a Child Protection Team. We know what we are about. It's a great model.

Although crisis teams work for some schools, many, such as the one above, found them too diverse. A Child Protection Team works in a similar manner in that specific staff meets when there is a suspicion or a report of child abuse or neglect. How an individual child protection team works can best be described by a teacher who reported to such a team.

Our school had just instituted a Child Protection Team that year. The team was staffed by our principal, two of the guidance counselors, the nurse, and two representative teachers. The team had already established a liaison with Children's Protective Services and they knew whom they could call with a question. We had all received training, early in September, on the CPT concept and how it worked. I absorbed the information and put it on file in my cluttered brain as I attended to the rest of beginning the school year with my fifth grade class. It was November when I began to be concerned about Eileen. She was not herself. She had always been a quiet child but in early November, her grades began to slip and she seemed like she was falling asleep all the time. I tried to talk with her but she was very evasive. I was talking to Jennifer, a friend of Eileen's one day and asked Jenn if Eileen was okay. All of a sudden Jennifer started crying and said that Eileen's new stepfather had "been messing with her" and she did not know whom to tell. I asked Jennifer to have Eileen come to me. To make a long story short, Eileen finally agreed to talk with me and told me that she was being sexually abused by her mother's new husband. I was shook! I had been told how to report abuse cases and trained about the symptoms but here was a real situation. Remembering the CPT, I quickly called the chairperson, Bud Hawley who was one of the guidance counselors. The Team met that day and I told them what I knew. They agreed that the situation should be reported. Chrisinda Black, another of the guidance counselors, had had some suspicions and now we realized that these were based in fact. The call was made by Bud then and there and at one point I talked with the Children's Protective worker as well.

CPS assured us that they would come out in an hour or two to talk with Eileen. I agreed to explain to her what was happening and Chrisinda urged me to send her down to her office if I felt that Eileen needed extra support. It was emotional, but the whole process went so smoothly. It was so good to have colleagues who support and respect your opinion.

Each Child Protection Team may operate slightly differently, but the support given the reporter is usually similar. The reporter feels as though he or she is not standing alone, but has other professionals to back up his or her decision that intervention is needed.

The Formation of the Child Protection Team

The Child Protection Team is an extremely useful and important tool, but its composition and method of functioning must be well planned and executed. Several issues must be considered when a school decides to institute a Child Protection Team. (The following adapted from Crosson-Tower, 1998, p.5).

1. *How many members will be on the team?* It is important for the size of the team to not be so large that it is difficult to get everyone together, but have enough staff to ensure a representation and diversity of opinion.

2. *Who will the members be? Who decides who will be on the team?* It would seem natural that team members might be chosen by the roles that people play within the school. For example, most teams would want a member of the administration represented. In addition such roles as guidance, the school psychologist or the school nurse might be in a position to see a cross section of children and therefore be more familiar with many of them. There may be those in any of the above roles or among the teaching staff who have had more training in child protection or crisis intervention and their input might be most helpful. In short, the composition of the Team will be an individual school decision. As far as who makes the decisions about CPT members, this will also depend on the individual system. Some schools have left such a decision to the administration while others have sought volunteers and chosen from these. The important piece is that members of the Team be level-headed individuals who do not panic and who have the best interests of the child at heart.

3. *Should the Child Protection Team have a representative from the child protective agency on the team?* It is important to have contact with the child protective services agency. That way, if there is a question about the report, there will be someone with expertise who can advise the CPT. Child protective workers might not have time to meet with a CPT on a regular basis, especially if the meeting is an emergency and scheduled on short notice. However, most pro-

tective workers would rather answer questions and offer guidance if it would ensure that the reports that were made by schools were more complete and therefore could be acted on more efficiently.

How does one secure a liaison with the local child protective agency? The best suggestion is to call and ask for either the director of the agency or the supervisor of the Intake Unit. Explain that your school is setting up a Child Protection Team and to ensure that you and your colleagues will be able to provide the best possible information to the agency and to establish a smooth working relationship in the interest of children, you are interested in a liaison with your CPS who might answer questions. It is helpful if this is one person or one unit so that the lines of communication are easier. Often, the Intake Supervisor will agree to perform this role with his or her unit as backup. If the agency is helped to understand that your interest is in making their job easier and in doing the best for children, they will surely comply with this request.

4. *When, where, and how often will the CPT meet?* Again, such a question must be decided by individual schools. Some CPTs like to touch base on a monthly or bimonthly basis to ensure they are up-to-date on what has been happening and possibly to plan and implement new training for the staff. The more positive visibility the CPT has, the better the likelihood of staff accessing the Team in a crisis. The point is for the CPT to be seen as a helpful service rather than one that makes decisions, sometimes difficult ones, only in a crisis. One excellent way to remain visible and helpful is to sponsor training on a variety of subjects throughout the school year. There are numerous topics that lend themselves easily to the prevention or intervention in abuse issues. For example, workshops on working with the student from the substance-abusing family or the divorced family or the family with high expectations might be useful. It is also vital to do frequent training on different aspects of child abuse reporting so that the staff continues their awareness of the symptoms and issues.

5. *What role will the CPT take? Will they merely review cases or will they also be responsible for making the report?* While all CPTs review a report of child abuse or neglect, there are several models for making the report. Some CPTs, once they have heard the facts, will make the actual report to the child protective agency. Others, on the other hand, prefer that the original reporter call child protective services with the support of the CPT. Either option can be effective.

6. *If the CPT does file the actual report with child protective services, which member will do this?* Once again, although an individual school's decision, there can be variables that come into play. Some schools have the chairperson of the CPT file the report and may rotate that position from year to year. Others value the contact between an individual Team member and the child protective liaison and those are the two who work together on every report. There are those who find dealing with an authoritative agency with the power of the child protective agency to be intimidating. These people might not be comfortable making the report. On the other hand, making such a report to an intake worker might help them to realize that the child protective worker is as interested in children and doing the best for them as are the schools.

7. *What type of feedback can the educator who reports to the CPT expect and in what manner will this feedback come?* When one reports a difficult situation to the CPT, one hopes for some feedback. Was the case reported to child protection? Will they investigate? There are actually two levels of feedback if a case is reported to the CPT and later to the child protective agency. There certainly should be a mechanism for the CPT to get back to the reporter. Was the case reported to the protective agency or not? If not, why not? The CPT may also be in a position to support the reporter emotionally, assuring him or her that the right thing was done by bringing the situation to the attention of the CPT. In addition, the CPT might offer suggestions to the reporter on what might happen next or how to deal with the child's anxiety over the situation.

The second level of feedback comes from the child protective agency. What have they chosen to do about the report? How much schools are told about the cases they have reported differs significantly from state to state and agency to agency. Many agencies will offer the original reporter or the CPT an assurance that the case will be addressed as need be. Some agency regulations, regarding confidentiality prohibit them from doing even this. On the far side of the continuum, other agencies choose to continue their work with the school and therefore may keep them as up-to-date on the case as the confines of the client's right to confidentiality would allow. So much depends upon the size of the community, the state laws, the agencies' regulations and the individuals involved that it is difficult to predict the feedback one will get. It might be helpful for the CPT member(s) dealing directly with child protective services to find out up front the policy on feedback of that particular agency.

8. *What if the reporter feels the report should be passed on to the child protective agency and the CPT does not? What recourse does the reporter have?* There may be situations when you, as an educator, believe that a case should be reported to CPS but your Team does not agree. According to the law of most states, an educator is a mandated reporter even if those above him or her do not agree to report. As we discussed in Chapter 1, failure of a mandated reporter to report to children's protective services can involve a fine (up to $1,000) or even a short jail sentence. However, with the advent of Child Protection Teams, a few states have instituted policy that says that an educator is no longer held liable to report if he or she has reported to a CPT and they have decided not to report to the child protection agency. If you have or form a Child Protection Team, they should find out if this is the case in your state.

Why might a CPT decide not to report when you feel that they should? First, with more experience in reporting such cases, the Team members may recognize that you do not have enough information to report. In this situation, documentation might have been helpful. If you can organize your thoughts and document all the pertinent facts, it might help the Team to see things as you do. Since most states indicate that all that is needed is suspicion, a great deal of information is helpful rather than vital. And also for this reason, most CPTs will recognize that, if your suspicion is strong enough, a report should be made.

The CPT, because it is made up of a collection of individuals in different roles, may realize that this is not abuse, but some other problem. Hopefully, they can let you know this without breaching the child's or family's right to confidentiality. One hopes that the CPT will not refuse to report for fear of political pressure, but it will sometimes happen. Hopefully, you can help the Team to recognize that the first obligation is to ensure the welfare of the child.

What recourse do you have if, despite your best efforts at convincing them, the CPT does not want to report? Within your school's protocol, if you do have a CPT, should be a statement indicating that an educator has the right to report independently if, after consulting with the CPT that chooses not to report, that reporter still feels it is warranted. There should be no penalty for doing this.

9. *When the CPT does make the report to the child protective agency, what role will the Team assume after the report has been made?* Most CPTs see their role as continuing to support the reporter and continuing to be involved in the case, albeit often on the sidelines. Many maintain contact with the protective agency for updates if they are forthcoming. Some CPTs, on the other hand, turn the responsibility for future protective agency contacts back to the individual reporter. The reporter should be able to depend on his or her CPT colleagues for support, however.

10. *Will the composition of the CPT change?* Certainly there will be changes in the CPT makeup. Positions may change; individuals may leave or lose interest. Most Child Protection Teams are able to invite new members when others leave. Or members may be appointed by the administration. "New blood" can actually be helpful and sometimes old members are asked to help to train the new.

11. *What type of training will be needed for the school staff and for Team members to effectively implement protocol?* Training is vital to the effective implementation and functioning of a Child Protection Team. Because it is so important, an entire section will be devoted to it.

The Importance of Training

So often a school department will feature an hour's training on reporting a case of abuse and neglect. Sometimes these training sessions are done by neophyte protective services workers who were recruited to "come out and talk with a group of teachers." Sometimes the training is squeaked between other administrative details in otherwise boring meetings and is almost lost. Yet, it is effective training that may make the difference in how well school staff will respond in a crisis.

When thinking about training, it will be important to consider several factors.

1. *How much time will be allotted to training?* Ideally, there should be frequent training sessions. If kept sufficiently interesting, these sojourns can revitalize staff and help them to perform their jobs more effectively. If training sessions are presented as an opportunity rather than an obligation, even if they are required, the equation tips toward the positive. Training sessions at least once a month are preferred. When this training is undertaken also becomes a crucial issue. Most teachers are tired at the end of the school day and may not be that receptive to staying an extra hour or two for training. Rather, half day or full day release of students to enable educators to attend training might be more effective. One school had an extended lunch/free time period every other week during which the students were organized into teams and, under the supervision of much fewer staff, played a variety of games. This extra hour enabled half the teachers on a rotating basis to attend planned training sessions. There are a variety of creative plans to ensure that all staff are able to attend necessary training sessions.

2. *What should be the content of training?* To deal effectively with child protection issues, there are several topics that should be touched on. First, *what are the responsibilities of educators regarding the reporting of child protection issues?* This should include the fact that they are mandated reporters, under what circumstances they must report, and so on. Second, *what is the protocol of the school?* Is there a Child Protection Team? If so, how does it work? To whom should cases be reported? Then, *staff need to know how a report will be made to the child protection agency and by whom?* It will also be helpful for them to know *what facts need to be included in the report* in order to best aid the agency in its investigation. What information specifics should they have? Concerned reporters will also want to know, *what happens once a report has been made?* What steps will CPS take in abuse and neglect cases?

To best help the child, training should include a segment on *what can be done for the child after the report has been made.* And last, but certainly not least, it is vital that educators *receive extensive training on prevention.* These are the topics only specifically related to child abuse and neglect, but there are many others that indirectly affect maltreatment. For example, the book *No Such Thing As a Bad Kid,* by Appelstein was mentioned in Chapter 2. This book helps teachers to recognize how children speak through their behavior and not always in the ways that we think. Helping teachers to understand the meaning of behaviors and to recognize that problematic behaviors might be cries for help would be an excellent training. Some schools have provided training on Posttraumatic

Stress Disorder (a condition frequently resulting from being traumatized by something like abuse), the connection between abuse and disabilities, substance abuse, and a variety of other topics that dovetail with abuse. A poll of the staff might bring to light interest in a myriad of interesting subjects.

A common misconception about training is that it involves throwing a piece of information at the trainee and expecting that he or she will emerge "trained"—whatever that is. In fact, effective training requires interaction with the trainee. While children may learn from a pedagogical model (have the information given to you and being expected to absorb it), adults learn very differently. In order for us to fully integrate new material, we must not only hear and see it but also try to use it. Thus, training adults should include an opportunity for hands-on experiences such as problem solving or walking through a hypothetical case using the new material. This is important to remember when planning the content and the time frame for adult training sessions.

3. *Who should do the training?* Although the budget and time a school has to devote to training often causes planners to choose the least expensive method and the most available people to provide training, this might be a mistake. Not everyone is a good trainer. Some people are boring; some are ill-informed or cannot handle groups. Some can actually do harm. Consider the following example:

> One school decided that it was time to do some training on sexual abuse and opted to add sexual harassment by peers. One teacher volunteered her brother who was an attorney in a nearby city. He was not schooled in child welfare law, a type of law that is quite different in outlook, but rather did a smattering of contract law with a few divorce and adult sexual harassment cases thrown in. He agreed to do the training as a favor and quickly boned up on the child abuse statutes. The school was pleased that this training would cost them nothing. His training, presented for children K–6th grades emphasized the fact that no one had the right to touch you in any way that you did not want. If they touched you in a way that was inappropriate, he told them, it was sexual harassment. You could report it and the offender could be prosecuted. The children absorbed all this and the teachers, most of whom left the room during training, had no idea of its content.
>
> Several days after the training, a young boy who had special needs hugged one of his classmates. Remembering the training the girl reported that she had been touched inappropriately. Her parents, sure that their daughter had been molested by a classmate, threatened the school and the child and reported the incident to the police. The result was that the special needs child was suspended and the case was blown incredibly out of proportion. Only a few

people traced the problem back to an unprepared trainer who gave somewhat distorted information to a group of impressionable children.

Although, hopefully, most adults are more discerning about what they hear than are impressionable children, the fact remains we are all guilty of tending to take the word of those we assume to be experts, especially in a subject that is either new to us or emotionally disturbing. Therefore, we must ensure that whomever we get to train does have expertise in the subject. The best bargain is not always the person who will come for free, although some experts do devote some of their time at a reduced rate when there are children involved. How do we find people who are up-to-date and skilled in training? There are a variety of resources. Most states have a Children's Trust Fund that is in touch with a variety of speakers. The child protection agency might be of help in identifying experts as might the crisis hotlines or other family services agencies in the area. Do not be afraid to contact authors and writers of articles on abuse who live in your area. A few teachers have also written requests for grants that have supplied the funds and some contacts for training.

The local child protection agency is a resource for speakers especially if you are establishing a relationship with them. Although many workers may have the information necessary, you are interested in someone who can also train effectively. Ask your contact person for an individual who can really engage a group, as your hope is that this training will greatly enhance the working relationship between your school and the CPS. Handouts that staff can refer to for future reference are also helpful and might be requested. It is better to take time and perhaps spend a bit of the budget to ensure that the staff of your school are well trained than to rely on someone who is easy to get but not as well informed.

4. *Who should be trained?* Training for the entire school staff will be mportant. Most of the personnel will need to know symptoms, some idea of when to report, and how to do this. Any additional training topics will be helpful, but not necessarily vital to make a report. More specialized training should be available for the Child Protection Team members, however. This more advanced training might be in-house or members could benefit from college courses or seminars presented on child maltreatment issues. Again, the local child protection agency might know of such seminars or colleges that offer courses in various aspects of child abuse. Many social service agencies also receive notification of various trainings. You might ask local agencies to keep you informed. The Internet also has listings of conferences and workshops. Organizations like the International Society of Child Abuse and Neglect, the Child Welfare League of America, the National Center on Child Abuse and Neglect, and the Children's Defense Fund often list conferences on their web pages. The information on training is out there. Sometimes a bit of creativity might be needed to find it.

Some schools arrange training for parents as well. Many parents are receptive to training on parenting skills and such training might help them not to be abusive parents. There are a variety of ready-made curricula available in this area. Training sessions based on handling such issues as ADD and learning disabilities, discipline, substance abuse in children, and a variety of other topics might help parents to deal with issues that put stress on them as parents.

Prevention training for children is also vital. This will be discussed in depth in Chapter 11. In addition to training, many schools keep a resource library of pertinent books, journals, and newsletters that pertain to child abuse and neglect and can be accessed by the school community. A partial list of suggestions for materials that might be included in such a resource library is included in the Appendix.

In short, training is what keeps us informed and educated so that children can best be protected and educated. For something this important, we should be making a substantial investment in time, creativity, and perhaps money.

How Do I Communicate with the Abused/Neglected Child and the Family?

We may have little trouble talking to children or their parents until it comes to a subject like suspected abuse or neglect. Hopefully the following will be of help to you as you undertake these tasks.

Talking with an Abused or Neglected Child

Talking with children about being abused or neglected is not always easy. What does one say? The subject may feel sensitive; the educator may feel ill-prepared. There are three basic things to remember when talking with a child. First, keep in mind that in most states *you need only suspicion to report the abuse.* It is not up to you as an educator to investigate or validate with certainty. Second, it is vital that you *do not lead the child.* Child abuse or neglect cases may reach the point where they are involved in the court system. Many a case, including some much-publicized ones, have been lost in court because it was alleged that an interviewer led the children to say what they did (see Poole and Lamb, 1998). Instead of questioning the child, listening is your best alternative, with gentle nonspecific questions or observations thrown in. And finally, children who are being abused or neglected may want attention and conversely be afraid that attention will uncover their secret. Therefore, it is important *to indicate gently that you are available to talk, but not to press the child unduly.*

If we suspect abuse, our first inclination might be to want to talk to the child and find out if they were in fact abused. This may not be advisable for several reasons:

1. The child may be afraid to tell the truth about being abused because of:

- Fear of being further hurt by the abuser if he or she tells.
- Belief that "people go to jail for abuse." This may have been threatened by the abuser if the child told. (Admittedly, in some states a "jail" or prison sentence could be a reality for the abuser, but hopefully the child can be helped by the social worker or a counselor to deal with this when the time comes).
- Fear that something, like removal from the home, will happen to him or her. (Again, a reality in some cases, but careful casework will prepare the child for this.)
- Loyalty to the parent—no matter how bad the situation might be.

2. The child may feel that the abuse is deserved.

3. While some children may be relieved by the outlet of talking to a sympathetic adult, others may be threatened and withdraw from you.

4. Neglected children may know nothing but neglect.

The best approach again is to assure the child that you can be approached when they are ready to talk. For example:

> Harley's teacher became concerned about the bruises that he had come into school with over the last few weeks. When asked what happened, Harley always had quick robotically-delivered answers, many of which did not fully fit the injury. Finally the teacher explained in a caring manner, "You know, sometimes kids have things happen that they do not know quite how to handle. I hope that, if that ever happens to you, you will talk to me about it." A week later, Harley asked to stay after school to help the teacher feed the gerbils. Harley finally shyly recounted her words saying that she could be of help. He told her that his new stepfather was out of work and drinking a lot. He would order Harley to do chores and when Harley would not do then quickly enough, he would beat him. The stepfather would then give Harley an explanation for the bruises that the child was supposed to tell anyone who asked. Harley was afraid to tell his mother because the day she married the stepfather she said to her son, "You better like him and not give us no trouble! You'll lose your happy home if you do!"

For Harley, the assurance that there was someone who would listen was enough to get him to disclose his plight. Some children cannot do this and it may be necessary to report on the suspicion that you have by observation, documentation, and deduction.

Children can be inspired to tell you about their abuse in a variety of other ways. Often prevention programs will elicit reports to teachers or other educational staff. Schools that have used prepackaged prevention material like Kids and Company, the Personal Safety Curriculum, or the Child Abuse Prevention Program and other such tools have found a significant increase in reports by children (Finkelhor and Daro, 1997). There are also a variety of books that can be read to all children in a classroom setting. These books (partial list in Appendix) are designed to educate all children about abuse/neglect situations, but in so doing they often give abused/neglected children the confidence to disclose.

We have been talking about inspiring children to disclose their abuse, but what of a child who spontaneously approaches an educator to disclose. How does one react? There are several pointers that might be helpful. First, *do not act shocked.* Studies show that the reaction of the first person that a child tells is important to the child's ability to handle the events that will follow. A calm, accepting attitude will help and support the child. Second, *tell the child that you believe him or her and that you are glad that he or she told you.* Children will often immediately regret disclosure and it is important that you let them know that what they did by telling was right. But what if you do not believe the child? When it is a question of the credibility of an adult we know versus a child, it is not uncommon for us to believe the adult. But again, remember, it is not up to you to determine if the child is telling the truth. If he or she is not (which is not that likely) you can deal with that at a later date. For now, the child needs to feel believed. After all, what if it is you who is wrong and the child who is telling the truth?

The child also needs to know that *children are not responsible for abuse and neglect; adults are.* A child never does anything to warrant maltreatment by an adult. Even if they are difficult to handle, there are other alternatives to abuse (see Appelstein, 1998). *Despite how you might feel about the abuser after hearing the child's story, do not speak disparagingly of him or her.* Remember that the abuser may be the child's parent—one half of who the child sees him- or herself to be. And, not all abusive parents are abusive all of the time. The child may feel close and nurtured by this parent when not being abused. Or the abuser may be a friend or acquaintance of the child, possibly someone who has given the child the only real attention he or she has ever had. It would stand to reason that the child's feelings about this person might be in conflict. Making this person seem like the monster you feel that he or she is might alienate or totally confuse the child and rob him or her of some of the positive strokes received.

Do not tell the child that you can keep his disclosure a secret. Let the child know that, *in order to get help, you will need to consult another professional.* You can suggest that only those who must know, (e.g., other professionals) will be told by you. He or she will probably have a multitude of fears like "will they take me away?" or "will they send my Dad to jail?" You cannot tell the child if any of these things will come to pass. You do not know. *Assure the child that things might be tough for a while, but things are more likely to get better in the long run if they all get some help.* Also, explain to the child that *now that the story has been told, it is important that it be stuck to.* There may be others who will ask the child to forget or deny what happened (very common for perpetrators in sexual abuse to compel the child to recant). Assure the child (and ensure that you are able to do this) that *you will give him or her support in the process or ensure that the child is immediately connected with someone who can* (e.g., guidance counselor, social worker, or counselor.). If you have talked with the child protection agency and know what will happen next, *tell the child what you have been told will happen.* This is called *anticipatory guidance* (Sgroi, 1982). For example, say "a social worker will come to the school this afternoon and talk with you." Many social workers will allow a concerned adult to accompany the child if that adult takes no part in the interview or does not influence the child. Even if you cannot attend the interview, *the child should know that someone will be available for support after the interview is completed.*

Imagine that you have just told a secret that you feel will destroy your whole world. Can you think how you might feel. Helpless to stop the rolling ball? Afraid? Alone? Powerless? Then you have a small inkling of how a vulnerable child might feel. For this reason, the more calming and supportive you can be after disclosure and in the months to come, the more comfort you will be to the child.

Talking with the Parents of an Abused or Neglected Child

If you suspect that a child has been abused or neglected, at what point should you talk with the parents? For many of us, the first inclination is to call the parents and see what they have to say. We are often sure that they will have a logical explanation. Others of us are convinced that they hurt this child and you want to confront them with it. Such action may pose several problems. Consider what might happen in some cases of maltreatment. In a neglectful situation the lifestyle may be chaotic and the roots few. A neglectful parent who feels threatened may flee. The same might be true in abuse situations. One well-meaning teacher found this out the hard way.

> Allen was frequently dirty and often smelled when he came to school. Concerned about the child who also seemed to be doing more care-taking of his younger siblings than seemed healthy, his teacher called Allen's mother to voice her concerns. She was met at first with disinterest and then with hostility. After enduring the mother's insults, the frustrated teacher said that she would be referring the matter to the child protection agency. She then called the agency and a worker assured her that they would get out there the

next day. The teacher had little sleep that night worrying if Allen would be all right. Shortly after noon, she again called CPS wondering if anyone had been out. "I just came back from there," the worker told her, "they cleared out lock, stock, and barrel. That's the last we will see of them until they surface someplace else. If they leave the state, we have no way of tracking them. Our data system is only statewide."

In addition to flight, there is also the possibility that knowledge that a report is to be made will increase the danger to the child, especially if it was the child who disclosed the maltreatment. Abuse is associated with control and the parent who feels desperately out of control may strike out. The introduction of the social service system in the family's life creates an even more vulnerable situation. If the parent feels threatened, the child may suffer even more abuse.

Sometimes when a parent learns that a child has told someone that there is abuse in the home, that parent will do everything possible to get the child to take back the story. One mother, after being called and told by a guidance counselor that her daughter had reported that mother's boyfriend was abusing her, stormed into the school and insisted upon seeing her daughter. Before anyone could intervene, she dragged the weeping girl into the guidance office saying "Tell her [the guidance counselor], you little liar! Tell her what you said was all in your head!" It was later confirmed by her siblings that the girl was being abused, but the trauma of her mother's act made testifying in court an impossibility for the victim. The boyfriend never was successfully prosecuted and drifted out of this family's life probably to molest another girl in some other family.

Other phenomena operate in cases of sexual abuse. For both victim and perpetrator (especially in cases on incest), there is a high risk of suicide immediately after the report has been made. Therefore, once the situation comes to light, the case *must* be handled swiftly and with expert timing.

Certainly parents must know that the abuse and neglect has been or is to be reported. In fact, the way in which this is presented to them may affect their ability to work with the school in the future. Social workers differ in their advice as to when to inform the parents. Considering the possible parental reactions mentioned, some feel that educators should report before informing the parents, but that the parents should subsequently be approached by those who are specifically trained to deal with them. Knowledge of such support should be reassuring to teachers.

Other social workers feel that the parents are owed an explanation before the report is made for the following reasons:

1. The situation may be a misunderstanding and once all the parties communicate, a report may be deemed unnecessary.

2. Parents may feel less threatened, more amenable to cooperation and therefore more willing to seek help if they are approached before involvement with the social service system. Considering that control is a central issue, especially for abusive parents, it is important to deprive them of as little control as possible.

Because of the differences of opinion among social service personnel concerning parental rights, cooperation, and the child's safety, educators may want to consult the local child protection agency for specific advice on how this contact should be handled.

In many cases, once the report has been made, you may have an opportunity to talk with the child or the parent about the report. By this time you will have the support of other professionals. Whether or not you see the parent may depend largely on your role in the school, whether you have a Child Protection Team, and your desire, if any, for further involvement.

Reporting a child maltreatment case is not an easy thing for educators emotionally. Many, although desiring to help the child, feel unsure of their own position and also the effect the report will have on the future relationship with both the child and the family. Some educators fear repercussions from the parents. In most cases, the physically abusive parent is dangerous to the child but not to adults. Some families may try to "fight back" legally but teachers who have acted in good faith are legally safe. The worst fear of many educators is that the family might strike out emotionally by making threats to them or false statements to others. However, anyone can be a victim of this type of behavior—from the vindictive neighbor to the family reported for abuse. The support of colleagues can enable educators to better handle such annoyances. One young teacher learned this lesson well.

> I was a new teacher, right out of college, when I first encountered Helene's parents. The Wagner's were a prominent family who knew all the right people. I suspected that Helene's father was sexually abusing her long before I had the nerve to report it. I talked to several other teachers who finally assured me that reporting was the best thing to do. So I did. When the local congressman called my principal, I was panic stricken! I was sure that I would lose my job and my reputation. Fortunately my colleagues supported me, and the social worker from CPS was a great help as well. Eventually the Wagners got the help they needed. The look in Helene's eyes and her new vitality and interest in school were enough to convince me that I had done the right thing.

What then, if the parents withdraw the child from school or from your classroom? This is always a possibility. But at least you will have involved the family members with the social service system so that the child may be helped. If you are able to talk with the parents and assure them that you wish to be an ally, you may be able to help in their treatment. Typically, parents about whom a report is made to protective services feel persecuted and alone. Knowing that your report was made out of concern rather than punishment will appeal to some.

Remember, abusive families cry for help in a variety of ways and often erect smoke screens to cover their cries. Many times no one hears until a child is badly hurt or even killed. Educators may be in a position to hear these cries for help a little sooner than other members of society. You may be the key to early intervention and a turning point in the life of the family.

Educators might also be in the position of having parents talk to them so that they might better deal with the child. For example, parents whose children have been abused outside the home might inform a teacher of this fact anticipating that the child might have reactions as a result. So often, when a parent is obviously trying to pave the way for an easier time for his or her child, we forget that the parent too might be in a great deal of distress. Parents whose children have been abused (usually sexually by friends, relatives, or strangers) experience a myriad of emotions. They may feel guilt, feeling that they should have supervised the child better. They may feel anger at the perpetrator or even at the child in the misperception that he or she may have allowed or instigated the abuse. They may also be grappling with their own conflicts if they were abused children or if they feel that they somehow contributed to the child being abused. Listening to the parent with an awareness that this is also difficult for him or her no matter how in control he or she might seem will go a long way toward helping the healing for both parent and child.

Whether the parent is the abuser or the nonabusive parent of an abused child, try to put yourself in that parent's shoes. No matter how heinous his or her acts may seem to you, the parent is someone who is hurt and in need of help. Sometimes, this may be harder to see than at other times.

The Importance of Confidentiality

In our world where sensationalism sells newspapers, hikes ratings, and sometimes seems to be worshipped like a minor deity, it is important to make extra mention of the importance of confidentiality. There appears to be nothing more sensational, especially in a small town school, than a particularly messy child abuse case. When you have just reported a prominent citizen who is abusing his daughter and the media gets hold of it, the tendency is to seek others for support or even to let your friends know that you were the one who uncovered the whole story (let's face it, it's human nature!). But this is a time when you should stop and think. How would you feel if you were a child who was sexually violated by a parent and whose world had just been blown apart? How would you feel if you were the mother who sincerely did not know that her husband had violated her daughter? The shame, the embarrassment she also must feel. And no matter what our feeling about the perpetrator, it is a person with a severe problem. Having the world know about it will only make admission more difficult.

When we speak of abuse, we are talking about a family—the delicate balance of relationships—that is at its best designed to nurture and prepare children for adulthood. Whether the abuser is someone within the family or outside, there will be trauma associated with the abuse. Whether it is normal functioning or trying to recover from an issue like abuse, the family will do better with some degree of privacy and the intervention of caring professionals. Healing is about growth and expansion into new attitudes and ways of handling old problems. Being surrounded by sensationalism will not help them have the courage to expand and grow. Instead they may turn inward in a psychological attempt to protect themselves. This makes it difficult for them to be reached or helped.

For some abused children, school has been a haven—a place where they have felt secure and safe. When the abuse or neglect is disclosed, it will be especially important for these children to continue to feel as though school is a friendly place. When their classmates and teachers all know about the abuse, they may feel that there is nowhere that they can find refuge.

For all these reasons, it is vital that we as educators to whom the abuse is disclosed or who have recognized it enough to report it, protect as much of the child and family's confidentiality as possible. The only people who should be told about the case are those who are in a position to intervene or who must know by virtue of their position. Certainly we all need support and the opportunity to vent about upsetting or difficult situations. This is where a Child Protection Team can again be helpful. If you do not have a CPT, try to use for support those colleagues who have reason to know about the case already.

By the same token, it is important not to make the child feel as though he or she is surrounded by a big, dark secret. Encourage the child to talk to appropriate supports as well. Some children, once they have initially disclosed and in their attempt to make sense of the abuse, will blurt out their story to anyone, child or adult, who will listen. It is up to concerned adults to help the child to recognize when further disclosure is appropriate and when it is not. Our own recognition of when it is appropriate to talk about specifics of abuse and when it is not can provide a model for children as well.

The bottom line is that the abuse or neglect that a child suffers is an intimate part of themselves. If they choose to share it, they have a right to the judicious use of this information in a way that can get them help rather than expose them to further emotional trauma.

How Do I
Make a Report?

Much of the content of a chapter on reporting child abuse and neglect will be dependent on whether or not the school has a Child Protection Team. For this reason, this chapter is divided into sections on making reports without a Team in place and with a Child Protection Team firmly in place.

Making a Report without a Child Protection Team

Making an effective child abuse report to the appropriate agency necessitates knowing some of the information discussed in Chapter 6. Does your school have a protocol that dictates to whom a report should be made within the school? Does that same protocol indicate who will call the child protective agency? If, for example, you need only tell your principal of your suspicions and he or she makes the formal report, then there will be little to consider. If the principal decides not to report, then you are still legally liable and must make the decision if you will report without his or her permission.

Let us say that you have told your administrator who agrees that you should report to CPS and assigns the task to you. What must you consider? Reporting to the designated protective agency (usually a division of the state or county social service agency) usually begins with a phone call to give the agency the necessary information they need to begin their investigation. State laws usually require at least the following information:

- Names of child and parents
- Address
- Age and gender of child

- Type and extent of child's injuries or complaints
- Evidence of prior injuries
- Explanation of injuries given by the child
- Name and telephone number of the reporter
- Actions taken by the reporter (such as detaining the child, talking with the child, and so on)
- other pertinent information

Many social services agencies now have a risk matrix that defines criteria that they feel will put the child at the most risk. The intake worker might ask you what you know about some of these factors. For example, the worker might ask you such questions as: Do you know if the perpetrator lives in the home? (higher risk if yes); Do you know if there is substance abuse in the home? (higher risk if there is); Do you know if the family has friends or neighbors with whom they are involved? (may be lower risk if there is a healthy support system). Careful documentation on your part before making the call will help in your being able to answer these questions. However, do not feel as though you must have the answers to all of these questions. Investigating a child abuse situation is not unlike a case of detective work. The worker looks for every piece that might fit into the puzzle making a total picture.

What is the timing of making a report? If you suspect abuse it is one thing, but let us say that a child has just come to you and told you that he or she is being abused. The first inclination is to prevent the child from going home until you make the report. Some types of abuse are more volatile than others. Neglected children have probably been neglected for sometime and their immediate safety is not in danger. Physically or sexually abused children might be in more danger if the parent knows that the child has talked with you. Ask the child if he or she feels safe in going home. If not, let CPS know this. It may be possible to detain the child after school by assigning a project. Make sure that the parents know that the child will be staying after school. A note of caution to educators: *Do not take the child to your own home.* Such an act may seem to provide the temporary protection the child needs, but it may place you in legal jeopardy. If your state does not give you a legal right to detain the child by taking him or her off school grounds, you could even be charged with kidnapping. It is better to work within the social service system than to put yourself in a legally precarious position.

If you call the agency at the end of the school day and the child refuses to wait at school or is fearful that the parents will be angry if he or she is not home immediately, tell the agency and urge immediate action. If the child is indeed afraid, social service agencies will usually consider these emergency situations and should be able to act quickly. In the meantime, it is important to explain to the child what is happening.

One of the advantages of developing a good rapport with the local child protection agency is so that you will learn to trust their judgments. Usually the worker can tell from your report if the case is indeed an emergency—that is, if the child is at immediate risk. If you have been involved in only a few child abuse reports, you may feel that every one is a risk. But the veteran worker has learned that the child whose eye has just been blackened by a drunken father who is still in the house is in more immediate danger than the child who has been neglected and whose teacher is now reporting it. The neglect case can probably wait until morning while the worker must respond immediately to the child of the drunken father. Therefore, it will be important to trust the worker's judgment, being sure to tell him or her of any circumstances that make you feel that your case should be attended to immediately.

Your phone call will be enough to have the agency begin the initial screening or investigation process. Some states will require a written form as a follow-up and this will usually be due in a day or two. Be sure to check on the agency's requirements or ask at the time of your initial report. Blank forms for states that require them should be kept in the school office so that they are readily available when needed. Reporters should keep a copy of any form they submit for the school's or their own records. Of course this information should be kept confidential.

Once the agency receives your report, staff members determine if there is sufficient evidence to warrant an investigation, or in the case of an emergency, immediate action. This decision and screening process may be completed instantly, or it may take a day or even a week depending upon the emergency nature of the case. A decision to screen in the case means that a social worker or team of social workers will investigate it. Here again, the nature of the case will determine how soon action will be taken. Most states mandate investigation within a week or two, or sooner in an emergency—such as when a child is severely threatened or when a delay would cause some immediate danger to the child.

A note of appeal for busy social workers is in order. Having been on the front lines and supervising many students and workers who are, I can tell you that there are peak times when you are convinced that every one is in the process of abusing their children. Holidays and school vacations as well as a string of snowy or rainy days bring in the abuse reports. Most of the social workers I have known are extremely conscientious but there are times when high caseloads and a peak in reports will mean that the waiting time for an investigation will be longer. It is especially important at these times that the intake worker know any concerns you have for the safety of the child. And after the report, we must have faith that the worker would not be in child protection if he or she did not want to see children protected and will get out on the case as soon as is possible.

When calling in a report, you may want to ask about the timetable of the agency. You can also assure the social worker of your continued cooperation and asked to be kept informed of the progress of the case. In some states, social workers cannot divulge the results of an investigation without a signed affidavit from the alleged abuser, but they may be able to assure you that the case has been looked into. Also, even though some social workers may not keep a reporter informed, others do—especially if they feel that an educator can continue to be a resource in helping the child and the family.

Reporters often complain that they feel as though the child protection agency has done nothing about the abuse report they filed. In addition to time constraints, it is important to realize that the child protection agency operates under a legal mandate from the state or county. The legal framework often requires that social workers provide certain facts to justify the validation of abuse. If those facts are not available, the case may have to be screened out (i.e., the agency cannot act without further information). As a teacher in contact with the child daily, your documentation may help the social worker to intervene. If a case is screened out and then you are able to document further abuse, do not be afraid to file another report or encourage a colleague who is close to the situation to file. It may be the second or third filing that gets results.

If you do not understand what is happening in the case, feel free to call the agency. Even though they may not be able to give you specific information, it may be reassuring to talk to someone about the case. Social workers may be difficult to reach because they spend much of their time out in the field and usually only a day or two a week in the office. The worker's supervisor, who is

Educator's Checklist for Preparing to Report

1. Have you documented your data and written down the information to organize it in your own mind?
2. Have you analyzed your data? What causes you to suspect abuse/neglect? List the symptoms—physical or behavioral.
3. Have you been able to observe the parent/child interaction as worthwhile or different and/or to hard to handle?
4. Have you spoken with other professionals within the school? Do they have reason to suspect abuse/neglect? Why?
5. Do you know the reporting policy of your school? Do you know to whom you should report?
6. Do you have the necessary information required for a report?
7. Do you (or does the school) have the exact telephone number and address of the agency to which you should report?
8. Have you talked with your administrator about the support you will receive once the report is made? What if the parents try to remove the child from your class? Will you have the support of the administration?
9. Does your school have on hand the necessary report forms?
10. Have you set up a support system for yourself with other teachers or administrators? (After the report is made, you may feel vulnerable and need to talk.)

usually in the office on a regular basis, is also a good resource if you want a bit of reassurance that the case is being addressed. Like educators who find it easier to respond to a concerned parent than a critical one, social workers and supervisors will be more likely to answer questions and share what information they can when they perceive that the educator is expressing concern rather than suggesting incompetence.

Perhaps the best way to ensure communication with the child protection agency is through personal contact. This can be done through a Child Protection Team or by asking that the agency allow one worker or supervisor to act as a liaison with the school. If your school is not receptive to this suggestion, call the agency yourself. Say that you are a concerned educator who would like to talk with a social worker or a supervisor about your role in the reporting process.

Remember that the helping teams need to present a united front as a model for the child who may be suffering from the confusion brought about by a disorganized, abusive, or neglectful family.

As you consider all the suggestions made above, the following checklist may help you to feel more prepared.

Making a Report Through a Child Protection Team

If teachers knew how much easier it is to report through a Team than it is to make a report alone, every school would have one.

Indeed, reporting through a Child Protection Team can be much easier than being on one's own. It is comforting to know that one's impressions are shared by others, and that someone else will be helping you to remember all that it takes to make a good report.

To report through a CPT, you will first need to know whom to contact. Hopefully you have received training on the formation of the CPT. In most schools, a reporter may speak to any member who will then initiate the convening of the CPT. This may be after school or during a brief connection in the school day. Team meetings need not be cumbersome affairs but rather a somewhat informal opportunity for you, the reporter, to share your data and the CPT to determine what to do. Having several people ask questions or discuss the case with you will often jog your memory about details you may have forgotten. Usually, if the CPT decides with you that a report is warranted, a CPT member will do the reporting to the child protection agency. Some CPT members who call in the report will ask the original reporter to sit with them to answer additional questions. Others times you may be told that either the CPT or the child protection agency will get back to you with future questions. Be aware that, even if you report through a CPT, you may expect a social worker from the child protection agency to contact you for additional information.

Let us say for a moment that you know who to contact during school hours but a situation suddenly arises after school when everyone appears to have left for the day. Again, your training should have informed you how to contact Team members after hours or how to proceed. If you happen to be at an evening meeting, in addition to knowing how to contact CPT members, it is important to also know that, in an emergency, child protection agencies have phone numbers that can be accessed when it is not during the working day. Your CPT members should have this number available to them.

One nice aspect of having a CPT is that you will have a support system right at the school who can talk with you after the report has been made. You might be able to get emotional support for your feelings surrounding the report, or the CPT members might know if child protection has had an opportunity to go out and begin investigating. Sometimes when the child protection agency is dealing with one individual (designated CPT member) regularly, they may be more forthcoming about follow-up information.

Child Protection Team members may also be resources for additional information on child abuse and neglect issues. Check out whether they have instituted a library for further reading. Or is there some type of training that would help you to recognize or deal with abuse situations? Ideally, CPT members will have had additional training and may act as consultants if you have questions about child maltreatment or about the process of reporting. Telling the CPT members of your needs will greatly help them to help you in your job as a concerned educator.

Tips for Child Protection Team Members

If you have decided to volunteer or have accepted the appointment as a Child Protection Team member, you are obviously intensely interested in the safety and protection of children. To do an especially effective job toward that end, there are some issues to consider and some preparations to make. Many of these were discussed in Chapter 6 when discussing setting up a CPT, but repeating a few of them might be helpful. First, *how will your Team function? What roles will the members play?* Once you know this, *preparation is a key factor.* Be thoroughly prepared before a report ever comes into you. For example, *do you have the phone number of the child protection agency and perhaps a contact person easily accessible? Do you have the after-hours number of child protection and do you carry it with you when you leave school? Do you know what will happen at the child protection agency's end when a call is made after hours?* For example, some agencies have their own crisis line that will beep a social worker on call. That person will usually get back to you right away. Other CPS agencies contract with crisis hotlines or other social services providers to take the after-hours calls. These providers will then contact a social worker on call. Knowing how your local child protection agency handles after-hours calls will be helpful.

Another prime consideration (see Chapter 6) is that of training. Have you trained staff members so that they know of your existence and how to make a report to the Team? Have you educated the staff on what symptoms to look for when they suspect abuse or neglect? Written material is extremely important and should be a significant part of your budget. You should generate a sheet that gives the names of the members of the Team and how to reach them both during school and after hours. One school contracted with a company that made magnets for businesses and had magnets made with pertinent names and numbers that teachers and guidance counselors could attach to their desks or file cabinets. That way the number was always accessible without having to find that paper that may have been misplaced or filed. Because they had enough magnets made for every staff member, the cost was minimal and the company was glad to redo the magnets from year to year as team members changed.

Staff might also appreciate a handout of clues to look for in trying to determine if it is abuse, or a teacher's checklist for making a report. A number of these checklists and guides are included throughout this text and could help you to generate appropriate handouts. Remember that many people are visual in their learning and memory recall. If they see something, it is easier for them to remember it.

Once you have fully prepared by defining roles, going through training, and determining where and how often you will meet, you will be ready to receive reports. The more visible your Team is in a positive helpful manner, the easier it will be for your colleagues to come to you with a report. When a report does come in, remember it is your role to help the teacher/educator. A meeting with the CPT should be comforting rather than intimidating. One teacher explained her experiences with a newly formed and somewhat overzealous Child Protection Team.

> All of the people on our Team were my colleagues. I had just finished having lunch with two of them. And then a child came to me with a report. I called a CPT member and asked to speak with the Team. A meeting was set up immediately as I was most concerned about this child. The student teacher took my class and we met in the guidance office. Suddenly I was having questions fired at me as if I were at the Inquisition. Did I know this? Did I try that? Finally I said "Wait a minute! I came here for support not interrogation!" The tone completely changed and we were able to discuss this child's problem in a manner that was really helpful to me. We decided that a report to the child protection agency should be made and all went well from there. My advice to CPT members is: "Remember that your role is one of support as well as determining whether a report should be made!"

The CPT members learned a valuable lesson from this teacher. When we are caught up in a job, we often forget that it may be difficult for the reporter who deals with the child on an everyday basis. *The roles of the CPT members at the meeting should be twofold: support the reporter and compile the information. Both roles are equally as important.*

Knowing who will actually make the report to the child protection agency in advance is also helpful. Most CPS agencies would prefer to deal with one person on a Team, but contacts can rotate if this better suits your needs. Look over the Teacher's Checklist earlier in this chapter to determine if you have all the necessary data. Be sure to find out about the agency's timetable on action and the policy on feedback. The reporter will probably be interested in feedback and it will be helpful if you can provide some idea of when it will be.

When teachers and other staff come to the Team to discuss their suspicions about child abuse and neglect, it is important to remember that these are individuals who bring with them their own histories and feelings. Some may have been abused or neglected themselves as children and making this report may bring up old memories for them as well. As one school nurse explained:

> I went to the Child Protection Team meeting full of concern for this poor little girl that I felt was being sexually abused. And as I began to talk about my suspicions, I suddenly saw myself thirty-eight years ago when I would desperately have loved to tell someone what my father was doing to me. All of a sudden I burst out crying. I was so embarrassed. I couldn't stop the tears. Someone handed me a tissue and someone else talked soothingly to me until I got control. It was then that I realized that I was doing for this child what I wished that someone had done for me—get help. Then I had to try to separate the facts of my abuse from hers. It wasn't easy, but the Team members were wonderful. The act of making that report was actually therapeutic for me and for the child who had come to me.

Remembering that you may not know, in every situation, the background of the reporter or what he or she is feeling, may help you to remain aware of the reporter's reactions. Does he or she need extra support or perhaps a referral for his or her own counseling. (It is also helpful to have names of possible referral sources for adult counseling that you can provide to a staff member who needs them.) Sitting on a Child Protection Team is not just about making decisions based on available information and making a report. It is about helping people with their own issues and conflicts to intervene on behalf of the children they seek to educate. You own caring attitude may model the emotional support that they are then able to give to the child.

Although the task of being on a Child Protection Team can be a significant one, you will also be in a pivotal role to help both the children you serve and your colleagues to better do their jobs as well. It is the careful, caring, thoughtful, and well-planned intervention that will enable the child and his or her family to take the first step toward healing.

What Happens Once the
Report Has Been Made?

Once a report has been made to the child protection agency and the decision made by them to screen it in, a whole series of events is set into motion. First, the intake social worker, often in conjunction with a supervisor or the intake unit, will need to make several important decisions, discussed in detail below.

Does the Case Warrant Further Investigation?

When a case comes into the Intake Unit, it is usually assessed on the basis of risk to the child. As previously mentioned, many agencies now use a risk matrix that tells them how urgent it will be to begin a more in-depth intervention. If the risk seems great, the intervention is likely to begin as soon as a worker can get out on it. If the risk is not as high or even low, the case may be attended to when the more high-priority cases have been handled.

Once the investigation is initiated, the worker assigned will be observing the parents' reactions, attitudes, and motivation throughout the process. In some cases the very fact that there is intervention from CPS will create improvement in the family situation. At the other extreme, the social worker may receive no cooperation from the parents, yet have insufficient evidence to ensure court involvement. Some parents are well enough acquainted with the social service system to know exactly what to say and how to look, so when the social worker visits the home, everything appears to be acceptable. In such cases, it is as frustrating for the social worker as it is for the teacher to close a case without rendering any help. It should also be mentioned that some states require intervention by the law enforcement agency. A police officer might accompany the social worker or may even be the one to make the first contact. If this is so in your state, the child protection agency will know the role the law enforcement agency plays in these cases. In addition, some cases in some states will involve mandatory referral to the District Attorney's office.

If the case is referred to court, the judge will usually appoint an investigator who will undertake a detailed investigation of the case and return, in a prescribed amount of time, a written report outlining his or her recommendations for the case. In some states this investigator will be appointed from the child protection agency. But in other states it is seen as a conflict of interest that a social worker from an agency assigned to treat a family performs the investigation to determine if there should be treatment and what type. Therefore, some states appoint an independent investigator who may be an attorney who investigates as a sideline or a worker from another agency (Crosson-Tower, 2002).

Thus, decisions made about further intervention on behalf of the child may, in fact, be joint decisions of two or more agencies and several professionals.

Is it Safe for the Child to Remain in the Home?

Throughout child welfare history, professionals have vacillated between keeping children in their own home and placing them in a foster home. Children feel greater security in their own home, however dysfunctional it may be. Studies have shown that foster home placement does not necessarily ensure a happier life. In fact, for children who are returned to their own home after foster home placement, the situation may deteriorate faster than it would have without placement. Another more recent alternative in some agencies is to place children in the homes of extended family members referred to as *kinship care* (see Hegar and Scannapieco, 1999), although this tends to be used more for long-term placement than for the placement necessary during an investigation. There are several advantages of these kinship placements even at the point of investigation. First, the child is given some security in that he or she is placed with familiar people with whom there already is a relationship. In addition, placement with relatives may mean that the child remains within his or her own cultural group which again adds security. Second, because they are family, these kin are usually more committed to the child than people in an unrelated foster home would be. And, relatives can be excellent motivators for parents who need a push to cooperate with the agency or to begin to take responsibility for their parenting roles (Berrick et al. 1999).(The possibility of foster care placement will be discussed further in a later section of this chapter.)

In some cultures, the community plays an important part in whether the child can be kept safe (see Ledesma and Starr, 2000). Hopefully the social worker involved with the case will recognize the cultural implications and assess these in the decision to leave the child in the home or cultural community.

Although the best plan for the child may seem to be removal from a difficult home situation, the social worker may well decide to have the child remain at home and to try to work with the family while it's intact. Even in cases of sexual abuse, it is more advisable to remove from the home the perpetrator rather than the child. This cannot be done, however, unless the nonabusing parent agrees to and is capable of protecting the child from contact with the perpetrator. The child would never be left in a home where it was felt that he or she was unsafe or in immediate danger.

Will the Family Accept Help Willingly?

We all know how difficult it can be when someone tells us that we need help. It is not surprising that a family would have difficulty accepting that they need help in parenting, especially in a society where we assume that to be a parent is everyone's right. Thus when an agency comes along and says in essence "you are not doing your job," families are understandably resistant. In addition, some cultural groups protest by silence or withdrawal (see Prater, 2000; Ledesma and Starr, 2000), and it may be difficult to communicate that our system expects them to act on their own behalf.

Families may agree to accept help from the child protection agency for several reasons:

- They may sincerely want help and have, in fact, been asking for it by their behavior
- They may fear the legal consequences if they do not agree to be helped
- They may comply to "get the social worker off their back"
- Some cultures are sufficiently intimidated by or respectful of authority figures that they agree to comply because they feel that it is expected

Whatever the motivation, if the agency feels that the family needs help and the family agrees to cooperate, the relationship will in most states, probably be voluntary. While this is the preferred treatment, it can sometimes be frustrating when the family does not keep appointments or the old problems begin to reappear. And there will always be the family who appears to cooperate with the child protection agency while they have no intention of making any real changes. If, on the other hand, the family refuses help initially, or at some point decides not to cooperate any longer, the social worker can opt for court involvement.

Particular instances that require court intervention are as follows:

- The child is in imminent danger of harm
- Attempts at treatment have failed, and parents have not made progress toward providing adequate care for the child

If there is a decision for court intervention, the child protection worker will usually file a petition in the juvenile division of the civil court requesting that the family be compelled to accept help or that the children be placed in foster care (Noel, 2000). This sets in motion a whole array of procedures that will be discussed later.

Whether or not there is court involvement or family cooperation, if the case is assessed to need more help, the agency works with the family. At this point, you may be asked to give reports to the social worker regarding your contacts with the family or the child's progress in school.

Exactly What Type of Treatment Does the Family Need?

Family treatment may take several forms:

- Concrete services such as financial assistance, medical assistance, housing assistance, day care (to relieve the parent of some stress)
- Referral to other services specific to the family's needs, such as services for counseling, budgeting consultation, family planning, substance abuse treatment, or help with special-needs children
- Advocacy services—helping the family to actually obtain the services for which they are eligible
- Legal aid services for situations like domestic violence or custody issues
- Culturally-based services (such as working through a Spanish Center for a Hispanic family) that will help the family to understand what is expected of them and communicate their needs
- Counseling services (most protective agencies are able to provide these in a limited way; if more in-depth counseling is needed, the family is referred to another agency that will often contract or work with the protective agency)

In general, "treatment" by the child protection agency is in the form of intensive case management or the agency assesses the family's needs, plugs them into other existing community services, and monitors their progress over time in an attempt to preserve the family unit (Savage, 2001) if that can be accomplished.

Who Will Be Involved in the Treatment of the Family?

The group of professionals concerned with the assessment or treatment of protective situations may vary depending on the family and their needs. Within the protective agency, the case is usually first screened or assessed through an intake process, possibly by a unit of workers skilled in investigation. Once a treatment plan has been devised and agreed upon, usually with the cooperation of the family, the case may be transferred to an ongoing unit and assigned to another social worker. Smaller agencies may assign a case to one worker from intake through termination but this is the exception rather than the rule. As part of the case management services, the assigned social worker may involve other community professionals such as health professionals, psychologists, psychiatric social workers or other mental health professionals, housing or legal assistance experts, substance abuse counselors, or other types of support services (such as daycare, or financial assistance). If the family is from a nonEnglish-speaking culture and they need either interpretative services or support in understanding norms that may different from their own, a culturally-based agency may become involved. For example, one Hmong (an area of Laos) family was totally confused about what was happening to them and required the help of an Asian Center that specialized in working with this population with somewhat unique mores. The protective agency may even call upon school personnel such as the child's teacher(s), the school nurse, the school social worker, or guidance counselor to be part of the treatment efforts. If placement is indicated, foster parents or relatives who serve as a kinship placement may become part of the equation.

One of the most difficult aspects of serving this family will be for the treatment team to keep open communication and work together. Professionals, each with their own area of expertise, may unwittingly get caught up in battles over "turf," forgetting that the child and the family are what it is all about. It is so important that the links in this therapeutic chain remain in positive contact with each other, bearing in mind that the primary goal is to help the family. This can become even more difficult for the professionals involved as some families may be skillful in building mistrust among professionals and in playing one against the other (referred to as "splitting"). Other families, not necessarily intending to pit their helpers against each other, may misinterpret the information that they are given, suggesting to one professional that another said something that would seem counterproductive. Thus, being on a therapeutic team requires frequent communication and an understanding of how families may react when they feel threatened by authority.

How Long Will the Treatment Take?

This is an extremely difficult question to answer. So much will depend on the family's willingness to cooperate and make changes, the agencies' protocol, the social worker's caseload, and how fast bureaucracy can move. Most child protection agencies will set up a treatment plan with clients that will have a timetable of betweeen a few weeks up to many months. These written plans are reviewed periodically by agency staff, sometimes with clients, and may be renewed if necessary. In the interest of *permanency planning*, a concept that seeks to find the best, most permanent solution for a child as soon as is feasible, many agencies are now under constraints to develop a permanent plan in a specific amount of time. For example, Massachusetts courts recently adopted legislation that affects some families giving them eighteen months in which to meet the stipulations of the treatment plan. If they are not able to comply during that time, the children could be removed by the child protection agency even to the point of having them adopted by someone else. Although this may seem harsh to some, the previous regulations allowed families, in some cases, many years to change often harming the children in the process. And, when in a study of former foster children done by Tower and Andrews (1992), these now-adults were asked what one change they would like to see in the foster care system, the response was overwhelming. Most felt that their parents had been given too many chances to change over too long a period of time, robbing these children of the permanency they deserved.

If the court becomes involved, hearings may be scheduled at regular intervals, from six weeks to six months. The severity of the family situation may also determine the length of treatment. If the family's progress toward the treatment goals is very poor and few gains are made, the children could be removed and placed in foster care. Sometimes progress is slow due to no fault of the family. For example, one family required a Cambodian interpreter. As there was only one such interpreter in the surrounding area, the meetings between social service staff and the family had to depend on when this individual was available. For this reason, the treatment stretched out much longer than it might have otherwise.

If, on the other hand, the family appears to really be benefiting from intervention, more time may be spent on teaching better parenting skills. For example:

Mila Honet had grown up in an institution. Though she was severely learning disabled, her parents had been convinced that she was mentally retarded and had placed her in an institution when she was quite young. She had remained there in the mentally retarded unit until she was eighteen. When she left, she had minimal daily living skills. Fortunately, she was placed in an industrial setting where several other girls, recognizing that she had more intelligence than was at first obvious, befriended her and taught her much of what she needed to know to maintain herself. She was invited to live with one girl and until her roommate was killed in an automobile accident several years later, all seemed to work well. By this time, however, Mila had met Jerome, a young man who was on the maintenance crew at the factory. They quickly became involved and married. The first child was not long in coming. For this new development, Mila was totally unprepared. She had no idea how to care for a baby. Jerome, somewhat limited himself, knew even less and started picking up extra hours to get away from home. When the baby was rushed to the hospital at several months old with severe pneumonia, the nurses felt sure that he was being neglected. They reported the case to the local child protection agency. After hearing Mila's background, it soon became clear to the child protection worker that this mother had not intended to neglect her child. Rather she had learned none of the skills necessary to be either a homemaker or a mother. What followed was intensive training in basic homemaking skills and parenting skills by both the social worker and an array of other professionals brought in for the task.

Whatever the cause, no abuse or neglect situation can be remedied immediately. Sometimes treatment can be terminated prematurely either by the family's action or because the time allotted for such cases has expired. If the family's insurance is used for services such as counseling or medical help, the allowed number of sessions or appointments may also run out. This premature termination is unfortunate but all too frequent in the world of social services. Hopefully, the future will see more emphasis on the completion of services rather than expecting that healing can take place in a prescribed number of visits.

At What Point Does the Family No Longer Need Services?

The obvious answer to the above question is that it depends on the family and the type of maltreatment. In an ideal world, the following are guidelines:

- In physical abuse cases, services are terminated when the abuser stops abusing the child and has learned another method of coping with aggressive feelings.
- In neglect cases, services are terminated when the parent can meet the child's basic needs adequately.
- In sexual abuse cases, services are terminated when the perpetrator is no longer involved sexually with the child and has learned more coping methods to prevent such involvement in the future.

In reality, the agency may need to terminate services when the abuse/neglect has stopped, hoping that the parent has learned to prevent any recurrence. As mentioned earlier, some agencies have arbitrary time limits based on the restriction of staff time and agency funds. If there is court involvement, the case continues until the judge determines that there is no further evidence of abuse.

Few professionals who work with these cases are pleased with the criteria used for closing their cases. But until we become more skilled in fully understanding and determining human motivation, these are the criteria that are in place. Even after a case has been closed by the child protection agency, if you suspect that the abuse or neglect is recurring, it is important to again report.

What Happens to the Child While the Family is Being Investigated and Later Treated?

To answer this question, we must consider both the logistical and the emotional aspects of the child's world. Logistically, the child will probably remain with the family while the investigation is being completed. After all, how can one assess the level of childcare the parents provide if there is no child in the home. As previously mentioned, this will be dependent on the child's safety and the parent's ability to cooperate. Many children remain at home throughout treatment as well. The mere fact that the parent knows that a social worker could arrive at any moment or that further abuse may mean that the child will be removed is enough to ensure that most children are safe in their homes as long as the child protection agency has an open case. Emotionally, the child may feel that he or she has caused the unrest and does not understand that the responsibility is with the parents. He or she may recognize that removal is a possibility and wake every morning wondering if this is the day.

If the home is too volatile to be safe, the child may be placed in foster care, as mentioned above. The attempt is made to keep the child in the same school district for some consistency, but that is not always possible. The advantage of a foster home is that the child is with people who have been trained to be a part of the therapeutic team and to work closely with the agency. The child is removed from the conflictual situation and has a chance—with space and nurturing—to heal to some degree. The disadvantages may be obvious as well. First, the child is separated from what is usually the only home and parents he or she has known and placed with total strangers whom he or she must learn to trust during a time when security and familiarity are what is needed. He or she usually knows that the placement is not permanent and may feel in limbo (Tower and Andrews, 1992). It can be a difficult time for many children.

Children placed in kinship care with relatives (mentioned above) have at least some of the security that a child placed in unrelated foster care lacks. That child may have an opportunity to see his or her parents in a relatively secure setting. It may feel good to kin that these children are invested in them and they care what happens on a very personal level. However, there are also some drawbacks that will affect the child. The fact that the parental home is "not good enough" for the child at this time, and the home of a relative is, may give rise to a variety of family conflicts between parents and kin. Parents may feel betrayed, resentful, and angry. Kin may assume a superior attitude, lauding over the parents that their (kin's) skills are better than those of the parents. And, the child might end up right in the middle of these dynamics. Relatives interested in custody might even jeopardized reunification efforts (Berrick et al. 1999).

It is also possible that the first placement for a child will not work out, and the child must be moved to another home. Obviously, each move is another separation and can create additional trauma. Hopefully, the social worker will be skilled in helping the child with this transition. Also, children may be placed in foster care or kinship care and then returned home. Despite the fact that this might be the intended plan, the transition may be difficult for all involved. The child has experienced a different style of parenting that may have been more functional at the hands of the foster parent. He or she may therefore become critical of the parent's style disturbing the parent's already shaky self-esteem. The child may test limits. Most children who are placed out of their homes misinterpret the gesture on some level as either abandonment by the parent or punishment because he or she has been "bad." Thus, when they return home, they may test to see if the parent will send them away again. Both parents and children will need a great deal of support during unification.

An entire book could be written about how a child feels when he or she is involved in abuse/neglect intervention and with the foster care system. But here you are, a classroom teacher, with a child who is experiencing all of this trauma. It goes without saying that the emotional impact of these changes and uncertainties will probably be seen in the classroom. One child may be overly compliant, perhaps afraid that the school will also send him or her away. This child is holding feelings inside and should be referred for counseling to help in dealing with a situation that he or she is afraid to face. Some children talk incessantly about what is happening and you may even wish that they would not. These children need a place where they can talk freely and try to make sense of the events in their lives. Children may act out in a variety of ways, from hostile behavior that gets them into trouble to striking out against other children. In short, if you know that a child is involved in the social service process, be conscious of his or her needs. Does he or she need a friend or a counselor? Are there ways that you can help to ease his or her burden. If you are especially concerned, it will be important to let the social worker assigned to the case know.

As we look at the myriad of feelings that children feel when they are involved with social services, a natural reaction might be "do I really want to put a child through all this? Perhaps I shouldn't report in the first place!" We all experience a variety of emotions as we wend our way through a crisis. But there are many crises in life that are necessary and worth going through for the end result. Is it not better for a child to be helped through the emotional turmoil of intervention rather than have him or her continue to be abused or neglected and face worse trauma down the road?

What Involvement Does the Educator Have in the Investigation and Treatment?

The last section indicates that you, as an educator, can be of help to the child by being aware of how he or she is doing and keeping the social worker up-to-date. But educators often wonder what else they might be called on to do during the whole intervention process. This may depend to some extent on whether or not you have a Child Protection Team. The Team members might be in contact with the agency and your time might not be required. On the other hand, if you were the original reporter or the child is in your class(es), you might be asked for an interview during the investigation period. The questions you will be asked will be an attempt on the part of the investigator to uncover pieces of the puzzle mentioned earlier and fit them together so that he or she might make a recommendation for treatment.

After the investigation has been completed and the family is in treatment, you may or may not be called on to be involved. This involvement, if you are asked, will probably entail keeping the social worker posted about your contacts with the child, his or her progress, and your contacts with the family. If you have information that you feel is important to the case and you have not been asked for it, feel free to call the social worker or the agency supervisor. Sometimes that little piece of incidental information may make a real difference in a case. For example:

> John, a social worker who was covering Intake, received a call about 4 PM that a child, Evan, had been quite badly abused. When he checked the files, he discovered that this was an open case but that the social worker assigned was in court that day. Concerned about the neighbor's evaluation of the severity of the bruises, John decided to go out and check it out. When he arrived at the apartment in a one story project, the mother was watching soap operas and said that the children were playing outside. John said that he would like to see the child in question. The mother went out and returned with an adorable blonde blue-eyed child who appeared not to have a bruise on him anywhere. John returned to the office, somewhat puzzled hoping to get in touch with the other worker whose case it was . But he was unable to do so.
>
> The next morning, Evan's teacher noticed that he had a few bruises on his neck. Concerned about them and his apparent difficulty moving, she asked the nurse to take a look at them. The nurse lifted the child's shirt and observed a whole series of severe and obviously painful bruises. Knowing that this was an open case, the teacher called the child protection worker who was assigned to it. He was out in the field and she happened to get John. She explained

the situation. John asked her to describe the child's appearance. "He is a very appealing child, she said. He has brown hair and very deep brown eyes." John told the supervisor who paged Evan's worker. Together he and John agreed to see Evan at school and then to confront the mother on how she had shown John the wrong child.

In this situation, it was the update by Evan's teacher that speeded up further intervention in the case and may have protected Evan from another beating.

A word about working with social workers. Having been a protective social worker for many years and then an educator, I can tell you that these roles are not that dissimilar. Both jobs can be high pressure and can have peak busy times. Yet both are interested in the welfare of the children they serve and in this there should be a comfortable meeting of the minds. For this reason, communication between these two professionals is very important.

I have heard teachers complain that social workers are unresponsive to their requests for information. The educator may therefore assume that nothing has been done on the case. But not unlike teachers who may attempt to give themselves with skill and understanding to their classes of thirty odd children, social workers too have very large caseloads often composed of very needy and demanding families. Often their attention goes—by necessity—from crisis to crisis with insufficient time for too many details on any one case. The neophyte social worker may feel overwhelmed; the overworked, experienced social worker may appear mechanical. But remaining in this profession requires a sincere concern for the welfare of one's clients.

" I may not always get back to teachers as I should," admits one experienced socal worker, "but I really do appreciate a phone call letting me know how the child is doing or if anything new has come up with the child and the family."

Although the social worker may be making major decisions that will affect the child's life, it is the teacher who "lives" with the child day after day and can be a vital resource in the agency's decision making. Of course, the decisions of the social worker are influenced not only by agency policy but also by the court system. A child may be returned to a natural family not because the social worker feels that it is the best plan, but because of insufficient evidence for the court to continue custody. In some cases it is the team of social worker and teacher who had carefully documented and communicated what is going on with the child, that can change the direction of the court when the case was about to be dismissed.

This is not meant to imply that responsibility for communication should be solely the educator's. It is mutual. Both professionals complain that they find it difficult to contact one another. However most social workers have a day in the office and teachers may have a free period during the day when they can be reached more easily. Those who are able to work together may find that this communication is a rewarding opportunity for both to feel that they are protecting the best interests of the child.

What if the Case Becomes Involved with Court?

> The first time it was necessary to go to court I was apprehensive. I expected to see the Perry Mason that I watched as a child, in all his glory. What I did see was a small courtroom—not unlike a formal classroom—with a desk for the judge and only a handful of people in attendance.

There are several types of court with which a protective case may become involved. The first of these, described above, is juvenile court known in some states as family court. It is also possible in some cases for the perpetrator to be prosecuted through criminal court or less frequently the case could be involved in probate court. Your chances of going to criminal or probate court on behalf of a child are extremely unlikely. The possibility of going to juvenile court are not very great either unless you are the original reporter and the case ended up in court right after the report was made, when there is more of a chance. But it is useful to know what will happen and to be prepared should you be asked to appear (see also Hobbs et al. 1999).

Protective cases are taken to juvenile court (as previously mentioned) if the social worker feels that the child is in real danger or the family will not co-operate. Prior to any court hearing, the child protection agency (or police) files a petition stating that the child is in need of the court's protection. There may be a pretrial hearing to determine if the case can be resolved without court intervention, or if there is, in fact enough evidence to go to court. The social service agency must then collect witnesses to substantiate the report. At this point, you may receive a subpoena to appear. In the juvenile courtroom there will be no jury, merely a judge, court officers, probation officers, lawyers (for the child and for the parents; sometimes there is a lawyer for the child protection agency), social service personnel, and witnesses. The parents will be in attendance and, for the first session, sometimes the children will be also, depending upon the regulations of the court. In a regularly-scheduled juvenile court, the courtroom itself is usually unpretentious, unless the juvenile court functions only a day or two a week and uses the regular courtroom facilities. A juvenile courtroom is closed to the general public and only those who are involved in the case are allowed to attend (Noel, 2001).

After a series of preliminaries—often so quickly done or muttered in such a way that one has difficulty knowing exactly what is happening—you will merely be asked to state your name, profession, and involvement with the case. One school adjustment counselor recounts her experience in court and makes some recommendations.

> As a representative of the school, I had the opportunity to be a witness at a child neglect hearing. I discovered that it is very important to bring documentation with you to the hearing. This may include

test scores, your own notes on observations of home conditions if you have been there, parent-child interaction in school or in the home (that you have witnessed), dates of documented abuse/neglect or dates of home/school contact. Try to answer each question as truthfully as you can, as you are under oath. In my case, I included not only the negative aspects of the home conditions and parenting skills, but also the positive aspects of the home environment. I was asked to answer only when spoken to and not give my personal opinion unless requested to do so.

When testifying, do not sound defensive. As a witness, you are not being judged and you need not fear being interrogated. Even if the proceedings become heated, remember that this is not about you but about the case. In my particular situation, I was briefed several weeks in advance of the hearing as to what types of questions might be asked of me. I was not allowed to hear other witnesses' testimony during the hearing and remained in a kind of waiting room before and after my testimony. I do not know if that is typical. When in the courtroom, I was encouraged to give my testimony slowly and not feel rushed.

Because I was dismissed before the hearing had concluded, I did not hear the outcome. I had been encouraged to call the social worker to find out whatever feedback she could give me. This she can do only within the rights of the clients confidentiality.

Tips on Going to Court for Educators

1. Prepare! Jot down dates, facts, and other vital information for your testimony, but do not memorize it. You will usually be allowed to take a paper or a notecard to the stand.
2. Dress appropriately, tending toward the conservative.
3. Check with the social worker or attorney to see if there will be a briefing before the court date.
4. Speak slowly and concisely. Remember that the recorder is recording your testimony.
5. Do not be afraid to go slowly, thinking out each question.
6. Speak only when spoken to, remembering that the court is interested in facts, not opinion, unless it is asked of you.
7. If you do not know an answer, do not guess. Feel free to say that you do not know.
8. Do not let heated cross examination fluster you.
9. Remember that you are not on trial. You are there only to help the child.
10. Do not be afraid to call the social worker after the hearing to determine the outcome.

In addition to this educator's suggestions, it may also be helpful to:

- Dress appropriately, remembering that courts tend to be conservative
- Prepare ahead—the documentation of facts, dates, and so on that will help you to remember
- Not memorize your testimony—it should sound spontaneous

You may feel somewhat nervous; most people usually do, especially when asked to take an oath. Preparing yourself mentally to answer and concentrating on speaking both loudly and clearly will help (Hobbs et al. 1999; Caulfield, 1978).

The court will be recording your testimony so it is important to be clearly audible. If you do not know the answer to a question, do not guess; just say that you do not know. Although, as in the case above, you may be separated from other witnesses, in other situations, you may hear their testimony. It is vital that you not let this influence you and that you present your own story in an organized manner, not being afraid to admit your beliefs. Most attorneys in juvenile court are fairly low key. But occasionally you will find one who is especially intense about the case or who is the frustrated dreamer excluded from a television courtroom drama. Such attorneys sometimes fire questions at you in quick succession or raise their voices in such a way that it can seem intimidating. Do not become flustered. If you have documented your facts, you are less likely to get shaken by this performance.

In some situations, you may be asked to appear at a later hearing to update the court on the progress of the child. More than likely, however, this information will be included in later social worker reports and you will be required to make only one court appearance. But, no matter how many times you are asked to appear in court, it should not give you undue anxiety if you remember that you are not on trial. You are merely there to help the child.

What About the
Long-Range Picture?

The report has been made, the case has been investigated, and the family is in treatment or treatment may have been terminated. But you are still in contact with the child who was the reason for it all. Classmates may have learned about the abuse. And you may still be dealing with the parents or the child's foster home. How does it all fit together? How do you as the educator juggle all these balls and still teach or counsel or do whatever job you are assigned effectively? This chapter will give you some ideas to answer these questions.

Helping the Child Individually

Over the years, it has become clear that abuse and neglect take their toll on a variety of children, usually in similar ways. Abused and neglected children may:

- Have a very poor self-image, feeling that they do not matter or that there is something wrong with them
- Need individual attention
- Need to express frustration and anger
- Have unattended educational and medical needs
- Need to succeed—to do something right
- Need to know that they have rights too; those with poor self-image may not know that, in some instances, it is all right to say no to adults
- Have hampered development emotionally, physically, or sexually

Different types of abuse or neglect may result in different problems to overcome. For example, adults often do not realize that children who are victims of neglect might not understand the messages that teachers give to them. Cantwell (1997) comments on the issue of language in the neglectful home.

The neglected child may have heard only one-statement commands like "Sit down!" or "Close the door." Therefore, he or she will have not had an opportunity to develop more complex language that connotes more abstract concepts. Thus, when this child goes to school and is told by the teacher to "sit in your seat, put your feet on the floor, and take out your notebook so that you can copy the words I will write on the board," he or she is completely overwhelmed. Most children have learned through experience how to listen to, translate, and therefore obey a series of commands. Not this child. The result is that he or she may sit there and do nothing, or obey only the last command that was heard. Some children will cover their anxiety about not knowing what is expected by clowning to create a diversion. Some might even act out behaviorally. And in the middle of a busy lesson, we, the educator become frustrated and annoyed with this child's not realizing that the behavior is a message about what he or she has experienced.

Maltreated children have another problem with respect to student-teacher communication; Cantwell (1985) points out that children whose parents are loving and consistent develop knowing that they are cared for and believing that adults want the best for them. They learn to accept adult's commands on faith. Therefore, when a teacher gives a direction, these children will assume that it is for their own good and will comply. On the other hand, maltreated children, exposed to inconsistent parenting, may not be convinced that adults mean well. When a teacher makes a request, such children may refuse to respond because they are unsure if compliance will be in their best interest. It is only when this child learns to trust you and your consistency that he or she will not question your commands.

It is therefore important that teachers be alert to children's comprehension as well as their level of trust in adults. During the first few days of class, be especially conscious of how children react to commands. Does each child really seem to know what you want? Further, does a particular child seem to want to please you or seem to comply fearfully only to avoid punishment?

Some types of assistance for children are more obvious than others. Referrals for medical testing within the school as well as assessment for special needs can be made for any child. Perhaps the two biggest needs—both related to maltreated children are to improve their self-image and to help them feel as though they can "do something right." There is also a need to express anger at what has been done to them. Any tasks or exercises that can meet these needs will be helpful. For example, choose tasks that give the youngster a feeling of authority in the classroom or on the playground—something as simple as erasing the chalkboard or handing out materials. Or choose care-taking tasks such as feeding the gerbils. This enables the child to be the caregiver and to learn ways to properly care for something or someone as well as to feel important. And a quiet word of appreciation on completion of the task may mean a great deal to the abused or neglected child. It is of course important to rotate tasks so that one child does not seem to be favored.

High school students can also be given tasks of importance. In each class, the teacher has an opportunity to comment on the student's little successes as they are accomplished. One school instituted an "achievement notebook." The students were given a little notebook that they were asked to carry with them. When they had accomplished something that was commendable or noteworthy, a teacher or other staff member could write a comment in the book. This served to give students a way to look at their accomplishments. It also proved to have an unexpected result. Teachers discovered that they were pressed to think of the strengths of the more difficult students. In so doing, they learned to capitalize on these strengths.

For some older students sports is a natural outlet. Shooting a few baskets amidst quips about life and the happenings at school may be a perfect occasion for building trust and encouraging the youngster to focus on the positive and attainable elements of his or her life. The high school years also provide an excellent opportunity to help students assess their strengths in the interest of career goals—with coaxing perhaps from a guidance counselor, a concerned teacher, or a coach. Many schools now have computerized skills-assessment programs that help the student, by answering a series of questions, to determine the areas at which he or she might excel.

There may also be community-based programs that encourage students who are not focused on college or specific careers to consider these options. This might be something to which the student could be referred. These career-oriented programs may train students in such useful skills as job searching, resume writing, assessing strengths and areas to improve, interviewing, and getting along with others in a work setting. These skills are invaluable to a youth whose emotional growth and ambition may have been stunted by abuse and neglect. And many teens are so caught up in the residual feelings around their abuse that they cannot see a future for themselves. Such programs can be a real help.

The high school years seem to be a time when many young people are looking for a mentor. Studies have found that mentoring can be a powerful tool especially for those who questions their own abilities. Perhaps one of the greatest benefits the educator can offer this age group, other than helping them to discover themselves, is to be open and approachable as a person—that is to communicate that you will listen if they need to talk.

A high school teacher who was enrolled in a Master's Level class in Child Sexual Abuse, carried her text to school, at first unwittingly, intending to use her study period to do her own homework. Many of the students never noticed the book sitting on her desk, but several who did spy it asked questions about her course. By the end of the day, several had disclosed their own sexual abuse and were able to talk with her about it. Besides making referrals to help these youngsters, the teacher was able to stand by the students in a way that told them that she was there if they needed her.

Some students, teens or younger, are not so easily helped. The behavior of disruptive students may need to be dealt with firmly, but with increased understanding. Again, I refer you to Appelstein's book *No Such Thing as a Bad Kid* (mentioned in Chapter 2) for help with these students. Unfortunately, the school's frequent disciplinary action is suspension or expulsion, two of the worst things that can happen to an abused child. Once again, they feel abandoned and rejected. And they *need* help! Also, the use of corporal punishment—already prohibited in many states and discouraged in others—is also highly undesirable for abused children. It is merely a reinforcement that violence is the way to solve problems, and keeps children from learning that there are other ways to handle conflict. A more effective method of discipline is to point out the positive benefits of acceptable behavior, at the same time motivating the children to accept responsibility for their actions and also to feel deserving of any rewards that might result. Further, children benefit when they are helping to devise the consequences for their negative actions.

One aid in knowing what maltreated children need is a look back at Chapter 5 (pages 62–63) to Helfer's (1979) theory about what abusive parents have not gotten in their own childhoods. First, *the child can be taught how to recognize his or her own needs and how to ask to get them met.* In other words, help the child to recognize that having a temper tantrum or acting out will not get the child what he or she wants, but telling you how he or she feels and asking may. Second, *the child needs to learn to separate feelings from actions.* It is okay to be angry but it is not okay to hit another person. Another lesson is to *help the child master decision making.* When one is faced with the task of making a decision, there is a process that must be followed; one looks at the alternatives, the consequences of each, and makes a choice. A clearheaded approach to a decision makes it much easier.

Abused and neglected children may have a great deal of difficulty taking responsibility for their own actions. By the same token, they may also tend to take on the blame for everyone else's actions. Thus, an important lesson will be *helping them to sort out what is their responsibility and what belongs to others.* For example, suggest to the child: "If Johnny tells you to take a piece of candy from the teacher's desk, whose responsibility is it?" Hopefully the child's answer will be that Johnny should not have suggested it (his responsibility) but I should not have taken it (my responsibility). And finally, the abused child might not want to delay gratification. To this child, life has seemed stingy with its gifts, so that he or she has learned not to anticipate having good things come his or her way. Therefore, if this child wants something, the inclination is to take it whenever possible. These children will do well *to learn how to delay gratification.* This can be accomplished by a system of tokens that encourages them to save for something special or in a variety of other ways. Children who learn the above tasks will be greatly helped not to repeat the abuse of their parents, because learning such tasks gives one more control over one's own life.

Children who have been abused need to feel that they have alternatives, the ability to problem solve, and then be rewarded for their good choices. Or, whether destructive or withdrawn, they may just need time to talk about what has happened to them. The informed educator can be the child's best ally. Understanding through reading and/or training what has happened to the child can be of invaluable help in knowing what to do or say to this child. Sensitivity to clues that the child needs to talk—such as a change in behavior or attitude—is important.

Helping the Maltreated Child in the Classroom

The average teacher may not have time for more individual help or may not want to single out one child. It is possible, however, to help the abused or neglected child within the classroom with the resulting benefit to the whole class. Such help can accomplish several purposes:

- It enhances the self-image and feelings of worth not only of the abused or neglected child, but of classmates as well.
- It enables classmates to begin to understand the abused or neglected child.
- It stimulates other reports and educates children about abuse and neglect.

The exercise or experience used in a classroom may be generic or specific. For example, all children may participate in an activity designed to enhance self-image or they may learn about and discuss child maltreatment specifically. The following are some areas that might be addressed to help the abused child and his or her classmates.

Enhancing Self-Esteem and Feelings of Worth

In our fast-paced world that uses success as a measure of people's worth, it is not unusual for individuals, especially children, to be lacking in self-esteem. Whether a class has a maltreated child or not, all children can benefit from a lesson in self-esteem building. One way to build self-esteem is to help children to feel more capable in their everyday lives. Again, Helfer's tasks (see pages 62–63) might be adapted for the whole class. There are also some excellent exercises that might be integrated into a classroom activity. Wells and Canfield in their book *101 Ways to Enhance Self-Concepts in the Classroom* (1994) offer some excellent suggestions. Other exercises might be created on the spot. For example, what if children were asked to consider, "What is the best thing about me?" or if older students had to answer the question, "What have I accomplished about which I am the most proud?" These discussions are good ways not only to discern the quality of the individual student's self-image, but also to improve it. Class projects in which all class members take part are also useful in helping children feel needed.

How else can you help the child in the classroom? Use any activity that encourages children to think in terms of their own potential rather than of their limitations. Even though it may be difficult for some children, help them to look for their positive attributes and their strengths. A mental or written exercise of thinking of and recording one's individual strengths may work well with some children while others will need a great deal of prompting. Once you have a sense of the positive aspects of each of the children, encourage these features.

To help the students look at their positive points and accomplishments, one teacher had each child in her class write an autobiography, recognizing that there were a few for whom this would be very difficult. She would then help each child recognize the good points about themselves through their writing. One child had been severely neglected and ended up being the care-taker of his younger siblings. The teacher helped him recognize how important he had been to his brother and sister. She also helped him see how responsible he had been by continuing to come to school and learn despite all that was happening in his life. These may seem like small points and in the case of some children, they might be difficult to find, but it is worth the effort when you observe what this means to the child. Remember that abused and neglected children are often surrounded by negatives at home. Emphasizing their positive aspects may be a very new concept for them.

It may be more difficult for one teacher to help a high school student in the classroom setting because of the constantly changing environment—class membership, subject, and so on. Some subjects, however, lend themselves to self-exploration and enhancement of self-image. For example, you might use a literature course to look at the role of women in literature, emphasizing not only the author's message, characterization, and plot, but also the strengths portrayed by women. This can lead to an opportunity to help the female (and perhaps the male as well) class members assess their own strengths. Health or family life courses can lead more obviously to looking at the self and at human potential. It might be more of a challenge to figure out how to build self-esteem concepts into a math class, but I have known some very creative math teachers who are probably equal to the task.

Peer support groups are another vehicle to help teens with adolescent/self-concept messages. Adolescence, a natural period of self exploration, can be a perfect time to introduce positive concepts and role models.

We sometimes forget that enhancing self-esteem can be very easily accomplished just in the manner in which we relate to children. DARE, the police Drug Education Program developed a list of points for parents that I have adapted for teachers (page 142).

A Question of Touch

Over the last few years the issue of whether or not to touch children in school has become a controversial one. It saddens me that some schools have gone so

Ten Ways For An Educator To Raise A Child's Self-esteem

1. Reward the child. Give praise, recognition, special privileges, or increased responsibility for a job well done. Emphasize the good things, rather than the bad.
2. Define classroom rules and limits clearly so that everyone knows what is expected of them. Enforce them, but allow leeway within these limits when appropriate.
3. Be a good role model. Let the children know that you feel good about yourself. Also let them see, too, that you can make mistakes and learn from them.
4. Have reasonable expectations for children. Teach them to set attainable goals for themselves to achieve success. When they attain them, reward them, but also teach them how to reward themselves upon reaching their goals.
5. Help the children develop tolerance toward people with different backgrounds, values, looks, and problems.
6. Give children responsibility at their own developmental level. It will make them feel useful and valued.
7. Show the children you teach that you are interested in them and that they are important to you. Share as is appropriate your interests and activities while encouraging theirs. If you are able to attend a play, concert, game, or other activity that they are in, try to do so. It will mean a lot to them.
8. Talk about values, expressing some of yours but allowing the children freedom to share and develop their own. Describe experiences that may have shaped your values, decisions you made to accept certain beliefs, and reasons behind your feelings. Emphasize that values are very individual things that are influenced by your home, your culture, and your learning. Everyone should develop their own.
9. Use phrases that build self-esteem, such as "Thank you for helping," or "That was a great idea." Avoid phrases that hurt self-esteem, or demean the character of the individual, such as "Why do you never do what you are told?"
10. Show how much you care about the child. Do not be afraid to give physical appreciation such as a pat on the back or a hug with the child's permission. But, be sensitive to the fact that some children are negatively sensitive to touch. Take your cues from the child's reactions.

Adapted from "10 Ways to Help Raise Your Child's Self-Esteem," from Drug Abuse Resistance Education (DARE) St. Louis, MO. 1998.

far as to institute a no-touch policy, thus robbing children of an important part of learning. Studies have confirmed that human beings and especially children, need touch. Research on parenting and deprivation tell us that touching is vital to the first hours of bonding and throughout life. Human babies have actually been known to die from lack of touch (Levy and Orlans, 1998). Children suffering from attachment disorder (see Chapter 3) have often been deprived of positive touch early in their development. Abused children may have experienced only negative touch.

Looking at the above facts should make one recognize that positive touch is extremely important and touch during learning for children deprived of it early in their lives may actually have a restorative value. Of course, one must be particularly sensitive to children who prefer not to be touched due to the fact that their earliest experiences with the sensation have been so negative. But for other children, abused or not, a positive gesture of touch from an authority figure can be especially rewarding. A hug is associated with love and support; a gentle pat with pride in a job well done or a message of assurance. Both are symbols that someone cares. These can be important gestures for children.

Teachers need not be afraid of touching—if they first lay the groundwork. The groundwork involves some basic education for children. Although some of the later sexual abuse prevention materials indicate that we can not rely totally on children's ability to distinguish between touch that is "good," "bad," or "confusing," these concepts can still be useful. "Good touch" can be a hug or a pat— *if* that feels good to a child. "Bad touch is usually first described by children as hitting, punching, pinching, or any touch that hurts. This definition can be expanded to include "anything that doesn't feel good to the child." For example, adults may enjoy ruffling children's hair—a seemingly harmless gesture for the adults—but for children who do not like having their hair ruffled, it is "bad touch." "Confusing touch" is something one is not sure about. As an adult, have you ever been in the situation where someone has invaded your personal space or has touched you in a way that just makes you uncomfortable? For children, expected to respect adults and their gestures to them, this type of touch can be "confusing."

Teachers can also help children to realize that there are parts of the body that are private. Some prevention programs for younger children identify these as the parts covered by one's bathing suit. Children who are confused about specific types of touch or specific places on the body should be encouraged to ask adults about it. This distinction about parts of the body not being touched does become blurred for children who require help with hygiene. Disabled children for example, may require toileting help and can be violated in the act of this type of care. Still, if children feel uncomfortable with the way that individuals are touching them in the interest of their care, they must be helped to tell someone.

We have already gotten into the second part of the groundwork. After teaching children to recognize types of touch, they must be encouraged to express their feelings about these touches. Adults do not always want to hear these feelings. I remember being guilty of hair ruffling when my boys were little. When the oldest said "Mother!!" in a way that let me know that I was embarrassing him, I realized that this type of touch no longer felt good to him. But to me, it still meant something positive. If someone touches a child in a way that he or she does not like, that child should be encouraged to say so—preferably to the person who is touching them—but at least to another adult. If the little boy whose hair is ruffled does not like it, he should be given "permission" to tell the person who ruffled it his reaction. By the same token, the adult must respect the child's wishes. This will also encourage the child to acknowledge good touch and to express feelings such as: "I like it when you hug me, Miss Jones. It makes me feel warm inside."

Empowering children to recognize types of touching and to be able to express their feelings allows educators to touch with more confidence. Although there will always be children who do not like to be touched, they should be encouraged to make this known as well. Some teachers or other educators would prefer not to touch. That, too, is their personal choice.

What about high school students? How does touch come into play here? Although they may still appreciate touch when they are older, high school students may not need it as much. They have been taught by our culture that other types of praise and rewards feel good too. In addition, as students get older, it might be important to not put one's self in a position where touch is misinterpreted as sexual. Thus, although touching high school students should be an option, the educator should consider the impact and the necessity of the gesture, as opposed to other forms of praise. Secluding one's self alone, especially with a member of the opposite sex, might not be the best alternative, especially if touching comes into play. In high schools, if an open atmosphere is sought where students and faculty are encouraged to interrelate openly and kindly, touch often becomes a more natural and accepted practice.

Touching need not be a problem for educators. The key is to know how to have open communication with students about their feelings about being touched and educators' feelings about touching.

Violence Prevention and Mediation

In our world where children are surrounded by violence and sexuality (often seen as violence when it involves the sexual humiliation or exploitation of others), it is not surprising that they would manifest it in their daily lives. It is everywhere. Numerous studies have pointed to the media as one contributor to the desensitization of children to violence and sexuality (see Siegel and Senna, 2000). And yet, in a recent survey, 59 percent of those polled in a random sample of American viewers, felt that the constant portrayal of violence and sexuality on television was merely "harmless entertainment" (Poniewozik, 2000). As long ago as 1982, the National Institute of Mental Health reported that ". . . excessive levels of TV violence lead to aggressive, even violent, behavior in children" (Kinnear, 1995, 24). Since that statement, most will agree that there is even more violence on television and in the movies. Even our sports events have been publicized as arenas for violent behaviors as players and fans act out their disagreements (Kinnear, 1995: Hoffman, 1996). It should not be a shock that our schools have begun to reverberate with this violence (Siegel and Senna, 2000).

What can be done to stem the tide of violence that seems to drag children in its flow? Former President Bush was not far off when he suggested that we needed a "kinder and gentler America," but this is not necessarily easy to accomplish. Yet schools are in a pivotal position in violence prevention.

Many of the ways that educators can help to prevent violence are also involved in the prevention of abuse and neglect and will be discussed in Chapter 12. However, there are a few ideas that can be suggested here.

When considering prevention it is important to think about what causes violence, and what one achieves by violent behavior. First and foremost, violence produces in those who enjoy it, a sense of power. This has often been described as "power-over" (others). Power-over people are those who do not feel good about themselves. Without their power, they would feel inferior to others and helpless. It therefore follows that these folks could be helped in several ways: help them to feel more secure within themselves and help them to find positive forms of power that do not hurt others. Thus, as we bring this back to the classroom, all children, whether those who have already learned to be "power-over" people or those who have seen violence around them, can benefit by enhanced self-esteem. Further, we feel more in control when we can make decisions and master situations competently. Again, teaching the tasks suggested by Helfer (see pages 62–63) would, once learned, help to provide children to feel more in command of themselves. Looking inward for one's own strength has been referred to as "personal power." Thus, we must strive to help children develop their own "personal power." [above concepts adapted from *The Verbally Abusive Relationship*, Evans, 1992.]

Another concept that we need to know about violence and "power-over" behavior is that it is learned. Children see power-over attitudes at home, in the media, and at school. So how do we counteract these? The answer is by repeatedly identifying, negating, and replacing these negative messages with positive ones. For example, one child popped up in a discussion with the comment, "the only way to get what I want is to take it!" The teacher stopped and suggested that they do a role play. He had the class play out a situation using the boy's methods. They then analyzed the outcome, the feelings of all involved, and how the boy felt in the end. The class then redid the role play using negotiation and compromise. The student was actually able to recognize that, using the teacher's negotiation method, everyone won and he came away feeling more liked by the group. Using his own power-over way, the child discovered that he may have gotten what he initially wanted, but he was not well liked when it was all over. Being ostracized by the group gave him a great feeling of helplessness; a greater need to exert power, and thus the cycle was destined to repeat itself.

We often feel less powerful when we encounter differences or change. If we are taught that differences are to be appreciated, we will probably do so. But if we are taught that someone with a different skin color or who speaks a different language or who has a different sexual orientation is not acceptable, we will often strike out either verbally or physically. Education in appreciating diversity is fundamental in peaceful relations between people.

Violence and the need for power-over are also cumulative. The more you have, the greater your need in the future. Therefore, the earlier we break the need for power-over in children, the better off they are. With teens, it is more difficult as they are within a period when developing one's power is a developmental task. However, what we as educators have working for us in dealing with teens is their need to be accepted by their peers. Through negotiation exercises such as the above, teens can learn that they can feel power, albeit internal power, while still getting along with the group. No one said that this lesson is easy with every teen, especially one who has been exposed to a power-over mentality in all parts of his or her life, but it is possible to teach a more positive concept of power.

And finally, as we have alluded to above, violence and negative power alienate us from others. Even though hurt children may deny their need for others, the fact remains that the human animal is a sociable one. We need each other. One of the most positive steps that schools have taken in the last few years is peer mediation. In a world where children see their sports heroes fight other players, hear constantly that someone is suing someone else, and where marital strife between their parents may await them in their homes, they are ill-equipped to negotiate with others in a peaceful fashion. It is often something that they must be taught, by example and by constant repetition. When children can be taught to sit down, in a comfortable, nonthreatening atmosphere, with someone by whom they feel wronged or have wronged and discuss both feelings and solutions for the future, they will go a long way toward settling future conflicts in a nonviolent way.

If we are ever to change the climate of violence in our nation, it must start with the children. Educators can provide children with excellent opportunities to learn nonviolent solutions to life's problems. Through repetition of these principles from kindergarten through graduation from high school, we can make a difference that affects the future.

Helping Classmates Understand the Abused and Neglected Child

Children find it difficult to understand why a particular child disrupts a classroom or antagonizes peers. Even more incomprehensible to the more outgoing child is the quiet, withdrawn student who seems removed from the classroom environment. The way in which the abused or neglected child chooses to deal with peers may greatly affect the peers' responses.

Perhaps a starting point in bridging the gap between the abused/neglected child and his or her classmates is to educate the class about feelings and emotions, including what it feels like when others wrong us. This may be done simply by presenting an age-appropriate circumstance, such as, "What if a friend breaks your favorite toy? How does it make you feel?" or "What if your mother hits you very hard?" Obviously teens are capable of discussing much more complex situations. Once students explore the range of feelings in response to these statements, they will be better able to empathize with others.

For withdrawn students, you might encourage other students to include them in their play. Making such a request of a more outgoing or empathetic child may prove the most successful. In one middle school housing grades 6–8, the custom was to have eighth graders become "big brothers and sisters" to the incoming sixth graders.

The Child Protection Team worked closely with the elementary school and took charge of helping with the matching of sixth and eighth graders. When a child came in who was in need of self-esteem building, they were flagged as needing a special big brother or sister. They were then assigned to an eighth grader who had shown special promise in the areas of empathy, caring, and leadership. These eighth graders were often the ones who were looked up to by other students. Thus the sixth grader began his or her middle school career under the mentorship of an older student who was able to model in an effective, positive manner. Plus, being identified as a little brother or sister of a popular student often made the sixth grader feel special. The plan seemed to be quite effective.

If children are disruptive, the chances are that they are disturbing their classmates as well as being difficult for the teacher. Students in the classroom will frequently handle the situation themselves if given a chance, but a lesson in empathetic response can change the "Aw shut up you weirdo!" to "You're a nice kid and I hate to see everyone mad at you, so maybe you might want to listen a little more and then we can too." Children respond to the cues they get from their environment. When they see that a teacher is handling a situation in an empathetic manner, they are more likely to model this behavior.

Hygiene problems can also be handled by peers in many cases. In one situation, a high school students patiently counseled a peer in the need for bathing so as not to be excluded by friends. A few years ago, the norm was the "dirtier the better" but the popularity of designer clothes and other such fashions is more likely to promote a clean body. Thus, cleanliness can help students feel more acceptable.

Years ago, manufacturers used to promote their products through cute presentations done especially in elementary schools. The beaver who danced across the floor with his giant-sized toothbrush was especially popular in getting children to think about brushing their teeth. Although those infomercials are apparently no longer provided to the school, nothing prevents us from creating our own. One inner city school suggested that the theme of the science fair be "Promoting a Healthy Body: The Importance of Primary Prevention." In small project groups, the students researched every aspect of prevention, from gum disease through inadequate care, to the effects of different types of soaps on the body. There was also room for displays that addressed a variety of other topics, but with the encouragement of the teachers, hygiene issues became a popular central idea.

There are numerous creative ways to help everyone in the classroom understand the plight of the abused or neglected child without singling out anyone. Being made to feel accepted and as if they belong is so vital to healing for the abused/neglected child, that the small extra effort made to help classmates understand may make all the difference to the hurt child.

Stimulating Other Reports

Children who have been abused or neglected will often hold their secret festering inside of them until they perceive that there is a safe person to whom they might unburden themselves. Some children never find that safe person or a safe place and carry their wounds into adulthood.

Over the last decade or two, numerous programs have been developed to teach children about abuse/neglect and encourage them to tell someone if it is happening to them. A stroll through almost any bookstore, especially those geared toward educators, will uncover a variety of books and games designed to help children understand and report. There are also training programs available through a variety of agencies. For ideas on what is available in your area, contact the local children's protection agency, the nearest Children's Trust Fund, or Child Advocacy Center.

As a way of helping children to understand and encourage reports, children have been encouraged to write puppet shows or plays. One high school drama club, with the help of the local child protection agency, wrote a play about a girl whose friends tells her she is being abused. The club toured the schools, gearing the play to the particular age groups. Representatives from the CPS agency went along and acted as backups if there were questions that were too technical or if reports were made. The result was overwhelming. The door was opened. Not only was the class better informed, but several children were able to tell of their own abuse and get help.

Also useful in helping children to recognize that they are being abused and report is the teaching of healthy sexuality. Sex education is still fraught with controversy. Is it the responsibility of the parent or of the school? Will teaching children about sex make them act it out? It is actually the child who understands healthy sexuality, at an appropriate developmental level, who will know when something is wrong and is more likely to be able to resist being sexually abused? And the sexually abused child may be quite misinformed about sex due to an inappropriate indoctrination. By the abuse, they may have been taken beyond their years in sexual activity but lack normal developmentally-appropriate knowledge. It is sad that it is still easier to get permission from parents to teach a sexual abuse prevention curriculum in the classroom than it is to promote a course in healthy sexuality. Children need to learn age-appropriate information about sex before they can be expected to fully understand when it is misused by adults.

Helping the Foster Child in the Classroom

Many children who are abused and neglected each year are placed in foster care. A child in foster care may be one whose foster home location has kept him or her in your class or the child may be new to the class due to a foster home placement outside of his or her home school area. Children placed in foster care have a variety of special needs that must often be addressed at school. The most pressing issue for a foster child is that he or she is probably still working out feelings of separation and loss. No matter how problematic we may have viewed a child's home, it was still home. Suddenly he or she is "in the hands of strangers." No matter what the parents have done, the child still wonders about being sent away. Feelings of guilt are mixed with feelings of anger, helplessness, and often depression. The child may feel that if his or her parents could not love him or her and would send him or her away, how can anyone love him or her?

The expression of the child's sense of loss and abandonment may be expressed differently from individual to individual. One child may be sullen and withdrawn, another difficult, exhibiting behavior problems. Feelings of inconsistancy and instability may create a child who seems not to care. The best way to deal with an unfamiliar child is to contact the child's social worker and request a bit more knowledge of the child's background in order to better understand his or her needs.

Mostly, foster children are wondering if you will reject or abandon them as they feel their parents have. They may test you or tell wild, unbelievable stories to shock you. Knowledge of their background may help here, too. The need to know that they are all right, no matter what the family situation, is paramount for these youngsters. Again the educator can be not only an ally, but also an important source of information on the child's progress by keeping in close contact with the social worker and the foster parents.

Any discussion of help for foster children would be remiss without mentioning the importance of foster parents. These people as a group may be victims of misconceptions. The vast majority, greatly overworked and grossly underpaid, are concerned, dedicated individuals who take their job seriously. As one foster mother put it:

> When a child is placed in a foster home, the foster parents may take
> on many roles. Although the child's agency social worker and his or

her team are important, it is the foster parents who work with the child twenty four /seven. We make the majority of the appointments, we screen the child for possible problems, and arrange the treatment appointments after consultation with agency staff. Bypassing the foster parent's role in the treatment of an abused or neglected child is like bypassing an electrical outlet in any electrical apparatus. The foster parent is the link between the many forces that work for the child.

Fortunately, in the last few years social agencies have enhanced the training offered to foster parents so that they might be able to be a more informed part of the team.

As mentioned earlier, some children are placed with relatives in kinship homes. While these kinship parents may be related to the biological parents, it is important to recognize that the very fact that they have been chosen as a placement for the child means that their childcare standards differ from that of the natural parents. They are now a part of the therapeutic team.

Frequent contacts with foster or kinship parents can help the teachers understand what is happening in the child's home life and provide them with information concerning the child's progress in school. Through the foster parents, the teacher can learn any new treatments or interventions that may have altered the child's behavior in the school setting. A note, a telephone call, or an appointment with these caretakers can ensure the more harmonious orchestration of the child's already out-of-tune life.

Whether keeping in touch with the child's natural or surrogate parents, aiding the social service team, or daily contacts in the classroom, the influence of the teacher on an abused/neglected child can be profound. In many cases an educator becomes the second most influential person in a child's life—one whose membership on a therapeutic team is vital.

"No One Said It Would Be Easy!"

Anyone who thinks that teaching is an easy job should spend time in a classroom today. Problems seem more difficult and children seem harder to manage. Illusion or fact? Most veteran teachers would answer overwhelmingly, "fact!" So when a child who has problems appears in your classroom, often in the company of several others whose issues are almost as time consuming, it may cause the teacher to question his or her career choice. But there are some tips to deal with those difficult situations. My first suggestion is to read *No Such Thing As A Bad Kid*, by Appelstein (1998) which has already been mentioned several times. If you have not yet read the book, let me suggest a few ideas.

Humor, says Appelstein in one of your best tools. The lives of troubled children have often been mirth-free. Even the surprise element of an adult who can be humorous with them may get their attention. And, there is actually a healing power in humor for several reasons: First, humor ". . . sheds light on darkened landscapes"(100). Children who are troubled have what Appelstein refers to as "overcast minds"(100). Their negative experiences have caused them to shut out the light. Their minds have often closed to all but the negative. Humor can lighten the load and make them feel that there may be another way of looking at things. Second, humor ". . . memorializes acts of love" (100). Most of us remember the fun times of our childhood days, and these are often moments when we laughed. One mirthful memory often opens the door for others and makes us remember the good times. For children of traumatic childhood, there are rarely these "good times." By beginning to teach them to laugh, we can help them to begin to build moments when life was not so cruel to them.

In addition, humor can engage children who might otherwise be resistant. They may have been used to bucking adult authority but when an adults kid with them, they may not need to get involved in a power struggle. They can laugh too and go along for the fun of it. In fact, humor ". . . demystified the power of authority figures" (101) making them seem more approachable. In a laughing moment, a child can feel allied with the adult rather than in a battle of wills with the adult as "one up" and the child as "one down." Often beginning with humor when you first meet a child will lighten future interactions and set a more positive tone. This also serves to build a better relationship (102).

Humor also reduces tensions and smoothes the road for working together. And finally, humor serves to foster identity formation (105). Children with problems are often struggling with identity issues. When one can relax and loosen up one can often begin look at one's self. Then this struggle for identity becomes more of a positive journey toward the discovery of self. Appelstein (1998) does caution that the use of humor requires versatility and sensitivity to the child's reactions. If it is not working "don't push it!" It is also important not to rely on sarcasm and to remember that comments that hurt the self-concept are not funny to a child (106–7).

No matter how prepared you feel to deal with a difficult child, it is always the moment that you feel most vulnerable when the worst situation will arise. Appelstein (1998) suggest that some "pretalk" may help you to deal with the situation in a manner that will benefit all. First, *consider how you can engage this particular child* (134). He or she will not hear you if you have not connected. No matter how horrendous his or her misdemeanor, empathy for the child's plight is often a good starting point. After all, how would you feel if you realized that the whole class was furious with you because your actions had spoiled the field trip to which they had all been looking forward!

As a teacher doing your pretalk, you might then want to consider *how you are feeling or thinking* (134). You are probably quite angry with this child. You have had a rotten day anyway and this is the capping climax. But remember, reacting because of your own stress will not help the child. Remember how you feel about the parent who hits out of anger instead of considering appropriate discipline. *Considering how you feel about the child in general* may be helpful (134). Despite your feelings, the child has a right to be dealt with fairly and like the other children. It is important that your feelings not color your actions. Even if you try to curb your feelings, *are there nonverbal messages that you send* (135)? What are these? The way you look at the child, the way you approach him or her and the body posture you assume may give messages about your feelings. That message, if too negative, may have a detrimental effect.

Once you have looked at your own affect, consider *"What is the child's side of the story"* (134)? He or she may perceive the situation quite differently from you and this perception may be coloring his or her reactions to it. For example, if the child perceives that nothing wrong was done, there may be angry feelings about being singled out. You, on the other hand may be convinced that the behavior was planned, vindictive, and manipulative and be equally as angry. *Anticipate how you will deal with a defensive reaction*. The child may need to vent too, and not allowing this will only cause internalization of the anger for a later explosion.

When you decide what is to be done about the child's behavior, *consider if consequences are necessary* (135). If they are, think of a few consequences ahead of time that are acceptable to you. Then give the child an opportunity to think of consequences also. If the child comes up with one or more that you had thought of, let him or her think that the idea was original. He or she will feel more powerful and may learn more about moderate behavior in the future. If he or she doesn't come up with any that you feel are acceptable, you might want to suggest some of your ideas, while enabling the child to feel as involved as possible in the outcome.

Finally, *analyze your own contribution to the incident. Was there anything you could have done to prevent it* (136)? Often we set children up for misbehavior, sometimes not even realizing it ourselves. For example, when children are undersupervised in a volatile situation, mishap is almost surely going to occur. It is Friday afternoon after a very stressful week of rain. This is the first time the children are outside for recess; everyone is testy, and there is only one basketball that everyone wants to play with. To busy yourself in rapt discussion with a colleague while neither of your monitors are watching the children is almost asking for trouble. When it occurs, you will have to assume some of the responsibility. So often, we forget that children need our guidance. Without it, they may fall naturally into situations that then necessitate our disapproval. A bit more guidance up front and the negative situation might have been avoided.

When you actually intervene with a troubled child, it is important to have a set of strategies. Again, Appelstein (1998) suggests some classic helps. Support is important to abused/neglected children and supportive comments that let them know that you are in tune with their situation can start you both off on the best foot. Feedback is another vital piece and to let the child know that you have heard him or her, repeating the statement back is helpful. Periodically, an

Pre-Suggestions In Review

How can I engage this child?

What is on my mind?

How do I feel about this child?

What is the child's side of the story?

What nonverbal messages will I send?

How will I cope with a defensive reaction?

Are consequences necessary?

Was I responsible for this incident? If so, what could I have done to prevent it?

From: *No Such Thing as a Bad Kid*. C.D. Appelstein. Weston, MA: The Gifford School, 1998, pp. 134–136. Reprinted with permission.

adult talking with a child for the sake of resolution needs to be aware of how the child is feeling at all times. A feelings update, asking the child how he or she feels, is recommended. Children need to feel an adult's approval, even when they are being reprimanded. Thus, animated praise could be something as simple as, "I am really proud of you that you were able to tell me what you did!"(137–141).

Children need to know that adults are not infallible. We may yell or lose our tempers, and covering this up sends a message that it is okay to do so. Thus there may be times when we need to apologize to children. For example, "I am sorry that I yelled at you but what you did really frightened me." Earlier, we talked about the importance of humor. The worst confrontation can actually be easier with a bit of well-placed humor. Reasoning responses are those that use "what if . . . " and encourage the child to problem solve by presenting him or her with an opportunity to see the logic of the situation. For example, "what if I let all the children in the class call out an answer without raising their hands? No one would be able to hear anyone else." Connecting statements let the child know that you are both on the same side of an issue. You might say, "I agree with you on this point, but we just can't let everyone do exactly what they would like."(Appelstein, 1998, 142–145).

Most experts on children would agree that empowerment is important to their healthy development. Empowering messages are those that allow the child to feel some power in the situation. A good example was used above when it was encouraged that a child be responsible for thinking up some of the consequences that might be a result of his or her actions. Surface clarifications are those that seek to uncover bits of information that are not already apparent. If a child says, "she hit me!" a clarifier might be "exactly what happened before she hit you?" (146–148).

As the discussion is beginning to wind down, it is a good time for the two final types of statements. Explorative responses allow the adult and the child to get to some of the underlying agenda. For example, "You still look pretty unhappy even though you say that this is all resolved. Is there anything else bothering you?" And finally, having processed the experience and collected additional information, it is time for plan making. Plan making looks toward the future by helping the child to devise a plan, either verbally or in writing, that addresses how he or she can avoid making the same mistake again (Appelstein, 1998, 149–53). While such a step may not have worked in the beginning, thoughtful processing will probably result in a more favorable end.

Troubled children, those who have been abused or neglected, are not always easy to handle, and no one said that it would be easy. But a few simple preparations can make the job more of a win-win situation for both the educator and the child. The outcome is worth the effort!

Summary of Verbal Intervention Techniques

	Technique	Definition	Example	Key Principles
Beginning Phase	Supportive Comments	Statements that support a child's feelings	*I don't blame you for being so upset.*	Employ regularly to enhance the likelihood of engagement
	Repeated Statements	Remarks that echo back a child's previous comment	*So you're saying no one cares?*	Use sparingly to help the child feel listened to
	Feelings Update	A solicitation or verbal expression of feelings	*How does that make you feel?*	Conduct sensitively to facilitate the identification and expression of emotions
	Basic Animated Praise	Emphatic praise delivered with lively affect	*That was a really nice thing you said!*	Keep the animated approval coming!
	Balancing Animated Praise	Emphatic praise given to offset criticism	*You made a mistake by running off, but it was a great decision to come back.*	Express strategically to counteract defensiveness
Middle Phase	Apologizing	Openly admitting to mistakes	*I'm sorry I yelled at you. I apologize.*	Use regularly to model honesty, humility, and vulnerability
	Nonresponsibility Apology	Acknowledging false accusations without accepting blame	*I'm sorry you feel I yelled at you. I'll be more careful next time.*	Use to model sensitivity when you are not at fault
	Humor	The art of bringing on a smile	*If you don't want more homework, then laugh at this joke.*	Time it well and take it seriously!
	Reasoning Responses	"What if" statements that explain a forthcoming decision	*What if we let every kid . . .*	Employ readily to increase predictability and diffuse authority issues
	Connecting Statements	Reassurances that you are still in the child's corner	*Hey, it's not me against you. We're on the same side. I just don't like having to . . .*	Utilize in times of tension to demonstrate care and bridge opposing points of view
	Empowering Messages	Solicitations for input, which instills confidence and autonomy	*What do you think . . .*	Transmit generously to share the power
	Surface Clarifications	Questions asked to elucidate a situation	*What exactly happened?*	Conduct open-mindedly to hear the child's side of a story
	Explorative Response	An invitation to gently uncover underlying issues	*Is anything else bothering you?*	State sensitively to seek out the true sources of displacement
End Phase	Plan Making	Devising strategies to prevent recurring misbehaviors	*So we'll use a new "stop, think, and act" signal. This is a good plan.*	Conduct collaboratively to encourage appropriate functioning

From *No Such Thing as a Bad Kid*, C.D. Appelstein. Weston, MA: the Gifford School, 1998, p. 154. Reprinted with permission.

How Can We Prevent Child
Abuse and Neglect?

Over the last few decades we have put more and more emphasis on the prevention of child abuse and neglect before it happens. While some critics complain about the money spent for prevention efforts, statistics tell us that we are on the right track by making this a priority. How much is spent on prevention programs is very little compared to what is saved by circumventing the abuse before it happens. For example, in the area of sexual abuse several studies have found that funds spent on prevention efforts are miniscule compared to the cost of abuse once it has occurred. A 1987 Vermont study reported that in a sexual abuse case where the offender is convicted and sentenced, the investigation, court costs, cost of his incarceration without treatment, and the cost of treatment for the child would be between $138,000 and $152,000 out of the pockets of taxpayers (Pithers, 1992, as cited in Freeman-Longo and Blanchard, 1998). In Massachusetts a similar study found that the estimated cost for such a case would be $183,000 (Prentky and Burgess, 1990). And finally, Canadian researcher, William Marshall, based on his own study, felt that Canadians would be spending closer to $200,000 toward the intervention and treatment of a case of child sexual abuse (Marshall, 1992 as cited in Freeman-Longo, 1998). With current cost-of-living increases, one can see how such costs would have increased over the years.

Thus, it becomes clearer as we contemplate the figures that primary prevention—preventing something before it occurs—costs us less, both financially as well as emotionally than the response once abuse has become a reality. The figures do not reflect the residual effects on both the victim and the family when abuse has entered their lives. So what has been done in the area of prevention?

A Brief Look at Abuse Prevention Efforts

The history of abuse prevention is a long one, although we may not always have been aware of the efforts. Since the identification of the *battered child syndrome* by C. Henry Kempe, in the 1960s (see Helfer et al. 1997), social service personnel and child advocates have been searching for ways that abuse could be prevented. Early on, prevention efforts became categorized into three groups: *primary prevention* aimed at addressing the underlying causes of abuse such as poverty, media violence, inappropriate discipline and more and directed at groups of people to promote awareness; *secondary prevention* aimed at people who might be at risk for abuse or for abusing and attempting to remove those factors that put them at risk; and *tertiary prevention* designed to prevent abuse from happening again and focused on those who already have abused (Donnelly, 1997).

The problems of physical abuse and neglect were the first types of maltreatment addressed. In fact, it was not until 1979 that the public became aware of the prevalence of sexual abuse. Because physical abuse and neglect were by definition home based, early prevention efforts centered around teaching parents the skills they needed to parent and cope with this role in other than an abusive or neglectful manner. But when sexual abuse was "discovered" and we realized that it occurred in not only the home, there was a need to broaden prevention efforts to the education of the potential victim. Where better to educate children than in school? Thus, schools became the arenas for much of the sexual abuse prevention. It is perhaps this avenue of prevention that can be best traced due to the abundance of analysis and research that has been done on its efficacy.

Because of the controversial nature of what sexual abuse prevention addresses—sexuality, the protection of children, and the abuse of sexuality—the efforts of programs to promote prevention and awareness have not gone without challenges. The sexual abuse prevention movement was born and progressed not only through community awareness but also as a result of federal and state guidelines. Central to prevention programs in the school is the concept that children should be informed about sexual abuse and taught ways to avoid it.

Sexual abuse prevention efforts began a little over twenty-five years ago when the federal Child Abuse Prevention and Treatment Act of 1974 made available funds to establish prevention programs and promote awareness of the problem of child sexual abuse. This same law had mandated reporting of all types of maltreatment, but it seemed that the lack of knowledge in the community about child sexual abuse was the most distressing. Through funding from the National Center on Child Abuse and Neglect (NCCAN), states were invited to develop multidimensional programs to heighten the awareness of all members of the community. Most sought to direct their efforts toward the children—the potential victims—and those who were responsible for their care.

School-based prevention programs became the most popular mean of reaching these populations and, as a result, between the mid-1970s and the early 1980s, reports of child sexual abuse increased by 150 percent (Plummer, 1999).

A 1991 survey of those who led the prevention efforts asked what they felt had contributed to the increased interest in children and caused the child sexual abuse prevention movement to take on such momentum. They cited several factors as being influential: first, there had been several highly-publicized child sexual abuse cases that had attracted the attention of the public; second, the media had been publicizing the dangers of sexual abuse; third, the sexual assault movement had made efforts to educate people about the crime of rape and how it might be avoided; fourth, victims had become more vocal in speaking about their own abuse and the impact that it had had on them; fifth, the woman's liberation movement had encouraged all females, including children, to be more vocal and had raised the consciousness of society about the victimization of females; and finally, the newly-enacted mandatory reporting laws had increased the incidence of reporting to child protection agencies and alerted people to the fact that children, especially, must have knowledge to report (Riestenberg, 1997 as cited in Plummer, 1999, 80).

As individuals and groups saw the need for prevention programs, a variety of different ones were developed across the country with little attention to what other geographic areas were doing. In addition, in 1980, the National Center on Child Abuse and Neglect funded several programs designed to be demonstration projects to develop and evaluate prevention programs in the area of child sexual abuse. States too, encouraged the development of programs and numerous states led by New York and California mandated that schools be required to offer some type of sexual abuse prevention program during the child's years in grades K–6 (Plummer, 1999).

Another important response to the interest in prevention was the development by pediatrician and child advocate Ray Helfer of the concept of Children's Trust Funds. The first, begun by Helfer in his home state of Michigan in 1980 was followed by a movement that saw the development by 1990 of Children's Trust Funds in 49 of the 50 states (Plummer, 1999). Funded in a variety of different ways from state to state, many of these agencies are still extremely active in the implementation of prevention programs of various kinds.

But the early 1980s brought with them federal cutbacks of social service programs, and child abuse programs were also caught in the pinch. Thus, federal incentives were not as available and communities were often left to find their own funding for prevention programs when other seemingly important program advocates clamored to be heard. And, as the funds decreased, the voices of critics could be heard even more distinctly. There were numerous reasons, said the critics, why child abuse prevention programs did not work and were not worth funding.

The empowerment of children, in and of itself, was one of the first complaints critics levied against the implementation of such programs. First, it was felt that children should not be shouldered with the entire burden of protecting themselves against what is an adult responsibility. Yet, most well-conceived curricula added a component of parental involvement and did not imply that the responsibility for protection rested exclusively with the child. Further, adults worried that encouraging children to say "no" to adults might transfer to other arenas than sexual abuse. But, again, programs were designed to counter this concern by carefully stipulating when a "no" to an adult is appropriate and when it is not (e.g., when a child is told to clean his or her room). Some claimed that programs had been developed too quickly without a mechanism for built in evaluations. Still others felt that the content of the warnings given to children about being sexually abused would scare them and questioned the use of sexually-explicit terms (Plummer, 1999).

Partially as a result of the criticisms levied against sexual abuse prevention programs and partly because of the fact that developers of such programs had already realized the need for evaluation, numerous research studies were undertaken to determine the efficacy of such programs. Studies demonstrated that, in fact, the child sexual abuse prevention programs were beneficial. Collectively, studies indicated that children experienced an increase of knowledge, improved skills, and changed attitudes (Finkelhor and Dziuba-Leatherman, 1995; Wurtele and Owens, 1997; Rispens et al. 1997; Plummer, 1999; Casper, 1999). Further, they gained information, not only about abuse but also about a variety of other topics related to personal safety, self-esteem, conflict resolution, and adult-child relations (Donnelly, 1991). And, there appeared to be no negative effects on children who had gone through the programs (Finkelhor and Dziuba-Leatherman, 1995; Taal and Edelaar, 1997; Plummer, 1999; Casper, 1999).

There were other findings from the evaluation and research done on child sexual abuse prevention programs that should guide us in the future. Credence was given to the need to adapt the type of teachings to the specific age group or population, and to include active learning experiences in which the children can take part. Further attention should be given to the fact that a "one-shot" training session is not sufficient. Concepts must be reviewed at different times and age levels in order to be fully integrated. And despite the popularity of the Spiderman comic book on sexual abuse, studies showed that a one-time passing out of a comic book is not the best approach. We know too, that it is vital to include parents who can reenforce the learning of their children and quiet their own fears through education (Finkelhor and Dziuba-Leatherman, 1995; Taal and Edelaar, 1997; Plummer, 1999; Casper, 1999).

Abuse Prevention Today

We have learned a great deal about abuse prevention over the last few decades. We still have a great deal more to learn, but the findings to date can help us toward the future. We know that, in order to prevent child abuse and neglect, entire communities must be involved. In addition to the support of new or at-risk parents, parenting education for all parents, adequate health care screening, and a variety of support services within the community, schools can play a large part as well. Schools can be involved in the following way:

- By providing life skills training
- By aiding in the preparation for parenthood
- By sponsoring self-protection training
- By providing educational services for the community
- By aiding in the help given to at risk families (Crosson-Tower, 2002)

Life Skills Training

Children need a variety of skills to cope with the high-tech, stress-producing society in which we live. Children from other cultures, newly immigrated to this country, may need an additional piece of cultural awareness training. All of these tasks can be neatly incorporated into the curriculum in a manner that teaches them, but does not necessitate any extra time out of the already busy schedule. The most important tasks included in life skills have been mentioned earlier but will be reviewed here briefly. These are:

- Learning to cope with stress
- Learning to respond appropriately to crisis
- Learning to make decisions
- Learning socialization and getting along with others
- Building a positive self-concept (Crosson-Tower, 2002)

Our discussion of the use of Helfer's tasks to be learned (see Chapter 10) dovetails nicely with the learning of these life skills. When children learn how to develop problem-solving techniques, recognize their feelings and are able to communicate them, learn to make decisions, and learn to get along with others, they will feel better about themselves. People who feel good about themselves are not those who abuse others. Thus, we cannot only help children, but may also break the cycle of dysfunction and abuse.

Preparation for Parenthood

In our culture, we assume that anyone who can procreate can parent. And yet, we have learned that this is not the case. Preparation in certain areas can help children and teens grow up to become better parents. There are three areas that can be of special help:

- Learning about healthy sexuality
- Learning about child development
- Learning about parenting

The teaching of healthy sexuality is a highly overlooked piece of the curriculum, even when the school has a child sexual abuse prevention program in place. Yet, how can we expect children to truly comprehend what is wrong with sexuality until they know what is right? Knowing about one's body is as important as knowing about one's world. To leave out specific parts of the body or specific functions is to communicate that there is something wrong with those parts or functions. Is this the message we want to convey when children are barraged by inappropriate sexual messages daily in the media? Would it not be better to counter such messages with positive ones of our own?

Learning about child development is something that can be taught in age-appropriate ways. While a high school student could learn straight child development, younger children might be exposed to smaller doses. It might also normalize their feelings and reactions to things. And parenting skills can be taught at any age. Parenting skills are really lessons in responsibility, nurturing, empathy, and problem solving. For example, the egg or bag of flour exercise used in some schools can, if taken seriously by staff, teach children a great deal. In these exercises, children of almost any age are given an egg or a bag of flour that is to represent their baby. For a specific amount of time, they are to care for the "baby" and make sure that it comes to no harm. They may not leave it alone without an appropriate baby-sitter. Children learn a great many messages that new parents often learn in a more painful manner. And, nurturing skills can also help them to be more responsible baby-sitters as they grow to adulthood.

Self-Protection Training

Self-protection is necessary today for both teachers and children. For teachers, it is important to understand how not to put yourself at risk for accusations of impropriety against children while still giving the children the attention and concern that they need. By training children to recognize their own needs and feelings, teachers can often circumvent misunderstandings and communicate better with their students.

There is still a need for children to develop skills that will enable them, with the help and protection of adults, to protect themselves from abuse. The previous section (see a "Brief Look at Abuse Prevention Efforts") pointed out the benefits of prevention training as well as the fact that there appear to be few negatives. The next section (see "Implementing a Successful Prevention Program") offers suggestions about the type of program that will work for your school. Schools with Child Protection Teams have often used these teams to research the materials that are available and develop a plan for implementation that suits the needs of that particular school.

Most prevention efforts teach a number of concepts such as the recognition that one's body is one's own, the need to tell a trusted adult when there are situations that a child cannot handle, and the importance of knowing the resources available to one who perceives they are in danger/crisis. Such teachings prepare children for a variety of circumstances, including but not limited to, sexual abuse.

Educational Services for the Community

The prevention of child maltreatment necessitates, as has been mentioned, a community effort. Schools can support this effort by sponsoring workshops on abuse awareness, parenting skills, coping with children's difficult behavior, and a variety of other topics that will be of help to parents and other community members. In addition, schools are in the position to offer their facilities for other groups or training that will play a part in the eventual protection of children. For example, some schools make their rooms available for such self-help groups as Alcoholics Anonymous or parent support groups. Some schools donate space for self-protection classes or teen parenting groups. Such services encourage the community to join with the school in the effort to make the world a better one for children.

Help for At-Risk Families

In every community, there will be families who are at risk for child abuse and neglect. Schools are in a position to minimize the stress for these families, not only by offering programs as mentioned above, but also through providing after-school programs and evening programs for both children and parents. One high school instituted a crisis nursery designed for parents who needed respite from their infants or toddlers and used as a training laboratory for high school students interested in early childhood education and social services with at-risk families. The school also joined with the local social service agency that provided training to students in what to look for in abused or neglected children. Another school set up a program with the local battered woman's shelter, where students would help mothers with various tasks and errands that were needed on weekends. This was part of a community service project for the students and provided support and encouragement for the mothers, some of whom were not much older than their high school helpers.

There are a variety of ways that the school can be part of the community effort to prevent child abuse and neglect. It may require creativity and commitment, but it may also make the job of serving children an easier one during school hours.

Implementing a Successful Prevention Program

Let us say that your school has decided to offer a prevention program to children during school hours. You have searched out materials and now you and your colleagues feel overwhelmed by the magnitude of materials available and unsure of what you should implement. Based on the research done on the efficacy of prevention programs, good programs should have certain characteristics. The following are some tips that may help you to decide not only what program materials might be best for your school and your students, but also what additional steps you might take to make abuse prevention concepts a vital part of your teaching.

1. *Can the materials be integrated into the classroom curriculum?* A video or a segment on child abuse prevention shown for a half an hour during a year of study might be a beginning, but that alone will not significantly integrate the knowledge into the students minds. Prevention material can, however, be incorporated into a variety of subjects. For example, younger classes could benefit from talking about feelings and perhaps writing about them in journals. Science classes might include segments about the body as a "marvelous machine" including all parts and functions. This may help children to recognize the importance of their bodies and keeping them clean and safe. The fact that their bodies are their own might also be emphasized.

High school age students are a natural arena for health classes that again discuss the body and its functions. In English class, they might read books such as *Oliver Twist* and discuss the treatment of Oliver, using it to discus the treatment of children in the past as well as the present. Today, attempts are made to protect children from the type of abuse that Oliver suffered. This discussion might lead naturally into a look at how children are protected. It might be worth an invitation to the local child protection agency and perhaps other social agencies who might be willing to speak about their services, individually or on a panel.

Children of any age can be taught, at the level appropriate for them, that they, as well as adults, have basic human needs—for food, shelter, safety, love and affection.

> One creative teacher asked children to cut out a multicolored pyramid (resembling Maslow's hierarchy of needs, found in many psychology texts—see diagram below) and to label each segment according to the level of needs represented. For example, at the bottom of the pyramid was the need to be physically comfortable. Next we need to feel safe, and so on. The children learned that if they were physically uncomfortable (such as hungry or too tired) they had trouble doing less tangible things such as learning and creating.

As they begin to understand their own needs, children can realize where these needs are not being met consistently, and they may perhaps ask for help.

Problem solving is another skill that could be integrated into different lessons. Children learn problem-solving skills in simple math and algebra problems. Why not broaden these problems to include other life situations?

Maslow's Hierarchy of Needs

2. *Is the prevention material I want to use appropriate to the age of the students?* As in every other type of learning, children need to be presented with information that they can readily absorb at their particular developmental level. For example, children in early grades can be taught about their bodies being their own, and about good, bad, and confusing touch without going into the specifics of sexual abuse. Giving labels to children before they understand them serves no purpose.

High schoolers may be ready to understand more about how people treat children. One high school English teacher used classic literature to explore society's view of children. The class then contrasted current materials in magazines, newspapers, and novels to see how attitudes toward children had changed. A government class collected newspaper articles about the abuse and neglect of children and they studied all the federal and state programs designed to protect children from the Child Abuse Prevention and Treatment Act of 1974 to current federal/state/county social service agencies and the juvenile court.

3. *Does the material reach children with different experiences in ways that will be meaningful to them?* Every classroom and school has children and teens with a variety of experiences. Some have never been exposed to any behavior that could be considered abusive. Others have been approached sexually, may have been exposed to careless parenting that is not quite neglectful, or may have been subject to severe discipline falling short of any real physical harm to the child. Still others may previously have been or currently are victims of abuse and neglect. It is important that each child be able to receive something positive from the prevention materials used.

Some readings, lessons, video, or tapes for example, imply that abuse (especially sexual abuse) is the worst thing that a child can experience. Although adults may feel that sexual abuse is the worst thing that can happen to children, it is essential to remember that the kind of parenting or attention children have experienced in an abusive or neglectful situation may be all they know. Children therefore feel that to condemn the abuser is to cut an important emotional lifeline. For a child who is currently being abused, such condemnation of an important figure in his or her life may feel unacceptable. Consequently the child will accept the blame: "I must be bad—that's why Daddy has done this to me." Adults working with children should help them to recognize that the responsibility for hurting them is entirely the adult's, but give the youngsters the opportunity to recognize that adults are multifaceted. Although children have a right to be upset when an abuser exploits them, they may still care about the person.

Stay far away from any material that refers to an abused child as "damaged." Again adults often perceive this as the case, but abused children already feel they are somehow damaged goods. To have an adult confirm this can make them feel as if there is no hope.

An eighth grade girl who had been sexually abused by her father overheard two teachers talking. "It is so sad" one said to the other, "Melanie is damaged for life. All that innocence lost because of that brute." Melanie did not stay to hear any more. So convinced was she that there was no hope for her now that she swallowed a bottle of her mother's sleeping pills. Fortunately, she was discovered quickly and rushed to the hospital.

Children—especially those currently being abused—need help in recognizing that all persons—both adults and children—have both rights and responsibilities. Children have the right not to be abused or exploited; they should let a trusted adult knows if this happens to them.

Another concern for children who are currently being abused is the issue of saying "no." Some materials present stories about children who have said "no"—especially to sexual abuse—and who have escaped abuse. Youngsters who are being abused need to know that just because they did not say "no" or because their "no" was overruled by the abuser, they are not weak or at fault. Adults have many ways of impressing their wishes on children. Their very size and strength (as well as the child's love for them) may be enough. Children must be helped to see that it is never too late to recognize that the adults in their lives are harming them. Telling another trusted adult should be stressed.

Children who have been approached or who are the victims of severe parenting may also feel guilt or discomfort. A prevention program should emphasize that children should ask an adult if they are confused about what happened to them.

> Rosa came to a guidance counselor because she was confused about something that had happened to her. On a recent visit, an uncle had rubbed the child's upper leg in a way that made her feel uncomfortable. The counselor helped the girl speak to her mother about it. The mother assured the child that she should say something if the

uncle persisted. Rosa's mother also promised to be conscious of the uncle's actions on the next visit. The child came away feeling protected as well as empowered to act on her own behalf.

Some parents who are asked to consider prevention programs for school worry that their children will be exposed to too much inappropriate information at too early an age. If a child is a victim of abuse or has been approached by an abuser, such knowledge may help the child recognize that he or she could be exploited and then tell an adult. Prevention materials can also help a child who has never been exposed to abuse or neglect not only to recognize and resist possible future abusers, but in other ways as well.

Children differ in ways other than their exposure to abuse. Children are from many different cultures and this must be considered when choosing prevention materials. The materials used must take into account that they may be viewed by different cultural groups and not demonstrate any cultural bias. Increasingly, this is being built into many already developed programs.

4. *Does the material encompass a variety of teaching that empowers children to perform in numerous instances?* Preventive intervention in child abuse and neglect should be designed to guide children toward becoming healthy adults. Such growth requires many skills, both physical and emotional. Children must learn when they can and should do a task themselves, but they must also learn when to ask for help. A valuable component of a child abuse prevention program should be a section on whom to tell and when. It should consider fire, injury, being lost, and home emergencies, along with abduction, and being touched inappropriately by strangers or relatives. In an age of busy parents and latchkey children such information can be valuable to many parents and youngsters alike.

One mother reported that her children had indeed benefited from a child abuse prevention program. One of the concepts that the program taught was how to tell an adult when you are in trouble.

I came home from a meeting to find my eight and four year old at the neighbor's with their somewhat flustered babysitter. The fire trucks were just leaving my house that was still billowing smoke. In a panic, I asked what had happened. It seems that the babysitter had been talking on the phone and paying little attention to anything else. She had the kettle on and a pot holder, sitting too close to the fire had caught on fire. She became very flustered, and not being able to extinguish the small fire that had spread to the counter, she panicked. My eight year old, remembering what he had been taught in school about telling adults when there is a crisis, called the neighbor who called the fire department. My son then got his brother and the sitter out of the house. Fortunately the damage was minimal.

But I am so thankful that through a child abuse prevention program, my son learned other skills.

5. *Does the program elicit input from the children, encouraging them to try out what they are learning in a safe setting?* Everyone learns by doing, especially children. It is important that whatever material is presented, children have an opportunity to become involved. For example, when students can respond to incomplete stories or answer "what would you do in this situation?" type questions, they will get more from the experience and learn the lesson better. Reading a story to children, perhaps about abuse, and having them say how they think the characters are feeling is one type of involvement. Or, they might act out what else the character could have done. One class—after listening to a story about a child who was neglected—made a collage of feelings, identifying those that could be expressed openly and those that would be difficult to tell others.

Older children and teens might enjoy more extensive role play about feelings or about dealing with friends who tell them that they have been abused. One class created a directory for children, complete with annotations (especially useful for those who are at home while their parents work) to let other children know the dos and don'ts of being alone and the numbers to call when they need help.

The point of prevention is to empower children. There are a variety of unique and creative ways that educators can teach children how to feel empowered. Whatever the particular learning experience, the child should be a participant.

6. *Can the material be taught by a trusted adult—preferably the regular classroom teacher?* If prevention material is to be well integrated into the school program, it should be presented by someone with whom the child is familiar and whom the child trusts. There are a variety of programs that bring experts to the school and put on a session for children. These might be fine, but eventually the teacher should become involved. Experts can help teachers become comfortable with and knowledgeable about the material, but the relationship between individual teachers and the students in their classes is a valuable part of the children's training.

Not everyone feels totally comfortable with child abuse prevention material. Developing a comfort level may necessitate two things on your part. First, explore your own values and experiences. Read available books on abuse. In addition to providing valuable knowledge, some books are first person accounts of abuse and can give you insight into how a victim feels if you do not understand this. These books will also help you to recognize that early intervention is so necessary.

Some educators have had their own abuse experiences and therefore do not want to deal with the issue again. But, especially if you work with children, it will come up again and again. It might be time to seek a referral to a good therapist skilled in helping survivors to heal. You might be benefiting yourself as well as the children you teach. If you are totally uncomfortable with some of the aspects of teaching child abuse prevention, it may be helpful to have other school personnel—e.g., guidance—teach the materials. That way the children will still know them and you can be available as a resource. Some schools prefer to have the formal training done just this way to ensure that all the children get relatively the same message. Sometimes Child Protection Team members become the trainers. This also allows a small group of people to get advanced training on the subject.

If you plan to become involved in training your own class, there is another way that you might seek to prepare—by more training for yourself. Many schools are now appropriating money to see that educators are trained in the area of child abuse and neglect, both for their own ease in recognition and to help present prevention materials to students. Your local protective agency or college may have someone who is skilled in training educators. Increasingly, colleges and universities are offering courses in child abuse and neglect that can also be used for continuing education credits or toward an advanced degree. *Understanding Child Abuse and Neglect* (by Crosson-Tower, Allyn and Bacon, 2002), the first college level text (originally published in 1989) on the subject is used in many of these college courses. The book, in and of itself, provides an excellent resource to have available in the school. This text explains how to recognize various types of abuse, the reporting process, and how the case progresses from disclosure through involvement with social services, the court and possibly foster or residential care. It also includes a chapter on adults abused as children and on the role of the social worker in abuse/neglect cases.

Once you have more information, you may feel more confident to undertake a major role in a child abuse prevention curriculum with your class or school.

7. *Does the material lend itself to repeated use throughout the grades—to help children integrate the information?* If a program is suitable for the age of children in a particular classroom it may need to be modified to appeal to the following grades. But programs should be reinforced from time to time in order to sink in. Children need repetition and reinforcement of the materials at a more advanced level as they mature. Many of the currently marketed programs take this into consideration (see the Appendix for suggestions).

Many programs, although designed for a single session or two, can be spread out during the course of the school year. The following year, the information is repeated with slightly different emphasis and/or advanced concepts. Some curricula are spread out and designed to be presented every other year. Others address targeted grades—e.g., second, fifth, and ninth. Programs that are used through grades K–12 are designed to provide at appropriate grade levels, material to improve self-concept, a knowledge of important resources, the skills to seek out trusted adults, and the ability to recognize and resist potential abuse. Even though many of these programs are designed specifically for sexual abuse prevention, they can be used for the whole spectrum of abuse and neglect with thoughtful additions.

8. *Does the material prepare children to be healthier adults?* We live in a more complex world than the world in which most of us grew up. Stress and crisis become familiar to children long before we think they should be exposed to these. Therefore, we must prepare them to meet the future and to grow into healthy adults, able to take these unpleasant facts in their stride. Not only should they be helped to cope with stress that is everywhere in modern life, but they should also be helped to assume (if they choose to do so in the future) the most important role of adulthood—parenting. While people are trained for most other jobs, society assumes that when the first child is born, the parent(s) will somehow miraculously know how to parent. So thoroughly does this attitude permeate out culture that many young parents are afraid to admit their ignorance.

Preparation for parenthood is more than learning how to take care of a baby. Earlier in this chapter, I mentioned the importance of exercises (like the "egg exercise") that teach the specifics of caring for a baby. Since the problem for many abusive parents is too high expectations of their children, knowing what to expect might prevent later abusive behavior. Courses in human development (mentioned earlier) would also help them to recognize what is appropriate for children at specific ages. But parenting goes beyond these areas of concrete knowledge. Parenting is about responsibility and commitment, two characteristics that are often lacking in abusive parents. Parenthood is hard work and not just the fun of playing with a child.

As we consider parenting and healthy adulthood, I find myself again returning to Helfer's task (mentioned in earlier chapters). Without the ability to make decisions, get our needs met appropriately, delay gratification, take responsibility, and separate feelings from actions, it will be difficult to live a happy adult life let alone parent effectively.

Thus, as you consider the curriculum materials that you will use as part of your prevention program, assess their ability to teach these vital tasks.

9. *Is there a component of the prevention materials that involves parents in a significant manner?* It is not uncommon for a school system to prepare to present a prevention curriculum and after everything is in place, a parent meeting is scheduled or parental permission notices go out. School staff members are often surprised when parents object to what seems to them (staff) to be a well-thought-out and vital piece of prevention education. What is the problem here? It may well have been based on several factors. First, there is the age-old controversy: who should teach children about sex? The parents or the school? In the case of a child sexual abuse program, this argument almost always surfaces. And, if you plan to discuss controversial topics, parents want to have more than a cursory glance at the materials you intend to impart to their children. Here comes another myth: if children have too much information about sex, won't they act it out? This is a fear of many parents. Studies about sexual abuse have discovered that it is actually the better-informed child who is able to protect him- or herself, and children will experiment sexually when they would normally have done so, unless they are indoctrinated too early by something like sexual abuse.

Whether you are planning to use a child sexual abuse prevention curriculum or a hygiene component, or violence prevention material, parents have a right to be informed. But rather than informing them you might be more successful if you engage them. For example, one school decided to institute a program that they called "Building Healthier Adults." One of the teachers had built a clever model out of snap together blocks, depicting a person and labeled according to what an adult needs; e.g., a healthy body, good hygiene, ability to take responsibility, and so on. The teachers had prepared handouts—some collected from other sources and some their own creations—about the various concepts they would teach. They presented the concepts to parents at a special meeting, asking them what they thought and how they could improve the program. They also asked if the parents would agree to have input. One wife of a dentist (a dental hygienist herself) offered her time and perhaps her husband's to teach the fine points of dental health and nutrition. Other parents had other ideas. Segments were to be included in different areas of the overall curriculum. For example, hygiene might be in science, readings on prevention topics might be in English, and so on. Included in the total curriculum which would be integrated over the next two years (as a pilot) was a component on healthy sexuality and sexual abuse prevention. (Healthy sexuality was to be part of the science and health curriculum along with a piece about what could go wrong. The computer teacher would also be adding a piece on how not to be lured by the Internet.) So thorough was the effort that not one parent questioned the sexual material. By the end of the meeting, the parents were fully behind the school's efforts. Subcommittees agreed to work on various components. The school learned that an engaged parent is a helpful parent. There was also benefit to the children in seeing the school and their parents working together on curriculum for them.

10. *Can the program be connected to the community so that the learning is reinforced in other places?* Obtaining community support, especially for a program to prevent child sexual abuse, is not always easy. But enlisting the support of not only the parents but the community leaders will add more weight to the training of well-rounded adults. Has your school ever considered setting up a children's counsel to serve as a resource for the activities provided for children in your area? Such a group could also provide information to help the various children's organizations such as the Boy Scouts, the Boy's and Girl's Clubs and Girl Scouts or Campfire Girls. Many of these organizations have already designed and distributed their own prevention materials, especially in the area of child sexual abuse. Why not join with them to provide a more integrated perspective to children?

Another idea to engage the community in prevention efforts might be to assess and respond to community issues regarding children. For example, an abundance of teen suicides shocked one small community. The school's response was to organize a series of awareness and training for both teens and parents to help them understand such issues as peer pressure, danger signals when a teen might commit suicide, and the feelings of both parents and survivors. The six week effort called "Preventing Adolescent Suicide" was a great success not only in seemingly reducing the number of suicides, but also in joining together the community. At the same time as the program was being presented, high school students were discussing the issues in school. Because the simultaneous discussions facilitated communication between students and their parents, the parents wholeheartedly supported the school's efforts.

Another school enlisted the support of a community service organization to buy prevention training materials as a service project. Such groups are often glad to support the school's efforts if they receive specific information about what materials are needed and where they can be obtained.

We have considered the characteristics of an effective program in some detail and you will now be searching out materials. The checklist at the end of the chapter may help you to narrow down your search:

Finding Prevention Materials

Now that your school has perhaps decided to implement training in prevention, where do you find the materials? There are a number of agencies and organizations that are dedicated to providing materials for prevention efforts. Several particularly helpful agencies are Children's Trust Funds (see Appendix for listings or contact), Children Advocacy Centers (listing available through *http://www.nca-online.org.*); and the National Center for Missing and Exploited Children (found online at *http://www.ncmec.org/*). The National Clearinghouse on Child Abuse and Neglect Information also can provide a wealth of resources (at *http://www.calib.com/nccanch.*). In addition to these resources, there are a variety of clearing houses that carry a variety of material on abuse and neglect for both children and adults. Catalogues from such groups (available at libraries or local bookstores) can provide ideas for many different materials. In addition, teacher-oriented bookstores are beginning to carry more and more resources that can be helpful in putting together a prevention program.

Once you have ideas about the materials to use, consider them in the light of the previously mentioned criteria. Some resources may be excellent but do not fit your needs exactly. Can these be adapted for use? Some ingenuity on your part may be required, but joining with other teachers in the school may also help. For example, two teachers in a Massachusetts school system obtained a grant for training their colleagues and integrating prevention materials into the school system. Then they designed a ten-week course for teachers to learn how to detect, report, and prevent child abuse. Experts were called in for particular sessions, including the last few when teachers were taught, by demonstration, how to use the information in their classrooms. The school system collected resources from a number of places to be housed in the school library. Now teachers in that system not only have ideas about integrating materials into their classroom, but they also have a selection of books, videos, and exercises that they can use.

Funding can certainly be an issue and not every school can write for and receive a grant. There are free materials available from some prevention agencies (see above and lists in Appendix). In addition, try the Internet at <www.safe-anddrugfreeschools.htm> for more ideas about funding. Watch for grants and incentive monies available through community organizations, especially those with a national affiliation. Service organizations in communities have often gotten involved in prevention efforts once an advocate for such a program has enlightened them as to the need. Community programs such as DARE America (usually part of the community policing effort) may have their own programs that can be brought into schools. Some schools have worked through agencies that have United Way funding to obtain resources. Although prevention education is not easy to fund, there are funds available if one is creative enough to search them out.

However you accomplish the task, educators have opportunities—if not a duty—to educate children and teens in the prevention of child abuse and neglect. After all, prevention is the hope for the future!

Checklist For Choosing An Efective Prevention Program

	Yes	No

Does the program or material

1. Lend itself to integration into the regular classroom materials?

   How _____　____ ____

2. Lend itself to the age of my students?

   Can it be modified? How? _____　____ ____

   _____

3. Reach children with different experiences?

   those who were abused?　　　　　　　　　　　　　____ ____

   those who have been exposed to abuse?　　　　　____ ____

   those who have not been abused?　　　　　　　　____ ____

4. Be adapted for children of different cultural backgrounds?　____ ____

5. Encompass learning to empower children in numerous instances?　____ ____

   Can it be modified? How? _____　____ ____

6. Get children involved in their learning?

   List exercises that do this　　　　　　　　　　　____ ____

   _____

   _____

   _____

   Can it be modified to include more? How? _____

   _____

7. Seem comfortable for me to teach?

   What do I need to become more comfortable in doing so?　____ ____

   _____

   Reading materials I should read

   _____

   _____

   _____

continued

Continued

	Yes	No
More training? (How do I plan to get it?)		
_____		
8. Lend itself to being repeated in other years?	___	___
How can it be modified? _____		
_____		
9. Prepare children for a number of adult tasks?	___	___
Examples:		
Problem solving	___	___
Concerns of parenting	___	___
Human development	___	___
Stress reduction and coping	___	___
Problem solving	___	___
Self-reliance	___	___
Other? _____	___	___
10. Cover the following concepts?		
Body awareness	___	___
Rights and responsibilities	___	___
Saying no	___	___
Asking for help	___	___
Knowing whom to ask for help	___	___
Recognizing feelings	___	___
Expressing feelings	___	___
Separating feelings from actions	___	___
Taking responsibility for one's own actions	___	___
Handling anger	___	___
Making decisions	___	___
Feeling good about oneself	___	___

Not every program will include everything you want, but this will allow you to assess existing programs and modify them as necessary.

continued

Continued

	Yes	No
11. Does the material involve a sufficient amount of parental involvement?	___	___

How could it be modified?_____

_____

	Yes	No
12. Does it lend itself to integration in community programs?	___	___

References

Adams, C. and Fay, J. (1984) *Nobody Told Me It Was Rape*. Santa Cruz, CA: Network Publications.

Appelstein, C.D. (1998) *No Such Thing As a Bad Kid*. Weston, MA: The Gifford School.

Araji, S.K. (1997) *Sexually Aggressive Children*. Thousand Oaks, CA: Sage.

Asbury, J. (1999) "What Do We Know *Now* about Spouse Abuse and Child Abuse in Families of Color in the United States?" In R.L. Hampton. *Family Violence: Prevention and Treatment*. Thousand Oaks, CA: Sage 148–67.

Barnett, O.W., Miller-Perrin, C.L., and Perrin, R.D. (1997) *Family Violence Across the Life Span*. Thousand Oaks, CA: Sage.

Berrick, J. D., Needell, B., and Barth, R. (1999) "Kin as a Family and Child Welfare Resource." In R.L. Hegar and M. Scannapieco (eds.) *Kinship Foster Care: Policy, Practice and Research*. New York: Oxford University Press, 179–92. .

Browne, K and Herbert, M. (1997) *Preventing Family Violence*. New York: John Wiley and Sons.

Caffaro, J.V. and Conn-Caffaro, A. (1999). *Sibling Abuse Trauma: Assessment, Intervention Stategies for Children, Families and Adults*. New York: Haworth.

Cantwell, H. (1997) "The Neglect of Child Neglect." In M.E. Helfer, R.S. Kempe, and R. D. Krugman. *The Battered Child*. Chicago: University of Chicago Press, 347–73.

Cantwell, H. (1985) "Neglect: Responses and Solutions." Minicoures presented at the Seventh National Conference on Child Abuse and Neglect. Chicago, IL November 10.

Carnes, P. (1992) *Out of the Shadows: Understanding Sexual Addiction*. Minneapolis: CompCare.

Casper, R. (1999) "Characteristics of Children Who Experience Positive or Negative Reactions to a Sexual Abuse Prevention Program." *Journal of Child Sexual Abuse*. 7 (4), 97–112.

Caulfield, B. (1978) *The Legal Aspects of Protective Services for Abused and Neglected Children*. Washington DC: U.S. Department of Health Education and Welfare.

Chandy, J.M., Blum, R.W., and Resnick, M.D. (1997) "Sexually Abused Male Adolescents: How Vulnerable Are They?" *Journal of Child Sexual Abuse*. 6 (2). 1–16.

Coohey, C. and Braun, N. (1997) "Toward an Integrated Framework for Understanding Child Physical Abuse." *Child Abuse and Neglect*, 21, 1081–94.

Crittenden, P.M. (1999) "Child Neglect: Causes and Contributors." in H. Dubowitz (ed.), *Neglected Children: Research, Practice, and Policy*. Thousand Oaks, CA: Sage, 47–68.

Crosson-Tower, C. (1998) *Designing and Implementing A School Reporting Protocol: A How-To Manual for Massachusetts Educators*. Boston: Children's Trust Fund.

Crosson-Tower, C. (2002) *Understanding Child Abuse and Neglect*. Boston: Allyn and Bacon.

Cunningham, C. and MacFarlane, L. (1996) *When Children Abuse*. Orwell, VT.: Safer Society Press.

Davis J.R. (1982) *Help me, I'm Hurt: The Child Abuse Handbook*. Dubque, Iowa: Kendall Hunt Publ.

Department of Health and Human Services. Children's Bureau. (1998) *Child Maltreatment 1996: Reports from the States to the National Child Abuse and Neglect Data System*. Washington, DC: Government Printing Office.

Donnelly, A.C. (1991) "What we have learned about prevention: What we should do about it." *Child Abuse and Neglect*, 15, 99–106.

Donnelly, A. C. (1997) "An Overview of Prevention of Physical Abuse and Neglect." In M.E. Helfer, R.S. Kempe, and R.D. Krugman. (1997) *The Battered Child*. Chicago: University of Chicago Press, 579–93.

Dubowitz, H. (1999) *Neglected Children: Research, Practice and Policy*. Thousand Oaks, CA: Sage.

Edleson, J.L. (1998) "Responsible Mothers and Invisable Men: Child Protection in the Case of Adult Domestic Violence." *Journal of Interpersonal Violence*, 13, 294–98.

Evans, P. (1992) *The Verbally Abusive Relationship*. Holbrook, MA.: Bob Adams, Inc.

Faller, K.C. (1987) "Women Who Sexually Abuse Children" *Violence and Victims*, 2 (4), 263–76.

Feldman, K.W. (1997) "Evaluation of Physical Abuse." In M.E. Helfer, R.S. Kempe, and R. D. Krugman. *The Battered Child*. Chicago: University of Chicago Press, 175–220.

Finkelhor, D. (1984) *Child Sexual Abuse*. New York: Free Press.

Finkelhor, D. and Daro, D. (1997) "Prevention of Child Sexual Abuse." In M.E. Helfer, R.S. Kempe, and R.D. Krugman. *The Battered Child*. Chicago: University of Chicago Press, 615–26.

Finkelhor, D. and Dzuiba-Leatherman, J. (1995) "Victimization Prevention Programs: A national survey of children's exposure and reactions." *Child Abuse and Neglect.*, 19, 129–39.

Finkelhor, D., Mitchell, K.J., and Wolak, J. (2000) *Online Victimization: A Report on the Nation's Youth*. Arlington, VA: National Center for Missing and Exploited Youth.

Fisher, B., Berdie, J., Cook, J., and Day, N. (1980) *Adolescent Abuse and Neglect: Intervention Strategies*. Washington, DC: U.S. Department of Health and Human Services.

Freeman-Longo, R.E. and Blanchard, G. T. (1998) *Sexual Abuse in America: Epidemic of the 21st Century*. Brandon, VT: Safer Society Press.

Garbarino, J. and Collins, C.C. (1999) "Child Neglect: The Family With the Hole in the Middle" in H. Dubowitz (ed.), *Neglected Children: Research, Practice, and Policy*. Thousand Oaks, CA: Sage, 1–23.

Garbarino, J., Guttman, E., and Seeley, J.W. (1986) *The Psychologically Battered Child*. San Francisco: Jossey-Bass.

Gil, E. and Johnson, T.C. (1993) *Sexualized Children: Assessment and Treatment of Sexualized Children and Children Who Molest*. Rockville: MD: Launch Press.

Groth, A.N. (1982) "The Incest Offender" In *Handbook of Clinical Intervention in Child Sexual Abuse,"* S. Sgroi (ed.). Lexington, MA: Lexington Books, 215–39.

Harden, B.J. and Koblinsky, S.A. (1999) "Double Exposure: Children Affected by Family and Community Violence." In R.L. Hampton. *Family Violence: Prevention and Treatment*. Thousand Oaks, CA: Sage, 66–102.

Hegar, R.L. and Scannapieco, M. (eds.). (1999) *Kinship Foster Care: Policy, Practice and Research*. New York: Oxford University Press.

Helfer, M.E., Kempe, R.S., and Krugman, R.D. (1997) *The Battered Child*. Chicago: University of Chicago Press.

Helfer, R. (1979) Lecture given by Dr. Helfer in New Bedford, Massachusetts, March, 1979.

Hewitt, S. K. (1999) *Assessing Allegations of Sexual Abuse in Preschool Children*. Thousand Oaks, CA: Sage.

Hobbs, C.J., Hanks, H.G.I., and Wynne, J.M. (1999). *Child Abuse and Neglect: A Clinician's Handbook*. London: Churchill Livingstone.

Hoffman, A.M. (ed.) (1996) *Schools, Violence, and Society*. Westport, CT: Praeger.

Hughes, D.R. (1998) *Kids Online: Protecting Your Children in Cyberspace*. Grand Rapids, MI: Fleming H. Revell.

Hughs, D.A. (1998) *Building the Bonds of Attachment*. Northvale, NJ: Jason Aronson.

Janoff-Bulman, R. (1992) *Shattered Assumptions: Towards a New Psychology of Trauma*. New York: Free Press.

Johnson, J.T. (1992*) Mothers of Incest Survivors*. Bloomington, IN: Indiana University Press.

Johnson, T.C. and Feldmeth, J.R. (1993) "Sexual Behaviors: A Continuum." In E. Gil, and T.C. Johnson, T.C. *Sexualized Children: Assessment and Treatment of a Sexualized Children and Children Who Molest*. Rockville: MD: Launch Press, 41–52.

Kelly, L. (1992) "The Connection Between Disability and Child Abuse." *Child Abuse Review*, 1, 157–67.

Kinnear, K.L. (1995) *Violent Children*. Santa Barbara, CA: ABC-CLIO.

Korbin, J.E. and Spilsbury, J.C. (1999) "Cultural Competence and Child Neglect." in H. Dubowitz (ed.), *Neglected Children: Research, Practice, and Policy*. Thousand Oaks, CA: Sage, 69–88.

Laviola, M.(1992) "Effects of Older Brother-Younger Sister Incest: A Study of the Dynamics of 17 Cases." *Child Abuse and Neglect*. 16 (3), 409–21.

Ledesma, R. and Starr, P. (2000) "Child Welfare and the American Indian Community." In N. A. Cohen (ed.) and Contributors. *Child Welfare: A Multicultural Focus*. Boston: Allyn and Bacon, 117–43.

Leigh, J.W. (1998) *Communicating for Cultural Competence*. Boston: Allyn and Bacon.

Levy, T.M. and Orlans, M. (1998*) Attachment, Trauma and Healing*. Washington, DC: Child Welfare League of America.

Lynch, E.W. and Hanson, M. J. (1998) *Developing Cultural Competenece: A Guide for Working with Children and Their Families*. Baltimore: Paul H. Brookes.

Marchant, R. (1991) "Myths and Facts about Sexual Abuse and Children with Disabilities." *Child Abuse Review*, 5 (2), 22.

Marshall, W. L. (1992) "The social value of treatment for sexual offenders." Proceedings at the Canadian Sex Research Forum. *The Canadian Journal of Human Sexuality*, 1 (3), 109–14.

McLaughlin, J. F. (2000) "Cyber Child Sexual Offender Typology." *Knight Stick: Publication of the New Hampshire Police Association*, 55, 39–42.

McLaughlin, J.F. (2000 b) Personal Communication at Fitchburg, MA, November 15, 2000.

McLaughlin, J.F. (1998) "Technophilia:A modern day paraphilia." *Knight Stick: Publication of the New Hampshire Police Association*, 51, 47–51.

Monteleone, J.A. (1998). *Child Abuse*. St. Louis, MI: G.W. Medical Publ. Co.

Noel, J. (2000) "Court Services on Behalf of Children" In C. Crosson-Tower. *Exploring Child Welfare*, Boston: Allyn and Bacon, 266–87.

Pithers, W. (1992) "Estimated cost savings of sex offender treatment in Vermont in 1987: Recidivism Packet." Brabdon, VT: Safer Society Press.

Plummer, C.A. (1999) "The History of Child Sexual Abuse Prevention: A Practitioner's Perspective. *Journal of Child Sexual Abuse*. 7 (4) 77–95.

Poniewozik, J. (2000) "We Like to Watch." *Time*, June 26, 2000, Vol. 155 (26).

Poole, D.A. and Lamb, M.E. (1998) *Investigative Interviews of Children*. Washington, DC: American Psychological Association.

Prater, G.S. (2000) "Child Welfare and African American Families" In N. A. Cohen (ed.) and Contributors. *Child Welfare: A Multicultural Focus*. Boston: Allyn and Bacon, 87–115.

Prentky, R. and Burgess, A.W. (1990) "Rehabilitation of Child Molesters: A Cost-benefit analysis." *American Journal of Orthopsychiatry*, 60 (1), 108–17.

Riestenberg, N. (1997) Personnel communication. As cited in C.A. Plummer. (1999) "The History of Child Sexual Abuse Prevention: A Practitioner's Perspective. *Journal of Child Sexual Abuse*. 7 (4) 77–95.

Rispens, J., Aleman, A., and Goudena, P.P. (1997) "Prevention of child sexual abuse victimization: A meta-analysis of school programs." *Child Abuse and Neglect*, 21 (10), 975–87.

Rosenberg, D.A. (1997) "Munchausen Syndrome by Proxy: Currency in Counterfeit Illness." In M.E. Helfer, R.S. Kempe, and R. D. Krugman. *The Battered Child*. Chicago: University of Chicago Press, 413–30.

Rosencrans, B. (1997) *The Last Secret: Daughters Sexually Abused by Mothers*. Brandon, VT: Safer Society Press.

Rossman, B.B. and Rosenberg, M. S. (eds.). (1998) *Multiple Victimization of Children*. Binghamton, NY: Haworth Maltreatment and Trauma Press.

Rubin, S. and Biggs, J.S. (1998) *Teachers That Sexually Abuse Students*. New York: Scarecrow Press.

Russell, D. (1986) *The Secret Trauma*. New York: Basic Books.

Saradjian, J. (1996) *Women Who Sexually Abuse Children: From Research to Clinical Practice*. Chichseter, UK: Wiley.

Savage, J. (2001) "Family Preservation and Support Services." In C. Crosson-Tower *Exploring Child Welfare*. Boston: Allyn and Bacon.

Segal, U.M. (2000) "A Pilot Exploration of Family Violence Among Nonclinical Vietnamese." *Journal of Interpersonal Violence*. 15 (5), 523–33.

Sgroi, S. (1982) *Handbook of Clinical Intervention in Child Sexual Abuse*. Lexington, MA: Lexington Books.

Siegal, L.J. and Senna, J.J. (2000) *Juvenile Delinquency: Theory, Practice and Law*. Belmont, CA.: Wadsworth.

Simolinski, A.K. (1997) " Emotional Effects of Violence in the Family." In J.S. Grisolia, J. Sammartin, J.L. Lujan and S. Grisolia. (Eds.). *Violence: From Biology to Society*. Amsterdam: Elsevier, 125–29.

Stephens, D.L. (1999) "Battered Women's Views of their Children." *Journal of Interpersonal Violence*" 14 (7), 731–46.

tenBessel, R.W., Rheinberger, M. M., and Radbill, S.X. (1997). "Children in a World of Violence: The Roots of Child Maltreatment." In M.E. Helfer, R.S. Kempe, and R. D. Krugman. *The Battered Child*. Chicago: University of Chicago Press, 3–28.

Taal, M. and Edelaar, M. (1997). "Positive and negative effects of a child sexual abuse prevention program." *Child Abuse and Neglect*, 21 (4), 399–410.

Tower, C.C. (1988) *Secret Scars*. New York: Viking/Penguin.

Tower, C.C. and Andrews, T. (1992) *In the Hands of Strangers: A Look at Foster Care in America*. Unpublished manuscript.

Wang, C.T. and Daro, D. (1998) *Current Trends in Child Abuse Reporting and Fatalities: The results of the 1997 annual fifty state survey*. Chicago: National Center on Child Abuse Prevention Research.

Warshaw, R. (1994) *I Never Called It Rape*. New York: Harperperennial Library.

Watkins, S.A. (1990) "The Mary Ellen Myth: Correcting Child Welfare History." *Social Work*. 35: p. 500–05.

Wells, H and Canfield, J.(1994) *101 Ways to Enhance Self-Concepts in the Classroom*. Englewood Cliffs, NJ: Prentice Hall.

Whetsell-Mitchell, J. (1995) *Rape of the Innocent:Understanding and Preventing Child Sexual Abuse*. Washington, DC: Accelerated Development.

Wiehe, V.R. (1997). *Sibling Abuse: Hidden Physical, Emotional, and Sexual Trauma*. Thousand Oaks, CA: Sage.

Wiehe, V.R. and Herring, T. (1991) *Perilous Rivalry: When Sibling Become Abusive*. Lexington, MA: Lexington Books.

Worling, J.R. (1995). "Adolescent Sibling Incest Offenders: Differences in family and individual functioning when compared to adolescent non-sibling sex offenders." *Child Abuse and Neglect*, 19, 633–43.

Wurtelle, S.K. and Owens, J.S. (1997) "Teaching Personal Safety Skills to Young Children: An Investigation of Age and Gender Across Five Studies." *Child Abuse and Neglect*, 21 (8), 805–14.

Appendix

Suggested Reading

General

Appelstein, C.D. (1998) *No Such Thing As A Bad Kid*. Weston, MA: The Gifford School.

Araji, S.K. (1997) *Sexually Aggressive Children*. Thousand Oaks, CA: Sage.

Barnett, O.W., Miller-Perrin, C.L., and Perrin, R.D. (1997) *Family Violence Across the Life Span*. Thousand Oaks, CA: Sage.

Browne, K. and Herbert, M. (1997) *Preventing Family Violence*. New York: John Wiley and Sons.

Caffaro, J.V. and Conn-Caffaro, A. (1999) *Sibling Abuse Trauma: Assessment, Intervention Strategies for Children, Families and Adults*. New York: Haworth.

Carnes, P. (1992) *Out of the Shadows: Understanding Sexual Addiction*. Minneapolis: CompCare.

Crosson-Tower, C. (2002) *Understanding Child Abuse and Neglect*. Boston: Allyn and Bacon.

Crosson-Tower, C. (2001) *Exploring Child Welfare: A Practice Perspective*. Boston: Allyn and Bacon.

Dubowitz, H. (1999) *Neglected Children: Research, Practice and Policy*. Thousand Oaks, CA: Sage.

Finkelhor, D. (1984) *Child Sexual Abuse*. New York: Free Press.

Finkelhor, D., Mitchell, K.J., and Wolak, J. (2000) *Online Victimization: A Report on the Nation's Youth*. Arlington, VA: National Center for Missing and Exploited Youth.

Freeman-Longo, R.E. and Blanchard, G. T. (1998) *Sexual Abuse in America: Epidemic of the 21st Century*. Brandon, VT: Safer Society Press.

Garbarino, J., Guttman, E., and Seeley, J.W. (1986) *The Psychologically Battered Child*.

San Francisco: Jossey-Bass.

Gil, E. and Johnson, T.C. (1993). *Sexualized Children: Assessment and Treatment of Sexualized Children and Children Who Molest*. Rockville: MD: Launch Press.

Helfer, M.E., Kempe, R.S., and Krugman, R.D. (1997) *The Battered Child*. Chicago: University of Chicago Press.

Hewitt, S. K. (1999) *Assessing Allegations of Sexual Abuse in Preschool Children*. Thousand Oaks, CA: Sage.

Hoffman, A.M. (ed.) (1996) *Schools, Violence, and Society*. Westport, CT: Praeger.

Hughes, D.R. (1998) *Kids Online: Protecting Your Children in Cyperspace*. Grand Rapids, MI: Fleming H. Revell.

Hughs, D.A. (1998) *Building the Bonds of Attachment*. Northvale, NJ: Jason Aronson.

Janoff-Bulman, R. (1992) *Shattered Assumptions: Towards a New Psychology of Trauma*. New York: Free Press.

Johnson, J.T. (1992) *Mothers of Incest Survivors*. Bloomington, IN: Indiana University Press.

Levy, T.M. and Orlans, M. (1998) *Attachment, Trauma and Healing*. Washington, DC: Child Welfare League of America.

McLaughlin, J.F. (1998) "Technophilia:A modern day paraphilia". *Knight Stick: Publication of the New Hampshire Police Association*, 51, 47–51.

McLaughlin, J. F. (2000) "Cyber Child Sexual Offender Typology." *Knight Stick: Publication of the New Hampshire Police Association*, 55, 39–42.

Monteleone, J.A. (1998). *Child Abuse*. St. Louis, MI.: G.W. Medical Publ. Co.

Parent, M. (1998) *Turning Stones: My Days and Nights with Children at Risk*. New York: Random House.

Richrad, K. (1999) *Tender Mercies: Inside the World of a Child Abuse Investigator.* Washington, DC: Child Welfare League of America.

Rosencrans, B. (1997) *The Last Secret: Daughters Sexually Abused by Mothers.* Brandon, VT: Safer Society Press.

Rossman, B.B. and Rosenberg, M. S. (eds.). (1998) *Multiple Victimization of Children.* Binghamton, N.Y: Haworth Maltreatment and Trauma Press.

Seryak, J. (1997) *Dear Teacher If You Only Knew: Adults Recovering from Child Sexual Abuse Speak to Educators.* :The Dear Teacher Project.

Tower, C.C. (1988) *Secret Scars: A Guide for Survivors of Child Sexual Abuse.* New York: Viking/Penguin.

Wells, H. and Canfield, J.(1995) *101 Ways to Enhance Self-Concepts in the Classroom.* Englewood Cliffs, NJ: Prentice Hall.

Whetsell-Mitchell, J. (1995) *Rape of the Innocent: Understanding and Preventing Child Sexual Abuse.* Washington, DC: Accelerated Development.

Wiehe, V.R. (1997). *Sibling Abuse: Hidden Physical, Emotional, and Sexual Trauma.* Thousand Oaks, CA: Sage.

Wiehe, V.R. and Herring, T. (1991) *Perilous Rivalry: When Sibling Become Abusive.* Lexington, MA: Lexington Books.

Abuse by Trusted Professionals

Berry, J. (2000) *Lead Us Not Into Temptation: Catholic Priests and the Sexual Abuse of Children.* Chicago: University of Illinois Press.

Boyle, P. (1994) *Scout's Honor: Sexual Abuse in America's Most Trusted Institution.* Prima Communications, Inc.

Hyman, I. And Snook, P.A. (1999) *Dangerous Schools: What We Can Do About the Physical and Emotional Abuse of Our Children.* San Fransisco, CA: Jossey-Bass.

Jenkins, P. (2001) *Pedophiles and Priests: Anatomy of a Contemporary Crisis.* Oxford: Oxford University Press.

Plante, T.G. (1999) *Bless Me father for I Have Sinned: Perspectives on Sexual Abuse Committed by Roman Catholic Priests.* Westport,CT: Greenwood Publishing.

Rossetti, S.J. (1990) *Slayer of the Soul: Child Sexual Abuse and the Catholic Church.* Mystic, CT.: Twenty-Third Publications/Bayard.

Rubin, S and Biggs, J.S. (1998) *Teachers That Sexually Abuse Students.* New York: Scarecrow Press.

Books to Use with Children:

Bean, B. and Bennett, S. (1997) *The Me Nobody Knows: A Guide for Teen Survivors.* New York: Jossey-Bass.

Lindquist, S. (2000) *The Date Rape Prevention Book.* New York:Sourcebooks.

Moser, A., Melton, D., and Thatch, N.R. (1994) *Don't Rant and Rave on Wednesdays: The Children's Anger Control Book.* (ages 9–12).

Moser, A. and Pilkey, D. (1988) *Don't Pop Your Cork on Mondays: The Children's AntiStress Book.* (ages 9–12).

Moser, A., Thatch, N.R. and Melton, D. (1991) *Don't Feed the Monster on Tuesdays! The Children's Self-Esteem Book* (ages 9–12).

Warshaw, R. (1994) *I Never Called It Rape.* New York: Harperperennial Library.

Williams, M.L. and Burke, D.O. (1996) *Cool Cats, Calm Kids: Relaxation and Stress Management for Young People.* (ages 9–12).

Mandatory Reporters of Child Abuse and Neglect

State	Professions That Must Report					Others Who Must Report		Standard for Reporting	Privileged Communications
	Health Care	Mental Health	Social Work	Education/ Child Care	Law Enforcement	All Persons	Other[2]		
ALABAMA §§ 26-14-3(a) 26-14-10	✔	✔	✔	✔	✔		• Any other person called upon to give aid or assistance to any child	• Known or suspected	• Attorney/client
ALASKA §§ 47.17.020(a) 47.17.023 47.17.060	✔	✔	✔	✔			• Paid employees of domestic violence and sexual assault programs and drug and alcohol treatment facilities • Members of a child fatality review team or multidisciplinary child protection team • Commercial or private film or photograph processors	• Have reasonable cause to suspect	
ARIZONA §§ 13-3620(A) 8-805(B)-(C)	✔	✔	✔	✔	✔		• Parents • Anyone responsible for care or treatment of children • Clergy	• Have reasonable grounds to believe	• Clergy/penitent • Attorney/client
ARKANSAS §§ 12-12-507(b)-(c)	✔	✔	✔	✔	✔		• Prosecutors • Judges	• Have reasonable cause to suspect • Have observed conditions which would reasonably result	
CALIFORNIA §§ 11166(a), (c), (e) 11165.7(a) 11165.8	✔	✔	✔	✔	✔		• Firefighters • Animal control officers • Commercial film and photographic print processors • Clergy	• Have knowledge of or observe • Know or reasonably suspect	
COLORADO §§ 19-3-304(1), (2), (2.5) 19-3-311	✔	✔	✔	✔	✔		• Christian Science practitioners • Veterinarians • Firefighters • Victim advocates • Commercial film and photographic print processors	• Have reasonable cause to know or suspect • Have observed conditions which would reasonably result	• Clergy/penitent

(continued)

181

Mandatory Reporters of Child Abuse and Neglect Continued

State	Professions That Must Report					Others Who Must Report		Standard for Reporting	Privileged Communications
	Health Care	Mental Health	Social Work	Education/ Child Care	Law Enforcement	All Persons	Other²		
CONNECTICUT §§ 17a-101(b) 17a-103(a)	✓	✓	✓	✓	✓		• Substance abuse counselors • Sexual assault counselors • Battered women's counselors • Clergy	• Have reasonable cause to suspect or believe	
DELAWARE tit. 16, § 903 tit. 16, § 909	✓	✓	✓	✓	✓	✓		• Know or in good faith suspect	• Attorney/client • Clergy/penitent
DISTRICT OF COLUMBIA §§ 2-1352(a), (b), (d), 2-1355	✓	✓	✓	✓	✓			• Know or have reasonable cause to suspect	
FLORIDA §§ 39.201(1) 39.204	✓	✓	✓	✓	✓	✓		• Know or have reasonable cause to suspect	• Attorney/client
GEORGIA §§ 19-7-5(c)(1), (g) 16-12-100(c)	✓	✓	✓	✓	✓		• Persons who produce visual or printed matter	• Have reasonable cause to believe	
HAWAII §§ 350-1.1(a) 350-5	✓	✓	✓	✓	✓		• Employees of recreational or sports activities	• Have reason to believe	
IDAHO §§ 16-1619(a), (c) 16-1620	✓	✓	✓	✓	✓	✓		• Have reason to believe • Have observed conditions which would reasonably result	• Clergy/penitent • Attorney/client
ILLINOIS 325 ILCS 5/4 720 ILCS 5/11-20.2	✓	✓	✓	✓	✓		• Homemakers, substance abuse treatment personnel • Christian Science practitioners • Funeral home directors • Commercial film and photographic print processors	• Have reasonable cause to believe	

State & Statute						Standard of knowledge	Other persons required to report	Privileges
INDIANA §§ 31-33-5-1 31-33-5-2 31-32-11-1	✓	✓	✓	✓	✓	Have reason to believe	• Staff member of any public or private institution, school, facility or agency	
IOWA §§ 232.69(1)(a)–(b) 728.14(1)		✓	✓	✓	✓	Reasonably believe	• Commercial film and photographic print processors • Employees of substance abuse programs	
KANSAS § 38-1522(a), (b)	✓	✓	✓	✓	✓	Have reason to suspect	• Firefighters • Juvenile intake and assessment workers	• Attorney/client • Clergy/penitent
KENTUCKY §§ 620.030(1), (2) 620.050(2)		✓	✓	✓	✓	Know or have reasonable cause to believe		• Clergy/penitent • Christian Science practitioner
LOUISIANA Ch. Code art. 603(13) Ch. Code art. 609(A)(1) Ch. Code art. 610(F)		✓	✓	✓	✓	Have cause to believe	• Commercial film or photographic print processors	• Clergy/penitent
MAINE tit. 22, §§ 4011(1) 4015		✓	✓	✓	✓	Know or have reasonable cause to suspect	• Guardian *ad litems* and CASA • Fire inspectors	
MARYLAND §§ 5-704(a) 5-705(a)(2), (a)(3)		✓	✓	✓	✓	Have reason to believe		• Attorney/client • Clergy/penitent
MASSACHUSETTS ch. 119, § 51A ch. 119, § 51B	✓	✓	✓	✓	✓	Have reasonable cause to believe	• Drug and alcoholism counselors • Probation and parole officers • Clerks/magistrates of district courts • Firefighters	
MICHIGAN § 722.623 Sec. 3(1), (8) 722.631		✓	✓	✓	✓	Have reasonable cause to suspect		• Attorney/client
MINNESOTA §§ 626.556 Subd. (3)(a) 626.556 Subd. 8		✓	✓	✓	✓	Know or have reason to believe		
MISSISSIPPI § 43-21-353(1)	✓	✓	✓	✓	✓	Have reasonable cause to suspect	• Attorneys • Ministers	• Clergy/penitent

(continued)

Mandatory Reporters of Child Abuse and Neglect Continued

State	Professions That Must Report					Others Who Must Report		Standard for Reporting	Privileged Communications
	Health Care	Mental Health	Social Work	Education/ Child Care	Law Enforcement	All Persons	Other²		
MISSOURI §§ 210.11(1) 568.110 210.140	✓	✓	✓	✓	✓		• Persons with responsibility for care of children • Christian Science practitioners • Probation/parole officers • Commercial film processors	• Have reasonable cause to suspect • Have observed conditions which would reasonably result	• Attorney/client
MONTANA § 41-3-201(1)-(2), (4)	✓	✓	✓	✓	✓		• Guardian *ad litems* • Clergy • Religioius healers • Christian Science practitioners	• Know or have reasonable cause to suspect	• Clergy/penitent
NEBRASKA §§ 28-711(1) 28-714	✓	✓	✓	✓	✓	✓		• Have reasonable cause to believe • Have observed conditions which would reasonably result	
NEVADA §§ 432B.220(3), (5) 432B.250	✓	✓	✓	✓	✓	✓	• Clergy • Religious healers • Alcohol/drug abuse counselors • Christian Science practitioners • Probation officers • Attorneys	• Know or have reason to believe	• Clergy/penitent • Attorney/client
NEW HAMPSHIRE §§ 169-C:29 169-C:32	✓	✓	✓	✓	✓	✓	• Christian Science practitioners	• Have reason to suspect	• Attorney/client
NEW JERSEY § 9:6-8.10	✓	✓	✓	✓	✓	✓		• Have reasonable cause to believe	

State (Statute)						Who Must Report	Standard of Knowledge	Privileges
NEW MEXICO §§ 32A-4-3(A), 32A-4-5(A)	✓	✓	✓	✓	✓	• Judges	• Know or have reasonable suspicion	• Attorney/client
NEW YORK Soc Serv. § 413(1)	✓	✓	✓	✓	✓	• Alcoholism/substance abuse counselors • District Attorneys	• Have reasonable cause to suspect	
NORTH CAROLINA §§ 7B-301, 7B-310	✓	✓	✓	✓	✓		• Have cause to suspect	• Attorney/client
NORTH DAKOTA §§ 50-25.1-03, 50-25.1-10	✓	✓	✓	✓	✓	• Clergy • Religious healers • Addiction counselors	• Have knowledge of or reasonable cause to suspect	• Clergy/penitent • Attorney/client
OHIO § 2151.421(A)(1)(a)(b), (G)(1)(b), (A)(2)	✓	✓	✓	✓	✓	• Attorney	• Know or suspect	• Attorney/client
OKLAHOMA Tit.10 §§ 7103(A)(1), 7104, 7113; Tit.21 § 1021.4	✓	✓	✓	✓	✓	• Commercial film and photographic print processors	• Have reason to believe	
OREGON §§ 419B.005(3), 419B.010(1)	✓	✓	✓	✓	✓	• Attorney • Clergy • Firefighter • Court appointed special advocates	• Have reasonable cause to believe	• Mental health/patient • Clergy/penitent • Attorney/client
PENNSYLVANIA § 23-6311(a), (b)	✓	✓	✓	✓	✓	• Funeral directors • Christian Science practitioners • Clergy	• Have reasonable cause to suspect	• Clergy/penitent
RHODE ISLAND §§ 40-11-3(a)-(c), 40-11-6(a), 40-11-11	✓	✓	✓	✓	✓		• Have reasonable cause to know or suspect	• Attorney/client
SOUTH CAROLINA §§ 20-7-510(A), 20-7-550	✓	✓	✓	✓	✓	• Judges • Funeral home directors and employees • Christian Science practitioners • Film processors	• Have reason to believe	• Attorney/client • Priest/penitent

(continued)

Mandatory Reporters of Child Abuse and Neglect Continued

State	Professions That Must Report						Others Who Must Report	Standard for	Privileged
	Health	Mental	Social	Education/	Law	All			
SOUTH DAKOTA §§ 26-8A-3, 26-8A-15	✓	✓	✓	✓	✓		• Chemical dependency counselors • Religious healers • Parole or court services officers	• Have reasonable cause to suspect	
TENNESSEE §§ 37-1-403(a), 37-1-605(a), 37-1-411	✓	✓	✓	✓	✓	✓	• Judges • Neighbors • Relatives • Friends • Religious healers	• Knowledge of/reasonably • Know or have reasonable cause to suspect	
TEXAS §§ 261.101(a)-(c), 261.102	✓	✓	✓	✓	✓	✓	• Juvenile probation or detention officers • Employees or clinics that provide reproductive services	• Have cause to believe	
UTAH §§ 62A-4a-403(1)-(3), 62A-4a-412(5)	✓	✓	✓	✓	✓	✓		• Have reason to believe • Have observed conditions which would reasonably result	• Clergy/penitent
VERMONT Tit.33 § 4913(a)	✓	✓	✓	✓	✓		• Camp administrators and counselors	• Have reasonable cause to believe	
VIRGINIA § 63.1-248.3(A)	✓	✓	✓	✓	✓		• Mediators • Christian Science practitioners	• Have reason to suspect	
WASHINGTON §§ 26.44.030(1), (2), (3), 26.44.060(3)	✓	✓	✓	✓	✓		• Any adult with whom a child resides • Responsible living skills program staff	• Have reasonable cause to believe	

For a complete listing of individuals mandated to report suspected child maltreatment, *see* Department of Health and Human Services, Child Abuse and Neglect State Statute Elements: Mandatory Reporters of Child Abuse and Neglect (2000).

From National Clearinghouse on Child Abuse & Neglect at (nccanch@calib.com).

WEST VIRGINIA
§§ 49-6A-2
49-6A-7

Other reporters:
- Clergy
- Religious healers
- Judges, family law masters or magistrates
- Christian Science practitioners

Standards for reporting:
- Reasonable cause to suspect
- When believe
- Have observed

Privileged communications:
- Attorney/client

WISCONSIN
§ 48.981(2), (2m)(c), (2m)(d)

Other reporters:
- Alcohol or drug abuse counselors
- Mediators
- Financial and employment planners

Standards for reporting:
- Have reasonable cause to suspect
- Have reason to believe

WYOMING
§§ 14-3-205(a)
14-3-210

Standards for reporting:
- Know or have reasonable cause to believe to suspect
- Have observed conditions which would reasonably result

Privileged communications:
- Attorney/client
- Physician/patient
- Clergy/penitent

TOTALS, ALL STATES

State										
TOTALS, ALL STATES	51	51	51	51	51	51	18	N/A	N/A	26

State Toll-Free Child Abuse Reporting Numbers Resource Listing*

Each State designates specific agencies to receive and investigate reports of suspected child abuse and neglect. Typically, this responsibility is carried out by child protective services (CPS) within a Department of Social Services, Department of Human Resources, or Division of Family and Children Services. In some States, police departments also may receive reports of child abuse or neglect.

Many States have an in-State toll-free number, listed below, for reporting suspected abuse. The reporting party must be calling from the same State where the child is allegedly being abused for the following numbers to be valid.

For States not listed, or when the reporting party resides in a different State than the child, please call **Childhelp, 800-4-A-Child** (800-422-4453), or your local CPS agency.

Alaska (AK) 800-478-4444

Arizona (AZ)
888-SOS-CHILD
(888-767-2445)

Arkansas (AR) 800-482-5964

Connecticut (CT)
800-842-2288
800-624-5518
(TDD/hearing impaired)

Delaware (DE)
800-292-9582

Florida (FL)
800-96-ABUSE
(800-962-2873)

Illinois (IL) 800-252-2873

Indiana (IN) 800-562-2407

Iowa (IA) 800-362-2178

Kansas (KS) 800-922-5330

Kentucky (KY)
800-752-6200

Maine (ME) 800-452-1999

Maryland (MD)
800-332-6347

Massachusetts (MA)
800-792-5200

Michigan (MI)
800-942-4357

Mississippi (MS)
800-222-8000

Missouri (MO)
800-392-3738

Montana (MT)
800-332-6100

Nebraska (NE)
800-652-1999

Nevada (NV)
800-992-5757

New Hampshire (NH)
800-894-5533

New Jersey (NJ)
800-792-8610
800-835-5510
(TDD/hearing impaired)

New Mexico (NM)
800-797-3260

New York (NY)
800-342-3720

North Dakota (ND) 800-245-3736

Oklahoma (OK)
800-522-3511

Oregon (OR)
800-854-3508

Pennsylvania (PA)
800-932-0313

Rhode Island (RI)
800-RI-CHILD
(800-742-4453)

Texas (TX) 800-252-5400

Utah (UT) (not toll free)
801-538-4377

Virginia (VA)
800-552-7096

Washington (WA)
800-562-5624

West Virginia (WV)
800-352-6513

Wyoming (WY)
800-457-3659

*From National Clearinghouse on Abuse and Neglect at (nccanch@calib.com).

How to Start a Child Abuse Prevention Program in Your Community*

This fact sheet provides a starting point for community members who want to establish a child abuse and neglect prevention program. The steps described here are common to most prevention initiatives. Because each community is unique, the process will unfold differently in each. The three main phases of launching a prevention program are planning, implementation, and continuation.

Phase One: Planning

During the planning phase, community members need to take steps to mobilize support, assess needs, secure funding, and plan for evaluation.

Mobilizing community support. In some communities, a well-publicized and tragic incident catalyzes community efforts to prevent child abuse and neglect. In other communities, an individual or group might build on a general community awareness and concern to create a formal prevention program aimed at keeping children safe and families strong. Potential stakeholders in prevention efforts include educators, law enforcement officers, health and human services staff, community leaders (such as presidents of neighborhood associations), clergy and spiritual leaders, parents, local government personnel, and business leaders.

Assessing community resources. A community resource assessment gathers information about community assets as well as gaps in services. Identified stakeholders help assess the scope and quality of services by pooling information from their own organizations and agencies as well as gathering demographic data. Many colleges and universities provide technical assistance to communities conducting resource assessments.

Selecting the prevention program design. Prevention programs take many forms including family resource centers, home visiting programs, parenting education programs, and public awareness campaigns.

Planners will use the information gathered through the assessment to design a program appropriate for their community. Whatever design they select, planners need to ensure that the prevention program reflects an understanding of, and respect for, cultural norms that influence child rearing. One way that prevention programs can bridge cultural gaps is by delivering services and materials in languages other than English. Draw on a particular cultural community's strengths by involving members in planning the program. Involve parents in developing and delivering services as board members, task force members, and volunteers.

Securing funding. Some communities might have sufficient resources to launch a prevention program, but many communities will need to secure fund-

*From National Clearinghouse on Abuse and Neglect at (nccanch@calib.com).

ing, possibly from more than one source. The four main sources of funds for prevention programs are the Federal government, State governments, foundations, and corporations. Along with start-up funds, planners must consider how they will fund the program over the long haul.

Evaluating the program. Planners should build evaluation into the prevention program and budget. An evaluator should participate in program planning and be viewed by the community as an integral part of the program. Emphasizing evaluation right from the start can help persuade funding sources to commit financial resources to the program. Again, many colleges and universities can provide technical assistance in designing and implementing program evaluations.

Phase Two: Implementation

During phase two, the group recruits and trains staff, starts delivering services, and begins to use feedback to improve service delivery.

Recruiting and training staff. When recruiting staff, consider an individual's ability to understand and meet the community's expectations and to deliver services with cultural sensitivity and competence. The composition of the staff should mirror the community being served. Recruiting neighborhood residents as staff will bring credibility to program efforts. Consider serving as a training ground for neighborhood residents re-entering the workforce or a field placement for graduate students in social work and early childhood education. Remember that an important part of staff training is to treat community members with respect and dignity.

Ensuring access. Make sure that the program's target audiences have easy access to services. Locate programs in the community to be served. Ensuring access to public transportation, providing child care, and linking the program to established community programs and institutions increase the likelihood that residents will take part in the program. Get the word out about the program using materials and channels familiar to community members—notices in grocery stores, brochures in medical clinics, and advertisements in church bulletins and free community papers.

Using feedback to improve services. Build frequent opportunities for information updates and feedback into the program. Ask for feedback from community members who come back for services and from those who don't. Schedule staff retreats to review progress and update strategic plans. Look at both tangible and intangible results. Celebrate even the smallest success with the community as a whole.

Phase Three: Continuation

For programs to succeed in the long-term in preventing child abuse and neglect, they must become a permanent part of the community's public landscape and secure long-term funding. The keys to securing continuation funding are:

- Start early
- Establish a team that includes program personnel and community supporters
- Develop a plan that targets sources and has a step-by-step timeline
- Generate data showing the effectiveness of the program
- Work at continuation every day.

Program framers must solidify relationships with funding sources and develop a team of supporters that are knowledgeable about, and feel a sense of ownership of, the prevention program. Program staff, board members, volunteers, consumers, referral sources, and community leaders are all part of the team that will help embed the program in the community.

Utilization data (e.g., number of participants served, amount of services offered) are helpful, but outcome data are critical. What difference does the program make? If this program is not continued, what will the community lose? What costs, economic and human, will be incurred? Programs that last are able to show that they work.

Resources

Community Collaboration and Assessment
The Asset-Based Community Development Institute
Institute for Policy Research
Northwestern University
2040 Sheridan Road
Evanston, IL 60208-4100
847-491-8712
Web site: http://www.nwu.edu/IPR/abcd.html

Prevention Program Designs
The National Clearinghouse on Child Abuse and Neglect Information
330 C Street, SW
Washington, DC 20447
800-FYI-3366 or 703-385-7565
Web site: http://www.calib.com/nccanch/

Evaluation
The W.K. Kellogg Foundation
One Michigan Avenue East
Battle Creek, MI 49017-4058
616-968-1611
Web site:
http://www.wkkf.org/publications/evalhdbk

Funding
The Department of Health and Human Services
Children's Bureau

330 C Street, SW
Washington, DC 20447
202-205-8618
Web site: http://www.acf.dhhs.gov/programs/cb/policy.htm

The Foundation Center
79 Fifth Avenue
New York, NY 10003
212-620-4230
Web site: http://fdncenter.org

Continuation/Sustainability
The Community Tool Box
University of Kansas
Work Group on Health Promotion and Community Development
4082 Dole Center
Lawrence, KS 66045
785-864-0533
Web site: http://ctb.lsi.ukans.edu/tools/tools.htm

Federal Funding Resources for Prevention Activities*

Following are activities that several member agencies of the Interagency Work Group on Child Abuse and Neglect conduct that support prevention. Federal agencies typically award funding to States and/or individual programs and institutions through a Request for Proposal (RFP) process. Announcements for available funds are published in the *Federal Register* (http://www.nara.gov/fedreg). Where available, phone numbers and Web site addresses for funding information are provided.

Department of Health and Human Services
Hubert H. Humphrey Building
200 Independence Ave., SW
Washington, DC 20201
http://www.dhhs.gov
(202) 619-0257

The following DHHS agencies provide support for child abuse and neglect prevention activities.

Children's Bureau (CB)
Mary E. Switzer Building
330 C St., SW, Room 2068
Washington, DC 20447
http://www.acf.dhhs.gov/programs/cb/policy.htm
(202) 205-8618

The Children's Bureau is responsible for assisting States and communities in the delivery of child welfare services designed to protect children and strengthen families. Located organizationally within the Administration on Children, Youth and Families, the Children's Bureau administers the Foster Care and Adoption Assistance Program, Child Welfare Services State Grants Program, Child Welfare Services Training Programs, Independent Living Initiatives Program, Adoption Opportunities Program, Abandoned Infants Assistance Program, programs supported by the Promoting Safe and Stable Families Act, child welfare training projects supported by Section 426 of the Social Security Act, as amended, programs funded under the Child Abuse Prevention and Treatment Act (CAPTA), and programs under Title II of CAPTA for Community-Based Family Resource and Support activities.

The Children's Bureau administers five discretionary grant programs: Adoption Opportunities, Child Welfare Training, Child Welfare Research and Demonstration Projects, Abandoned Infants Assistance, and Child Abuse Prevention and Treatment Act (CAPTA) Research and Demonstration Projects. The Children's Bureau also administers nine State grant programs: the Title IV-E Foster Care program, Title IV-E Adoption Assistance program, Independent Living program, Title IV-B Promoting Safe and Stable Families program, Child Welfare Services program, Child Abuse and Neglect Basic State Grants, Medical Neglect/Disabled Infants State Grants, Community-Based Family Resource Program Grants, and Children's Justice Act Program.

Head Start Bureau
Mary E. Switzer Building
330 C St., SW, Room 2018
Washington, DC 20447
http://www.acf.dhhs.gov/programs/hsb/announce/fund
(202) 205-8572

Head Start promotes school readiness by enhancing the social and cognitive development of low-income preschool children ages 3 to 5 and provides comprehensive social services for their families. Services for children focus on education, socio-emotional development, physical and mental health, nutrition, and additional relevant issues determined by family needs assessments.

Grants for Head Start programs are awarded to local, public, private non-profit agencies, and for-profit agencies by the 10 ACF Regional Offices and the Head Start Bureau's American Indian and Migrant Programs Branches. Most of the Head Start program's appropriation funds local Head Start projects. The remainder is used for: training and technical assistance to assist local projects in meeting the Head Start Program Performance Standards and in maintaining and improving the quality of local programs; research, demonstration, and evaluation activities to test innovative program models and to assess program effectiveness; and required monitoring activities.

Administration on Developmental Disabilities (ADD)
Hubert H. Humphrey Building
200 Independence Ave., SW, Room 300F
Washington, DC 20201
http://www.acf.dhhs.gov/programs/add
(202) 690-6590

ADD funds State, community, and private sector efforts to protect the rights of people with developmental disabilities. The Agency administers four grant programs: the State Developmental Disability Councils Program,

Protection and Advocacy Program, University Affiliated Programs, and Projects of National Significance. Issues addressed under these programs include child development, abuse and neglect of persons with disabilities, day care, early intervention, and training.

National Center for Injury Prevention and Control
Centers for Disease Control and Prevention
Mailstop K58
4770 Buford Highway, NE
Atlanta, GA 30341-3724
http://www.cdc.gov/ncipc/res-opps/grants1.htm
(770) 488-4265

CDC's National Center for Disease Prevention and Control administers research grants and funding opportunities related to injury prevention, including injuries caused by child abuse and domestic violence.

Indian Health Service
Parklawn Building
5600 Fishers Lane
Rockville, MD 20857
http://www.ihs.gov
(301) 443-1083

IHS, an agency of the U.S. Public Health Service, operates a comprehensive health service delivery system for approximately 1.5 million of the nation's 2 million American Indians and Alaska Natives. IHS's many areas of special concern include prevention of violence and child abuse and neglect.

Office of Public Health and Science
Hubert Humphrey Building
200 Independence Ave., Room 738G
Washington, DC 20201
http://www.osophs.dhhs.gov
(202) 401-6295

The Office of Public Health and Science administers relevant grants and funding through several of its offices including the Office of Minority Health (http://www.omhrc.gov) and the Office of Women's Health (http://www.4woman.gov/owh).

Department of Education
400 Maryland Ave., SW
Washington, DC 20202
http://www.ed.gov/funding.html

Information Resource Center
Department of Education
600 Independence Ave., SW
Washington, DC 20202
http://www.ed.gov/offices/OIIA/IRC
(800) USA-LEARN

The Department of Education funds programs addressing child abuse prevention, abuse of children with disabilities, parent education, and research and training programs concerning child maltreatment and child welfare through its Offices of Elementary and Secondary Education, Special Education and Rehabilitative Services, and Educational Research and Improvement.

Office of Elementary and Secondary Education (OESE)
400 Maryland Ave., SW, Room 3W300
Washington, DC 20202
http://www.ed.gov/offices/OESE/program.html
(202) 401-0113

Within OESE, the Compensatory Education Programs Office, Office of Indian Education, Office of Migrant Education, and the Safe and Drug-Free Schools Programs Office address child abuse and neglect prevention, family support, and related child well-being issues.

Office of Special Education and Rehabilitative Services (OSERS)
Mary E. Switzer Building
330 C St., SW
Washington, DC 20202
http://www.ed.gov/offices/OSERS
(202) 205-5465

OSERS addresses child maltreatment and child welfare issues through its Office of Special Education Programs (OSEP) and the National Institute on Disability and Rehabilitation Research (NIDRR). These offices support programs for children from birth to age 21 with special needs, and support research to improve the lives of individuals with disabilities.

Office of Educational Research and Improvement (OERI)
Capitol Place
555 New Jersey Ave., NW
Washington, DC 20208
http://www.ed.gov/offices/OERI/funding.html
(202) 219-1385

OERI addresses child abuse and child welfare issues through the National Institute on Early Childhood Development and Education and the National Institute on the Education of At-

Risk Students. The office conducts research and demonstration projects funded through grants; collects educational statistics; distributes information, and provides technical assistance.

Department of Justice
950 Pennsylvania Ave., NW
Washington, DC 20530
http://www.usdoj.gov/08community

National Criminal Justice Reference Service Justice Information Center
PO Box 6000
Rockville, MD 20849-6000
http://www.ncjrs.org
(800) 851-3420

The Department of Justice supports activities related to child maltreatment and child welfare by collecting crime statistics, providing training in the investigation and prosecution of child abuse cases, training law enforcement personnel, and funding programs addressing child abuse and neglect, domestic violence, and prevention services for crime victims.

Office of Juvenile Justice and Delinquency Prevention (OJJDP)
810 Seventh St., NW
Washington, DC 20531
http://ojjdp.ncjrs.org/grants/grants.html

Juvenile Justice Clearinghouse
PO Box 6000
Rockville, MD 20849-6000
(800) 638-8736
http://www.ncjrs.org/jjhome.html

OJJDP administers State Formula Grants, State Challenge Grants, and the Title V Community Prevention Grants Program, and also funds projects through its Special Emphasis Discretionary Grant Program, the National Institute for Juvenile Justice and Delinquency Prevention, and the Missing and Exploited Children's Program. Recognizing the link between maltreatment and subsequent juvenile delinquency, OJJDP initiated the Safe Kids/Safe Streets and Safe Start demonstration projects, as well as programs for secondary analysis of childhood victimization data.

*Children with Disabilities Resource Listing**

The following organizations are among many that provide information on resources for children with disabilities. Inclusion on this list is for information purposes and does not constitute an endorsement by the Clearinghouse or the Children's Bureau.

American Association of University Affiliated Programs for Persons with Developmental Disabilities (AAUAP)
8630 Fenton St. Suite 410
Silver Spring, MD 20910
PHONE: (301) 588-8252
FAX: (301) 588-2842
E-MAIL: info@aauap.org
URL: http://www.aauap.org

AAUAP represents the national network of University Affiliated Programs (UAPs). UAPs work with people with disabilities, members of their families, State and local government agencies, and community providers on projects that provide training, technical assistance, service, research, and information sharing. AAUAP collects data on performance and results and brings its collective strength to bear on problems that are beyond the ability of any single UAP to solve.

ARCH National Resource Center for Respite and Crisis Care Services
Chapel Hill Training-Outreach Project
800 Eastowne Dr. Suite 105
Chapel Hill, NC 27514
PHONE: (888) 671-2594 or (919) 490-5577
FAX: (919) 490-4905
E-MAIL: YLayden@intrex.net
URL: //www.chtop.com/archbroc.htm

The mission of the ARCH National Resource Center for Respite and Crisis Care Services is to support service providers and families through training, technical assistance, evaluation, and research. Respite is a service in which care is provided to individuals with disabilities and other special needs; to individuals with chronic or terminal illnesses; or to individuals at risk of abuse and neglect.

Council for Exceptional Children (CEC)
1920 Association Dr.
Reston, VA 20191-1589
PHONE: (703) 620-3660 or (888)
CEC-SPED
TTY: (703) 264-9446
FAX: (703) 264-9494
EMAIL: service@cec.sped.org
URL: http://www.cec.sped.org

The Council for Exceptional Children (CEC) is the largest international professional organization dedicated to improving educational outcomes for individuals with exceptionalities, students with disabilities, and/or the gifted. CEC advocates for appropriate governmental policies, sets professional standards, provides continual professional development, advocates for newly and historically underserved individuals with exceptionalities, and helps professionals obtain conditions and resources necessary for effective professional practice.

Disability, Abuse and Personal Rights Project (DAPR)
Spectrum Institute
P.O. Box T
Culver City, CA 90230
PHONE: (310) 391-2420
FAX: (310) 390-6994
E-MAIL: dmora@doctor.com
URL: http://www.disability-abuse.com

DAPR conducts research and training regarding the sexual abuse of children and adults with disabilities, primarily developmental disabilities. In addition, DAPR coordinates the only national conference on this topic. Publications available through DAPR include a guide for parents on risk reduction, a guide written for survivors with developmental disabilities, and an interviewing guidebook. DAPR provides training to law enforcement personnel, child protective services workers, judges, and prosecutors on risk reduction, reporting, and interviewing. Services in Spanish are available.

ERIC Clearinghouse on Disabilities and Gifted Education (ERIC EC)
1920 Association Dr.
Reston, VA 20191-1589
PHONE: (800) 328-0272 (V/TTY)
E-MAIL:ericec@cec.sped.org
URL: http://ericec.org

ERIC EC gathers and disseminates professional literature, information, and resources on the education and development of individuals of all ages who have disabilities and/or who are gifted.

Family Village
Waisman Center
University of Wisconsin-Madison
1500 Highland Ave.
Madison, WI 53705-2280
E-MAIL: familyvillage@waisman.wisc.edu
URL: http://www.familyvillage.wisc.edu

Family Village Project integrates information, resources, and communication opportunities on the Internet for persons with cognitive and other disabilities, for their families, and for those who provide them with services and support. Family Village includes informational resources on specific diagnoses, communication connections, adaptive products and technology, adaptive recreational activities, education, worship, health issues, and disability-related media and literature.

National Early Childhood Technical Assistance System (NECTAS)
Frank Porter Graham Child

Development Center
137 East Franklin St.
Chapel Hill, NC 27514-3628
PHONE: (919) 962-2001
TDD: (919) 966-8300
FAX: (919) 966-7463
E-MAIL: nectas@unc.edu
URL: http://www.nectas.unc.edu

NECTAS is a national technical assistance consortium working to support states, jurisdictions, and others to improve services and results for young children with disabilities and their families.

National Fathers Network
16120 NE Eighth St.
Bellevue, WA 98008-3037
PHONE: (425) 747-4004 ext. 218
EMAIL: jmay@fatheresnetwork.org
URL: http://www.fathersnetwork.org

The mission of the National Fathers Network is to celebrate and support fathers and families raising children with special health care needs and developmental disabilities The National Fathers Network provides technical assistance to organizations and agencies, produces a twice-yearly newsletter (DADS), sponsors local and regional conferences, and develops materials in English and Spanish.

National Information Center for Children and Youth with Disabilities (NICHCY)
PO Box 1492
Washington, DC 20013-1492
PHONE: (800) 695-0285 (V/TTY)
(202) 884-8200 (V/TTY)
FAX: (202) 884-8441
EMAIL: nichy@aed.org
URL: http://www.nichcy.org

NICHCY is the national information and referral center that provides information on disabilities and disability-related issues for families, educators, and other professionals. NICHCY's special focus is children and youth (birth to age 22). Services include personal responses to questions, publications, referrals, database and library searches, and materials in Spanish.

National Parent Network on Disabilities (NPND)
1130 17th St., NW Suite 400
Washington, DC 20036

PHONE: (202) 463-2299 V/TDD
FAX: (202) 463-9403
E-MAIL: NPND@cs.net
URL: http://www.npnd.org

NPND provides its members with up-to-date information on the activities of all three branches of government that impact individuals with disabilities and their families. NPND's primary activities include advocating for, and supporting the development and implementation of, legislation that will improve the lives and protect the rights of children, youth, and adults with disabilities.

National Resource Center for Special Needs Adoption
Spaulding for Children
Crossroad Office Center, Suite 120
Southfield, MI 48075
PHONE: (248) 443-7080
FAX: (248) 443-7099
E-MAIL: sfc@Spaulding.org
URL: http://www.spaulding.org

The Center works with States, Tribes, and agencies to increase the number of children with special needs who are adopted and to improve the effectiveness and quality of adoption and post-adoption services provided to them and their families. The Center has developed and distributes a number of training curricula as well as publications, videos, and a newsletter.

Parent Advocacy Coalition for Educational Rights (PACER) Center
4826 Chicago Ave., South
Minneapolis, MN 55417-1098
PHONE: (612) 827-2966
TDD: (612) 827-7770
FAX: (612) 827-3065
E-MAIL: webster@pacer.org
URL: http://www.pacer.org

PACER's mission is to improve and expand opportunities that enhance the quality of life for children and young adults with disabilities and their families. PACER offers 20 major programs, including Parent Training programs, programs for students and schools, and technical assistance to parent centers both regionally and nationally. PACER's programs help parents become informed and effective representatives for their children in early childhood, school-age, and vocational settings.

Index